The Yachtsman's Pil
West Coast of Scotland
Crinan to Canna

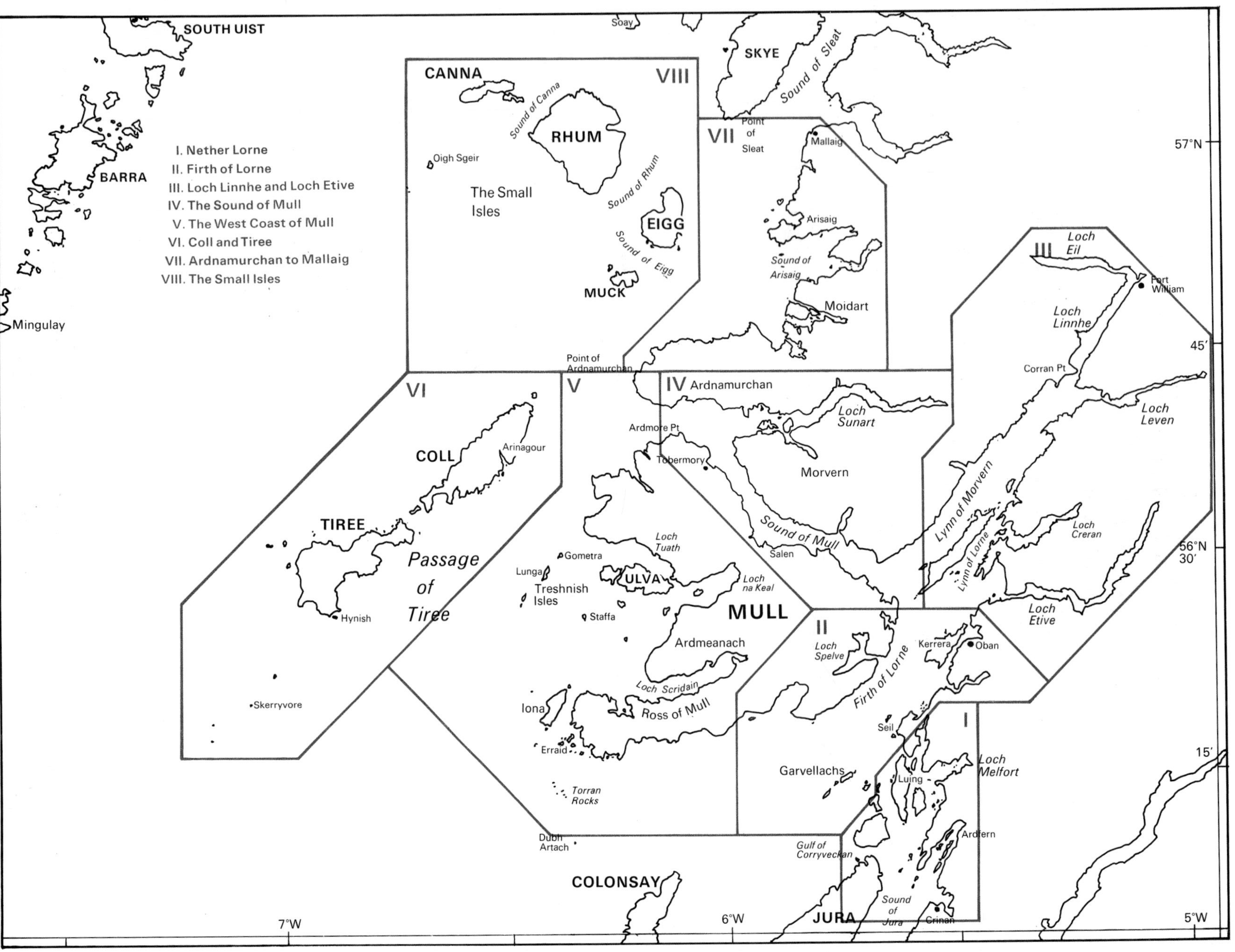

I. Nether Lorne
II. Firth of Lorne
III. Loch Linnhe and Loch Etive
IV. The Sound of Mull
V. The West Coast of Mull
VI. Coll and Tiree
VII. Ardnamurchan to Mallaig
VIII. The Small Isles
SOUTH UIST
BARRA
Mingulay
Soay
SKYE
Sound of Sleat
CANNA
RHUM
EIGG
MUCK
Sound of Canna
Sound of Rhum
Sound of Eigg
Oigh Sgeir
The Small Isles
Point of Sleat
Mallaig
Arisaig
Sound of Arisaig
Moidart
Point of Ardnamurchan
Ardnamurchan
Loch Sunart
Morvern
Ardmore Pt
Tobermory
Sound of Mull
Salen
Loch Eil
Fort William
Loch Linnhe
Corran Pt
Loch Leven
Lynn of Morvern
Lynn of Lorne
Loch Creran
Loch Etive
COLL
Arinagour
TIREE
Hynish
Passage of Tiree
Skerryvore
Gometra
Lunga
Treshnish Isles
Staffa
ULVA
Loch Tuath
Loch na Keal
MULL
Ardmeanach
Loch Scridain
Ross of Mull
Iona
Erraid
Torran Rocks
Dubh Artach
COLONSAY
Loch Spelve
Firth of Lorne
Kerrera
Oban
Seil
Garvellachs
Luing
Loch Melfort
Ardfern
Gulf of Corryvreckan
Sound of Jura
JURA
Crinan
57°N
45′
56°N 30′
15′
7°W
6°W
5°W

The Yachtsman's Pilot to the West Coast of Scotland
Crinan to Canna

MARTIN LAWRENCE

Imray Laurie Norie & Wilson Ltd
St Ives Cambridgeshire England

Published by
Imray, Laurie, Norie & Wilson Ltd
Wych House, St Ives, Huntingdon,
Cambridgeshire, PE17 4BT, England.

British Library Cataloguing in Publication Data

Lawrence, Martin
Crinan to Canna. – (The Yachtsman's Pilot to the West Coast of Scotland).
1. Pilot guides – Scotland
I. Title II. Series
623.89'29411 VK833

ISBN 0 85288 107 X

CAUTION
Whilst every care has been taken to ensure accuracy, neither the Publishers nor the Author will hold themselves responsible for errors, omissions or alterations in this publication. They will at all times be grateful to receive information which tends to the improvement of the work.

PLANS
The plans in this guide are not to be used for navigation. They are designed to support the text and should at all times be used with navigational charts.

The technical data in this work is correct to April 1987.

Set in Plantin by Cromwell Graphics Ltd, St Ives, Huntingdon direct from the Author's and Publishers' disks.

Printed at Tabro Litho Ltd, St Ives, Huntingdon

Contents

To the memory of M.E.L.

Preface

"This narrow strait" (the Sailing Directions said),
"Is full of rocks, and difficult to enter;
Whirlpools are common here at every tide;
There are uncharted reefs on every side
And currents (twenty knots) along the centre."
"Come," said the Skipper, "we will go in there."
(We went in there.)

"There is no sand" (the Sailing Directions said),
"The anchorage is thoroughly unsafe.
There is no shelter from the frequent squalls,
Save on the west, among the overfalls.
Boats should go on to Loch MacInchmaquaif."
"Come," said the Skipper, "we will anchor here."
(We anchored here.)

From *The Log of the Blue Dragon* (1903)

There has been no shortage of pilotage information for the west coast of Scotland over the last century or more, much of it in the form of personal accounts of cruises. Some of these make tedious reading but some are minor classics. Hugh Miller's *Cruise of the Betsey* of 1858 and John Inglis' *A Yachtsman's Holidays* of 1879 are early examples. Among the best are *The Log of the Blue Dragon* by C. C. Lynam, published in 1903 and describing ten years of cruising in a 25-foot centreboard yawl, both in winter and summer, and frequently single-handed. Next in chronological order were the articles written almost every year in *Yachting Monthly* by Robert Groves from 1906 onwards describing cruises in a small yawl, also often single-handed. Even now to read of Groves' and Lynam's experiences provides valuable insights into the character of individual anchorages.

The Admiralty sailing directions had been established many years earlier, building on a tradition going back to Alexander Lindsay's *Rutter of the Scottish Seas* of about 1540, but the first publication to provide navigational information specifically for yachtsmen on the west coast of Scotland was Volume 5 of Frank Cowper's *Sailing Tours* of 1896. Cowper sailed round the whole coast of Britain and the west coast of France (where he was regarded with suspicion as a potential spy) in a heavy 48-foot gaff cutter, with only a boy for crew – and no engine, of course. Cowper's *Sailing Tours* have, incidentally, now been re-published.

When the Clyde Cruising Club was founded in 1909 it began to publish pilotage information in its *Journal*. This material was gathered into one volume in 1923 as the first of many editions of its classic *Sailing Directions for the west coast of Scotland*. The 1930s produced a further crop of books about cruising on the West Coast, of which the two most useful are *Sailing Orders* by Capt. J. R. Harvey, and *Leaves from Rowan's Logs* by Dr R. B. Carslaw. Valuable information can also be found in the journals of the Royal Cruising Club and the Clyde Cruising Club (CCC).

Recently there have been several rather superficial sailing guides which have made no attempt to (and to be fair they do not claim to) cover the West Coast in comprehensive detail. In 1975 following the metrication of Admiralty charts, changes in the datum used, and impending change to the buoyage system, the CCC began the publication of a new series of sailing directions with new plans.

Yachtsmen's sailing directions for other waters have for a long time been well illustrated with photographs or drawings. Views from seaward, both of transits and for identification, used to be a feature of Admiralty charts and pilots; no doubt with electronic aids they were thought unnecessary, but their usefulness is being rediscovered and their value is undoubtedly much greater for the crew of a small yacht which does not, usually, have as many navigational aids as a warship. This pilot combines my experience in compiling much of the current edition of the CCC sailing directions with as many pictorial views as may be useful to a stranger who might be disconcerted by the relative lack of artificial marks.

I have had some excellent advice from Malcolm Robson, whose five pilots for the Channel Islands and the west coast of France are among the best yachtsmen's pilots anywhere. He uses drawings exclusively to illustrate his books and considers air photographs in particular 'strictly for the birds'; however I hope those included here will be found helpful. I have used drawings where they are clearer than photos.

The photos were taken mainly at low spring tides to reveal as many hazards as possible. However if coverage isn't as comprehensive and some of the photos not as clear as might be, this is because it takes many years to visit each place at a specific time of day and month, whether by sea, land or air – with no guarantee that conditions will be suitable for photography when one gets there.

Inevitably a book of this kind is flavoured by the author's outlook and experience; it may be of interest to know that I have a steel ketch of traditional character and perhaps take a slightly more light-hearted view of rock-dodging than would the owner of a less robust vessel. On the other hand *Erraid* is not so handy as most GRP cruiser-racers, and any place into which she can find her way should present little difficulty to a modern yacht of moderate size.

These directions can be no more than the sum of my own observations and a summary of all that I have read and gleaned from charts and air photos. There could well be hazards which I have missed by luck rather than good management, and in spite of all the efforts of the editorial team at Imray, Laurie, Norie & Wilson there may be simple errors which have been overlooked – even the supplements to the Admiralty pilot contain the occasional instruction 'for E read W'. Scepticism and checking against all other information available is the safest course to adopt – with any directions. If you find information which you think is inaccurate, or changes which have occurred since the publication of this volume, I should be very grateful if you would let me know, through the Publishers.

Acknowledgements

The initiative for this pilot came from Nigel Gardner, who also provided much detailed information. Much information also came from Ian Wallace and Hilary King. The production of the book itself owes an enormous amount to the work put in by various people: the text was made more readable by my wife's efforts to disentangle it; further order was introduced by the editor, Nell Stuart, who also meticulously checked every detail. The final form of the plans is due to the work of Imray cartographers, to whom I gave only the outlines and rough notes. The drawings of transits are by Harriet Lawrence. The aerial photograph of Corryvreckan is by John Dewar Studios.
The Publishers are grateful to Elizabeth Cook who compiled the index.

Martin Lawrence
Edinburgh
March 1987

Most of the plans in this book are based on British Admiralty charts with the permission of the Hydrographer of the Navy and the sanction of H.M. Stationery Office.

Introduction

This pilot sets out to provide as much information as may be useful for visitors to the west coast of Scotland in small boats, as clearly as possible. It is not trying to 'sell' the West Coast; anyone reading it is probably already considering sailing there. The upper limit of size for which it caters is a draught of 2 metres, and it provides information specifically for shoal-draught boats – centreboarders, trailer-sailers, twin-keel boats and multihulls, and of course motor cruisers, who tend to be forgotten by writers of 'sailing directions' who usually have sailing boats. Many West Coast anchorages have areas only accessible to shoal-draught boats, particularly those which can dry out fairly upright. In most other parts of Britain, indeed in most other parts of Europe, having a shoal-draught boat is the best way to avoid the crowds, and this is increasingly becoming the case on the west coast of Scotland which has traditionally been considered a deep-water area.

However, while the smallest boats, even cruising dinghies, may be at home in much of the area described in this pilot, they must be soundly equipped and competently handled by experienced crews. Except within some very sheltered lochs, and bearing in mind the need to keep well away from the entrance where there may be strong tides, the West Coast is no place for anyone who is unable to deal with adverse conditions which may arise unexpectedly. A good way to gain experience on the West Coast is to take a berth on one of the skippered charter yachts or instructional courses which are available.

Most of the waters covered by this volume are sheltered by islands or are within lochs which penetrate far among some of the highest hills in Britain. This shelter creates problems of its own, particularly the squalls which are generated in the lee of hills as well as the higher rainfall. With two reservations, however, anyone who is capable of managing a yacht at a comparable distance from the shore whether in the North Sea, the Baltic, the English Channel, the Atlantic coast of France or the Irish Sea will have little problem on the west coast of Scotland. The reservations are the lack of navigational marks (and the number of unmarked rocks), and the strong tides in some passages. To set against these are the relative absence of commercial shipping and also the visibility which is usually good – except in rain; fog as such is fairly rare. To complete a round of generalisations, the climate is wetter and cooler than, for example the south coast of England (although the further west you go, out of the lee of the hills, the drier the weather), but a compensating factor is the longer daylight in summer, so that you rarely need to sail at night.

One of the main attractions of the West Coast is the sheer variety of anchorages and passages which occur within quite a small area. The main body of this book is divided into 8 chapters, each covering waters of quite different character, from the almost land-locked pastoral country of Loch Melfort and the lower part of Loch Etive, to the dramatic scenery of Loch Sunart, and the white sand and pink granite of the Ross of Mull – all within an area about 60 miles square.

Charts This pilot is not intended as a substitute for Admiralty charts. Many of the plans in the book are at a larger scale than the charts, and include more detail, but only cover small areas, and it is essential to have plenty of charts. A complete list of current charts, and further discussion, including information on old charts and Ordnance Survey maps, is given in Appendix I, page 157. Some obsolete charts show more detail than any current one and sometimes at a larger scale, but with soundings in feet and fathoms, and these are referred to where appropriate. They should of course only be used to supplement current charts, not as a substitute for them. Although many people blithely observe that 'rocks don't move', new ones are discovered (sometimes the hard way), buoys are moved around, and new features are constructed. The more charts you have, the less anxious your pilotage will be.

Imray chart C65, whose boundaries correspond closely with the scope of this pilot, is ideal as an overall chart of the area.

Sketch charts published by the Clyde Cruising Club may be found more convenient but they show less detail than the Admiralty charts and are not corrected so frequently.

Maps Ordnance Survey maps at 1:50,000 or Bartholomew at 1:100,000 are well worth taking along to make up for the lack of topographical detail on current charts (see Appendix I).

Equipment should be as robust and reliable as for a yacht going a similar distance offshore anywhere in the English Channel or the North Sea. You should have at least two anchors, of the sizes recommended by anchor manufacturers or independent reference books, rather than those supplied as standard by boat manufacturers which are often on the light side. Chain rather than rope will prevent a yacht roving around in gusts, but if you do use rope it will help to have a weight which can be let down to the seabed on a traveller. So many yachts are now kept in marinas and only sail to another marina or to a harbour that anchoring is no longer an everyday operation, but on the West Coast it is essential that the crew is thoroughly familiar with anchor handling. It is no use relying on visitors' moorings being available; where they do exist they are quite likely to be already occupied.

Chartering Plenty of boats are available, both for bareboat and skippered charters, and also instructional cruises. Many of the operators are members of the Association of Scottish Yacht Charterers, whose brochure can be obtained from the Scottish Tourist Board, 23 Ravelston Terrace, Edinburgh 4 or the Yacht Charter Association, 60 Silverdale, New Milton, Hants BH25 7DE (☎ 0425 619004). Most operators, including some owners of individual yachts, also advertise in yachting magazines.

Travel

Transport Public transport in the area is probably better than it has been at any time during the last 30 years. There are rail and bus services to Oban, Fort William and Corpach, Arisaig and Mallaig. If a crew change has to be made on Mull, there are frequent ferry crossings, some of which are met by buses to Tobermory and to the Ross of Mull. Other ferry and bus services (as well as rail and air services, and local boat and car hirers) are included in the *Combined Timetable* which is published by the Highlands and Islands Development Board annually at a price (in 1987) of £1.50.

With the exception of Tiree no part of this area has a regular air service.

There are good roads to Crinan and Oban and places between them; also to Loch Leven, continuing to Fort William, but beyond Oban and Fort William they are tortuous in places.

Trailed boats can be launched at Oban where there is a concrete slip with a capacity of 5 tons. There are also slips at Ardfern Yacht Centre (Loch Craignish), Craobh Yacht Haven (Loch Shuna), Airds Bay (Loch Etive), Dunstaffnage Yacht Haven, Creran Moorings (Loch Creran), Ballachulish old ferry (Loch Leven), Salen (Loch Sunart), and Arisaig Marine. Several yacht centres have mobile hoists.

For Oban check by phone before arriving; either with the piermaster ☎ (0631) 62892, or boatbuilder D. Currie ☎ (0631) 62102. Otherwise phone the owners, listed under the relevant area in each chapter.

Passage making

Most passages covered by this volume are within sounds or lochs or along a shore entailing only short hops across open sea, so that navigation is, in the main, a matter of pilotage by eye and satisfying yourself that what you see corresponds to the chart. It is useful to pick out from the chart transits such as tangents of islands, or beacons in line with headlands to give you position lines from time to time. Check by compass bearings as well, starting from something unmistakable such as, for instance, the south tangent of Mull, so as to avoid wrongly identifying a whole group of islands.

Traditional clearing marks for avoiding unmarked dangers, based on transits of natural features, are often much easier to use than compass bearings particularly where there are cross tides. Bearings are given in the text as a check on identification.

At night most of the main passages are fairly well lit, at least for a passage under power or with a fair wind, but they aren't up to the standard of Scandinavian countries as there isn't enough traffic to justify more lights. A few anchorages or passages are very well lit for local commercial users. At least during June and July there is little need to sail at night unless you are making a longer passage, beyond the limits of this book.

Radiobeacons There are only two radiobeacons likely to be of any use.

Name	*Frequency*	*Identification*	*Range*	*Seq.*	*Position*
Hyskeir Lt, Oigh Sgeir	294.2 kHz	OR (———/·—·)	50M	5	56°58′N 06°41′W
Barra Head LtHo	308 kHz	BD (—···/—··)	200/70M	1	56°47′N 07°39′W

Tides

Within the area covered by Chapter I the tidal range is less than 2 metres but in several passages in that area tides run at up to 8 knots. Elsewhere the range is up to 4 metres. Tidal streams are strong wherever the movement of a large body of water is constricted by narrows and there are often overfalls at the seaward end of narrow passages, particularly with wind against tide. Overfalls also occur off many headlands, and eddies are formed, usually down-tide of a promontory or islet or even a submerged reef, but sometimes in a bay up-tide of the obstruction. There are also usually overfalls wherever two tidal streams meet such as, for example, the ebb streams from the Sound of Mull and from Loch Linnhe. These eddies and overfalls are too common to be mentioned individually.

Tidal streams The flood tide generally runs north and west, but in the mouth of the Firth of Lorne it runs northeast. At Crinan the stream turns up to 1½ hours before HW and LW Oban at Crinan and about an hour after HW and LW Oban in the Sound of Mull. This means that at least 8 hours of fair tide can be carried going north although of course at the expense of the return passage.

See also the paragraphs on *Tides* under each relevant area.

Anchorages

This heading covers not only natural anchorages but also moorings and berths alongside pontoons or quays. Many places are only suitable for a short daytime visit in settled conditions and the inclusion of an anchorage is no indication that it is suitable for all conditions. The skipper must decide whether to use an anchorage at all, and for how long, in the light of conditions at the time and all the information available. Even the most apparently sheltered place will sometimes have the crew standing anchor watches throughout the night.

Within some anchorages there are often several suitable places to lie depending on conditions and it is not always practicable to describe them all, nor to mark each one on the plans. In any case, an anchorage suitable for a shoal-draught boat 6 metres long may be inaccessible to a 15-metre yacht with a draught of 2 metres, and a berth which would give shelter for the larger yacht might be uncomfortably exposed for the smaller.

A few very general observations may be helpful. Steep high ground to windward is unlikely to provide good shelter; in fresh winds there may be turbulent gusts on its lee side, or the wind may be deflected to blow from a completely different direction. After a hot windless day there may be a strong katabatic wind down the slope, usually in the early morning – such conditions are by no means unknown in Scotland. Trees to windward will absorb a lot of wind and provide good shelter.

Rivers, burns and streams generally carry down debris, often leaving a shallow or drying bank of stones, sand or silt, over which the unwary may swing – frequently in the middle of the night.

Within any anchorage the quality of the bottom may vary greatly. Mud is common, (usually where there is little current) but its density may not be consistent and there are likely to be patches of rock, boulders and stones; also clay which tends to break out suddenly. Sand is also common, but sometimes it is so hard that an anchor, particularly a light one, will not dig in. Weed of all kinds appears to be on the increase, but it does vary from year to year.

Man-made obstructions Fish farms are increasing at an alarming rate, usually outwith the most popular places, but attempts are sometimes made to establish them in recognised anchorages as well. An application was made, for example, for permission to set up a fish farm in the southwest corner of Drumbuie, in Loch Sunart, and it might well have been approved had it not been for objections by the coastguard that the anchorage was a vital refuge for small craft.

Permission to establish any permanent fixture on the seabed, such as a mooring, has to be obtained from the Crown Estates Commissioners who own the rights to the seabed, and also the Department of Transport (Marine Directorate), who consult the RYA (Scotland), who in turn refer to the Clyde Cruising Club and the West Highlands Anchorages and Moorings Association (WHAM), which represents the interests of both yachtsmen and fishermen; the comments are then passed back up the chain and may or may not be taken into account.

Increasingly, moorings for yachts and fishing and other workboats, as well as fish farms, are being laid within established anchorages, preventing or restricting their use. The number of inshore fishing boats operating from some parts of the coast of Argyll has doubled in a few years. Preservation of anchorages is one of the main functions of WHAM who wish to hear about any unauthorised obstruction; the honorary secretary of WHAM is Mike Bolton, at 8 Grianach Gardens, Oban.

Few yachtsmen whose moorings occupy cruising anchorages would object to their being used by visitors, but any visitor must be certain that the mooring is capable of holding his boat, must take reasonable steps to find out whether the owner is likely to return, and be ready to move if he does.

Visitors' moorings These may be seen as a convenience, necessity or obstruction depending on your point of view. Some are provided by local hotels free of charge to yachts whose crews patronise their establishments.

HIDB moorings Visitors' moorings have been provided by the Highlands and Islands Development Board in several places to bring more business to local traders. They tend to be laid in the most suitable area for anchoring, and are arranged (as they have to be) to suit the largest boats likely to use them. The effect is to reduce the number of visiting boats which can use an anchorage. HIDB moorings have large blue buoys marked 'HIDB visitors' and '10 (or 15) tons'. There is no pick-up, and a rope has to be fed through a ring on top of the buoy. If your bow is so high that the buoy is out of reach and you cannot pass your rope through the ring, the best way to secure to one of these moorings is to lead a rope from the bow to the lowest point amidships, pick up the buoy there and take the end of the rope back to the bow. Beware of chafe at the ring and use chain if necessary.

Marinas and yacht centres are being established, sometimes obliterating the natural anchorages which are after all the main attraction of the West Coast. A berth or mooring will usually be found for a visiting yacht; the charges vary widely and cost-conscious skippers will do well to enquire first. At most of these places you will find a space to put down your own anchor if you are determined to. Some more enlightened establishments make no charge for a daytime visit.

Commercial harbours Only Oban and Mallaig come into this category, although the canal basins at Crinan and Corpach which are both entered through locks, should perhaps be included. Mallaig is controlled by a harbour board with a full-time harbourmaster. Oban has no overall controlling authority (so that VHF calls to 'Oban Harbour' usually go unanswered).

Piers and jetties, even in the most remote anchorages these should be treated in the same way as private moorings. Some are used by fishermen or workboats which may not treat an unattended yacht with as much delicacy as the owner would wish. Some piers are derelict and dangerous.

Eating ashore The prospect of eating and drinking ashore is a good deal less bleak than it was even ten years ago; hotels, restaurants and pubs are mentioned in the text, although not usually by name and without specific recommendations as management and standards may change rapidly.

Communications

Phone boxes are fairly well distributed and are referred to where known, but the 'rationalisation' of the telephone service may lead to a reduction in their numbers.

VHF radiotelephones The mountainous nature of this coast puts some areas out of range of either the coastguard or coast radio stations. The south side of Mull, for instance, is a blind spot for Oban Coastguard, and you can't usually contact the coast radio stations from anywhere between Ardnamurchan and the Sound of Sleat and the Small Isles; it is hoped to establish a branch transmitter/receiver for Islay Radio at the north end of Mull to fill this gap. Several yacht centres have VHF R/T, but they may not be continuously manned.

Place names Admiralty charts and sailing directions follow the Ordnance Survey convention of printing academic renderings of Gaelic names, with a variety of accents as they would appear in a Gaelic dictionary. Some of these are quite unpronounceable other than by Gaelic speakers (and, I believe, sometimes unrecognisable even to them). Both authorities sometimes use anglicised versions, or translations of Gaelic words, apparently quite arbitrarily; for example you may come across 'Old Woman Rock' among a patch of Gaelic names on a chart, or alternatively a Gaelic name alongside its equivalent anglicisation. The early surveyors often made up their own names, based on natural features, their own translations of the Gaelic, or events or personalities connected with the survey, and these names were used on earlier charts, but these have not often survived.

Place names need to be communicated verbally, for example between the navigator, helmsman and lookout, so I have used the popular form of a name where there is one, as well as the name which appears on current charts. The spelling of these names matches that on the Admiralty charts, less any accents. You may find some discrepancies, but I hope they will not be so great as to cause confusion. See Appendix II.

Emergencies

Serious and immediate emergencies (including medical ones) are usually best referred to the coastguard. If you don't have VHF R/T but are able to get ashore (for example, if a crew member is ill), phone the coastguard or police. For less serious problems, such as a mechanical breakdown out of range of a boatyard, mechanics experienced at least with tractor or fishing boat engines will often be found locally.

Coastguard The Marine Rescue Sub-Centre (MRSC) for the area is Oban Coastguard, ☎ Oban (0631) 63720; there are also coastguards at Tobermory, ☎ Oban (0631) 2200, and Mallaig, ☎ (0687) 2336.

Lifeboats are stationed, within the limits of this volume, only at Oban and Mallaig; outside the immediate area there are lifeboats at Port Askaig, Islay, and at Castle Bay, Barra.

Notes on plans and pilotage directions

Generally the conventions used on Admiralty charts have been followed so that this pilot may be used in conjunction with them. Please see *Charts* on page 1.

Bearings are from seaward and refer to true north. A few of the plans are not orientated with north at the top in order to make the best use of the space available, but reference to the north point on the plan will make this clear.

Distances are given in nautical miles and cables (tenth of nautical mile); less than ¼ cable is generally expressed in metres.

Depths and heights are given in metres to correspond with the current Admiralty charts. Depths are related to the current chart datum which is generally lower than that on older charts. It is the lowest level to which the surface of the sea is expected to fall owing to astronomical causes. If high barometric pressure and/or strong offshore winds coincide with a low spring tide the water may fall below this level, in which case there will be less depth than shown on the chart, or sketch plan.

Tides Heights of tides are represented by five figures; these are: Mean High Water Springs, Mean High Water Neaps, Mean Tide Level, Mean Low Water Neaps, Mean Low Water Springs. The word *Mean* is important because (for example) Low Water Springs in any particular fortnight may be substantially higher or lower than the mean. If you have tide tables which give heights of tides at Oban you will be able to relate the tide on any particular day to the mean figures there (4.0 2.9 2.4 1.8 0.7) and judge whether the rise and fall is greater or less than the mean.

The difference between times of tides at Oban and at Dover may vary by as much as 40 minutes, so that tide tables for Oban will give more accurate results than those for Dover. In addition to Admiralty tide tables and commercial almanacs, pocket tide tables for Oban are supplied by local chandlers, boatyards and marinas, and also by Glasgow chandlers.

Plans of anchorages and passages in this pilot are often at a larger scale than those on current charts, and the information in them is compiled from many sources. These include the Admiralty's original surveys; air photographs mostly of RAF origin; observations by (rather too few) other yachtsmen; and my own surveys, both from the air and by sea, as well as from the land. Some of them are based directly on British Admiralty charts, with the permission of the Hydrographer of the Navy.

Photographs and views from sea level are used to illustrate transits and clearing marks, or to help identify landmarks, while air and hilltop photos often show more detail than can be included in the plans. Transits are in some cases more clearly illustrated when the marks used are not actually aligned; where this is done the marks are indicated by pointers.

Key to symbols used on plans

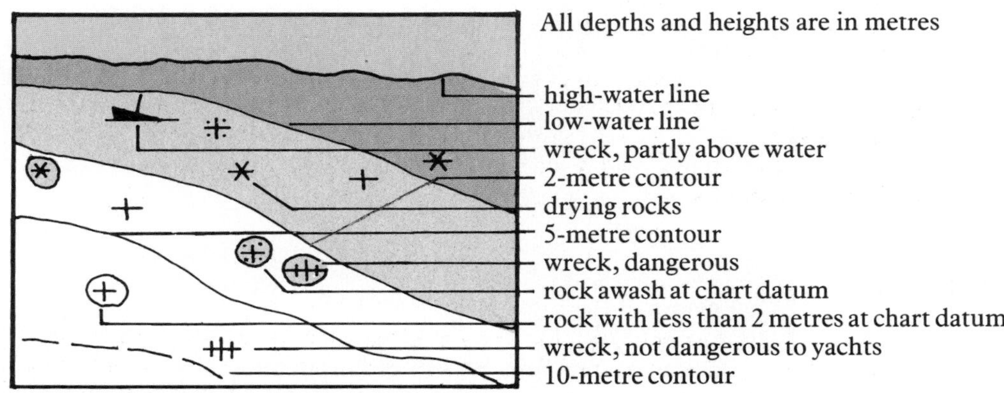

There are usually shoals at the mouths of the burns.

Grey Dogs.

I. Nether Lorne

Most yachts visiting the West Coast will pass through these waters unless they go to the west of Jura, and Admiralty chart *2326* at a scale of 1:25,000 is essential. There are probably more islands and passages in the area covered by this chart than in any equivalent area off the British mainland. Tidal streams in passages covered by chart *2326* are as strong as any around Britain; there are few artificial marks, and plenty of hidden dangers. However most of the passages are completely sheltered from the open sea and the hazards are easily avoided with care.

This used to be an area which everyone passed by in their hurry to get north, but several yacht centres of varying degrees of sophistication have grown up here in the last fifteen years and hundreds of yachts are now berthed in these waters. Inshore of a line between Ardnoe, the south point of Loch Crinan, and the south end of Luing the land is relatively pastoral, but the islands west of this line are bleak and rugged and almost uninhabited. The character of the tidal streams differs on either side of the same line; to the east the tides present few problems, but to the west they need close attention.

Tides

The tidal range inside Jura and the islands northward is little more than 2 metres at springs but to the west of Jura it is more than 3, so that the whole volume of water in the Sound of Jura has to pour out through a few narrow channels on the flood and back again on the ebb; each of these channels has tidal streams at springs of 6 to 8 knots. It is therefore essential to work the tides unless you have a really hefty engine.

The Sound of Luing

56°12′N 5°40′W

The main passage, the Sound of Luing, is straightforward enough but eddies and overfalls make it necessary to keep a very close watch on the course at all times but probably most of all under sail in light weather. It is very easy to be carried off course and although, as I've said, the hazards are easily avoided, they are there and a constant check on position must be kept. A branch of the flood stream runs towards Corryvreckan and you need to watch that you aren't being carried into this passage without realising it. In anything like heavy weather with wind against tide the Dorus Mor and the passage from there to the south end of Luing would be actually dangerous to a small boat. The photograph on this page was taken from Craignish Point looking west towards Corryvreckan with a flood tide and a southerly wind about Force 7 (that is, the wind and tide were running the same way), and the boat is a heavily built 50-foot motorsailer.

Corryvreckan

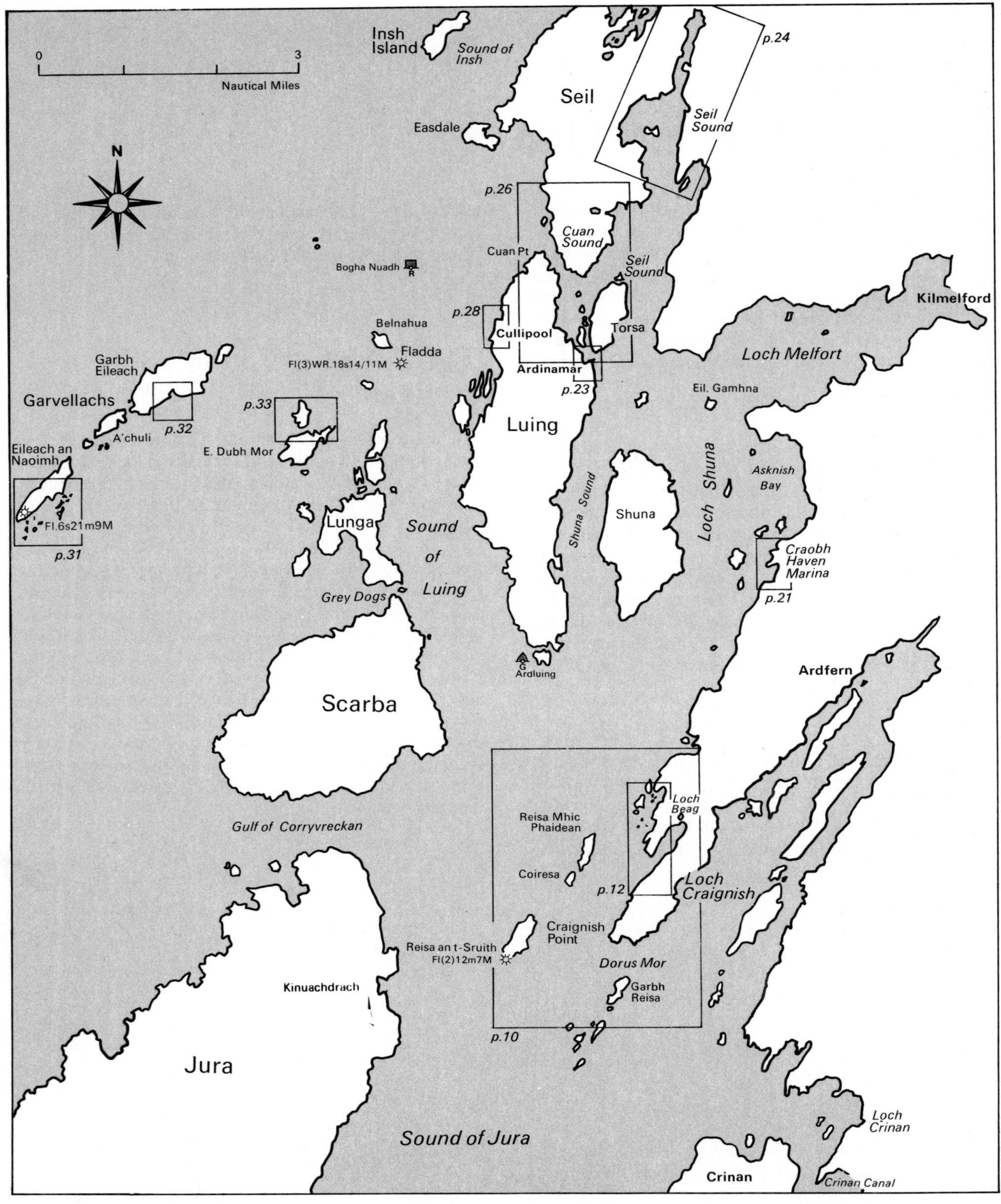
Insh Island
Sound of Insh
0
3
Nautical Miles
N
Seil
p.24
Seil Sound
Easdale
p.26
Cuan Sound
Cuan Pt
Seil Sound
Bogha Nuadh
R
Kilmelford
p.28
Cullipool
Torsa
Belnahua
Fladda
Fl(3)WR.18s14/11M
Ardinamar
Loch Melfort
Garbh Eileach
Garvellachs
p.23
Eil. Gamhna
p.33
p.32
A'chuli
Luing
Eileach an Naoimh
E. Dubh Mor
Loch Shuna
Asknish Bay
Shuna Sound
Shuna
Fl.6s21m9M
Lunga
Sound of Luing
Craobh Haven Marina
p.31
Grey Dogs
p.21
Ardluing
G
Ardfern
Scarba
Loch Beag
Reisa Mhic Phaidean
Gulf of Corryvreckan
Coiresa
p.12
Loch Craignish
Craignish Point
Reisa an t-Sruith
Fl(2)12m7M
Dorus Mor
Garbh Reisa
Kinuachdrach
p.10
Jura
Loch Crinan
Sound of Jura
Crinan
Crinan Canal

Tides

The flood tide runs northwards and westwards, beginning about +0430 Oban (−0100 Dover) at springs; +0515 Oban (−0015 Dover) at neaps. The ebb runs southwards and eastwards, beginning about −0145 Oban (+0515 Dover) at springs, −0100 Oban (+0600 Dover) at neaps.

A branch of the flood tide sets strongly across to Corryvreckan, and eddies form generally down-tide of any obstruction such as a point of land or a rock, with overfalls where eddies and main tide meet.

The flood tide sets northwest across the reefs to the NNE of Ruadh Sgeir at the north end of the Sound of Jura and this must be allowed for by any yacht coming from the Sound of Jura and making for Loch Craignish or the Dorus Mor. Likewise the ebb sets southeast at the same point. Northwest of the reefs NNE of Ruadh Sgeir there are heavy overfalls on the flood.

Marks

Unless it is obscured by cloud, the peak of Scarba is a convenient reference point. Other marks are Fladda lighthouse at the north end of the Sound of Luing, Reisa an t-Sruith light beacon to the west of the Dorus Mor, and a conspicuous white house on Shuna island (Shuna Cottage).

Passage notes

From the Sound of Jura the passage of the Sound of Luing is straightforward but, especially under sail in light weather, take care to avoid being carried towards Corryvreckan; keep to the east side of the passage. Identify the correct passage by reference to landmarks. Towards the north end of the sound there are two submerged rocks, one on either side of the fairway. These are unlikely to be of any concern except to a deep-draught boat at a low spring tide. The main passage is between Fladda and Dubh Sgeir light beacon.

From the north identify Scarba, and Fladda lighthouse will be seen to the east of it – yachts have been known to go west of Scarba by mistake.

Lights

At night, light beacons at Ruadh Sgeir and Reisa an t-Sruith kept in transit 188° provide a safe line when you are south of Ard Luing. Within the Sound of Luing the only guide is to take compass bearings on Reisa an t-Sruith and on Fladda and Dubh Sgeir light beacons at the north end of the sound.

Ruadh Sgeir Fl.6s13m8M
Reisa an t-Sruith Fl(2)12s12m7M
Fladda Fl(3)WR.18s13m14/11M. 169°-R-186°-W-001°
Dubh Sgeir Fl.6s7m6M

Anchorages

Kinuachdrach (Kinnochtie), 56°7′.5N 5°41′W, at the northeast end of Jura, either the bay north of the promontory (Port an Tiobairt) or south of it (Kinuachdrach Harbour) provides an occasional anchorage according to wind direction.

Lunga – Poll na Corran, 56°12′.5N 5°41′W, a bay on the east side of Lunga only exposed to the fetch across the sound. Enter north of the islet there and anchor off the beach.

Black Mill Bay, 56°13′N 5°39′W, on Luing will give better shelter in easterly winds; just south of the most westerly point on Luing, and north of a ruined timber pier.

Cullipool, see page 27.

Dorus Mor

56°07′.5N 5°36′W

This is the passage, about a third of a mile wide, between Craignish Point and Garreasar (Garbh Reisa), the most northerly of the string of islands and reefs to the SSW of the point. It is deep and clean and provides a direct route from Crinan and Loch Craignish to the Sound of Luing.

Scarba and the north end of the Sound of Luing from northeast. The Black Isles (Eileanan Dubha) are to the right, and the Garvellachs are out of the picture to the right. Luing is on the left, with Fladda in front of Luing and Belnahua in front of the east side of the Black Isles.

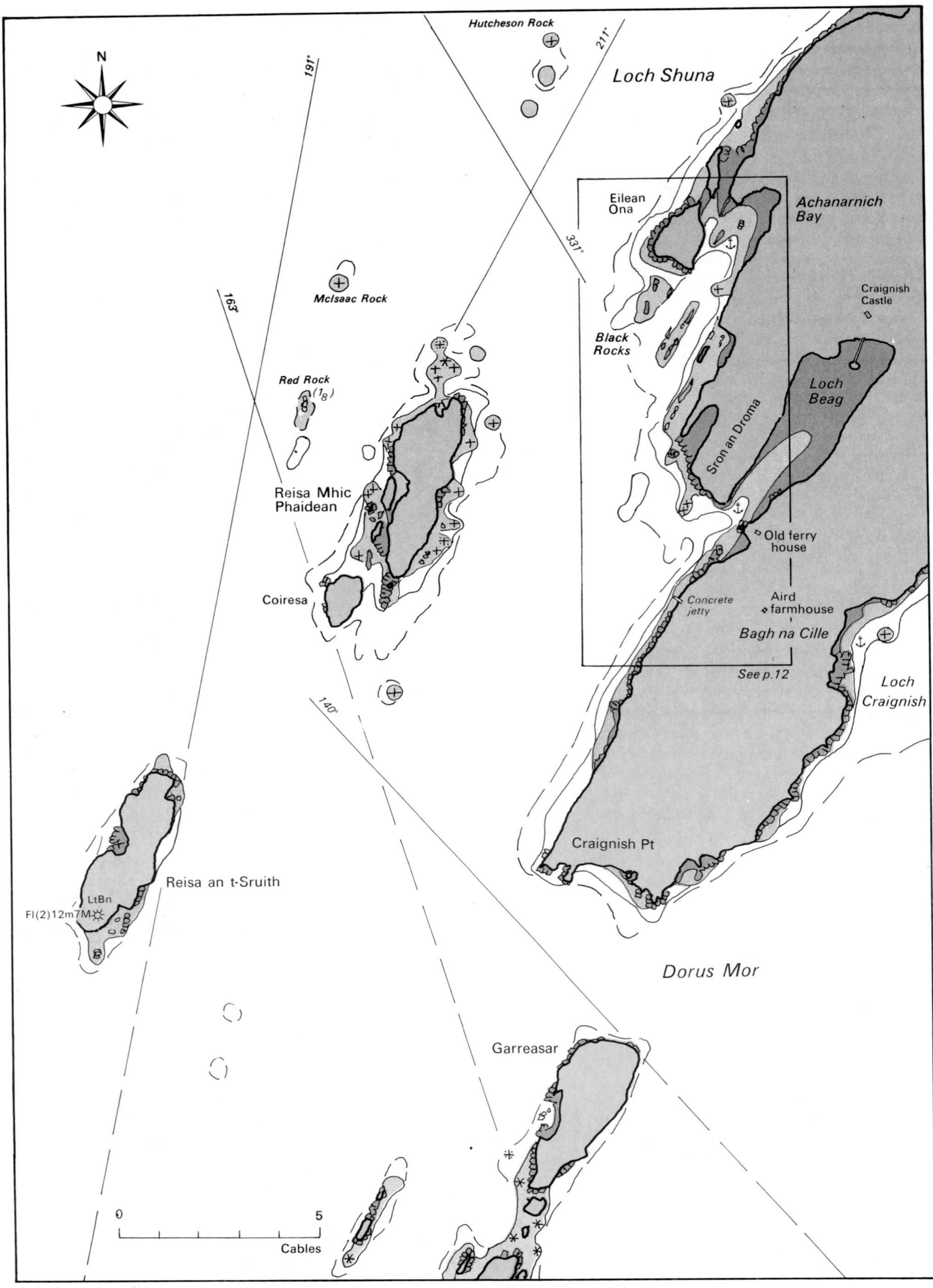
N
Hutcheson Rock
211°
191°
Loch Shuna
Eilean Ona
Achanarnich Bay
331°
Craignish Castle
McIsaac Rock
163°
Black Rocks
Red Rock
Loch Beag
Sron an Droma
Reisa Mhic Phaidean
Old ferry house
Coiresa
Concrete jetty
Aird farmhouse
Bagh na Cille
See p.12
Loch Craignish
140°
Craignish Pt
Reisa an t-Sruith
LtBn
Fl(2)12m7M
Dorus Mor
Garreasar
0
5
Cables

Dorus Mor

Tides

The main stream in the Dorus Mor runs at up to 8 knots changing as in the Sound of Luing, but at most states of the tide there are eddies, particularly on the north side, causing small whirlpools at the boundary between the eddy and main stream.

On the flood a strong branch of the stream sets across to Corryvreckan. At certain times, especially early on the flood, an eddy runs southwards on the west side of the Craignish peninsula. At the northwest point of Garreasar an eddy runs northeastwards close to the island. A strong eddy on the north side of the passage runs at the same rate as the main stream, with a sharp line separating them.

On the ebb there is an anticlockwise eddy to the south of the main passage, between Garreasar and Reisa an t-Sruith. As on the flood there is a strong eddy on the north side of the passage. In strong southerly winds there will be heavy overfalls on the ebb from Craignish Point to Ard Luing. In these conditions it would be best to wait for slack water before making this passage.

Dangers and clearing marks

Half a mile northwest of Craignish Point, towards Coiresa, is a submerged rock with 0.6 metres of water over it. Keeping the hotel at Crinan just open north of Garreasar, 140°, leads south of it.

A quarter of a mile west of Reisa Mhic Phaidean, Red Rock (Dearg Sgeir) dries 1.8 metres. McIsaac Rock, with less than 2 metres over it, is 3½ cables northward of Red Rock. These are cleared by keeping Ruadh Sgeir light beacon (to the south) touching or hidden behind the east side of Reisa an t-Sruith, 191°.

To the east of Reisa Mhic Phaidean various submerged and drying rocks on both sides of the channel are avoided by keeping near the middle of the channel. If tacking, careful chartwork will be needed.

Nearly a mile to the north of Reisa Mhic Phaidean is Hutcheson Rock with an unspecified depth, but less than 2 metres, over it; it may, in fact, be very much less. A long mark for passing southwest of it is to keep Rubha Fiola, the north end of the islands extending north from Scarba, open of the south end of Luing, 331°. An alternative line to pass southwest of the rock is to keep Aird farmhouse open of Sron an Droma at the west side of Loch Beag, 152°. To pass east of Hutcheson Rock keep Reisa an t-Sruith touching Reisa Mhic Phaidean, 211°.

Passage notes

Going north it is worth planning to be at the Dorus Mor as soon as, or slightly before, the tide turns northwards; 20 miles further north there is another tidal gate and with reasonable speed through the water a fair tide can be carried to Tobermory. Note carefully the various clearing marks described above, and take care to avoid being carried towards Corryvreckan, especially under sail in light weather.

Going south the tide presents fewer problems except in strong southerly winds when there will be heavy overfalls between Craignish Point and Scarba. If late on the tide at Dorus Mor a skilled helmsman may take advantage of the eddy by keeping close to Craignish Point.

By night or if arriving after dark at the end of a passage, Reisa Mhic Phaidean and Ruadh Sgeir light beacon in line 188° lead well clear to the west of Red Rock. You only have a few minutes to identify correctly the light at Crinan, which has a low range, and to turn to keep it in sight through the Dorus Mor. Failing this you have to go south of Ruadh Sgeir.

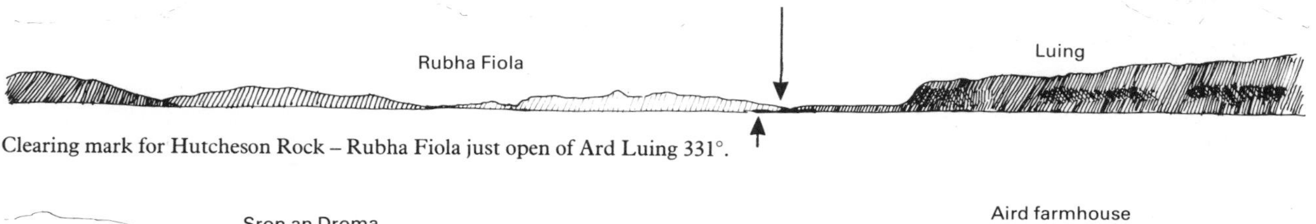

Clearing mark for Hutcheson Rock – Rubha Fiola just open of Ard Luing 331°.

Clearing mark for Hutcheson Rock – Aird farmhouse open of Sron an Droma 152° leads south of Hutcheson Rock.

Craignish Eilean Ona Reisa Mhic Phaidean Reisa an t-Sruith

Clearing mark for Hutcheson Rock – the east side of Reisa an t-Sruith touching the west side of Reisa Mhic Phaidean 211° leads southeast of Hutcheson Rock.

Anchorages
West side of Craignish Point

Loch Beag, a little more than a mile north of Craignish Point, is an occasional or temporary anchorage for settled weather. The greater part of the loch dries, so anchor just within the entrance off the old ferry house (not the concrete jetty with a red-roofed shed a quarter of a mile south of the loch).

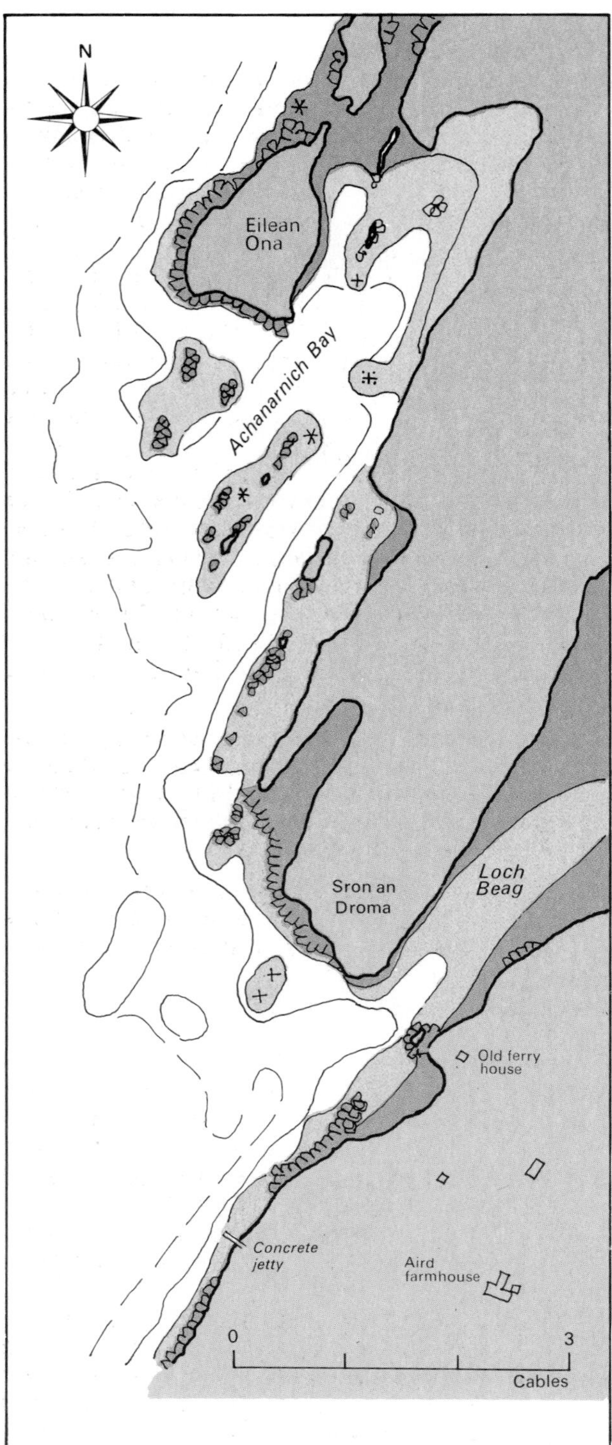

Loch Beag and Achanarnich Bay

Achanarnich

Tides run strongly across the entrances, there are many drying rocks, and the south entrance is difficult to identify. Find the passage between two lines of long low rocks and keep in the middle, on the line 025°; after passing the last rock above water on the west side of the entrance passage, alter course towards the shore to avoid a drying rock at the north end of the west line of rocks, the rock is east of the line, then head NNW towards Eilean Ona to avoid a rock awash near the shore. Anchor either side of the islet in the basin between Eilean Ona and the shore; there is a submerged rock, about 1.5 metres, half a cable south of the islet. Bottom is sand and weed.

Entering from the west by the south side of Eilean Ona the tide is more of a problem as it sets straight across the entrance. Keep 20 metres off Eilean Ona to avoid rocks close south of it; keep rather further off the southeast point of the island before turning north into the basin.

Bagh Ban nearly a mile NNE of Eilean Ona provides an anchorage in settled weather, with some shelter behind a 4-metre islet north of the middle of the bay. There is a drying rock near the north point of the drying bay east of the islet.

See also *Loch Craignish*, page 17 and *Loch Shuna*, page 20.

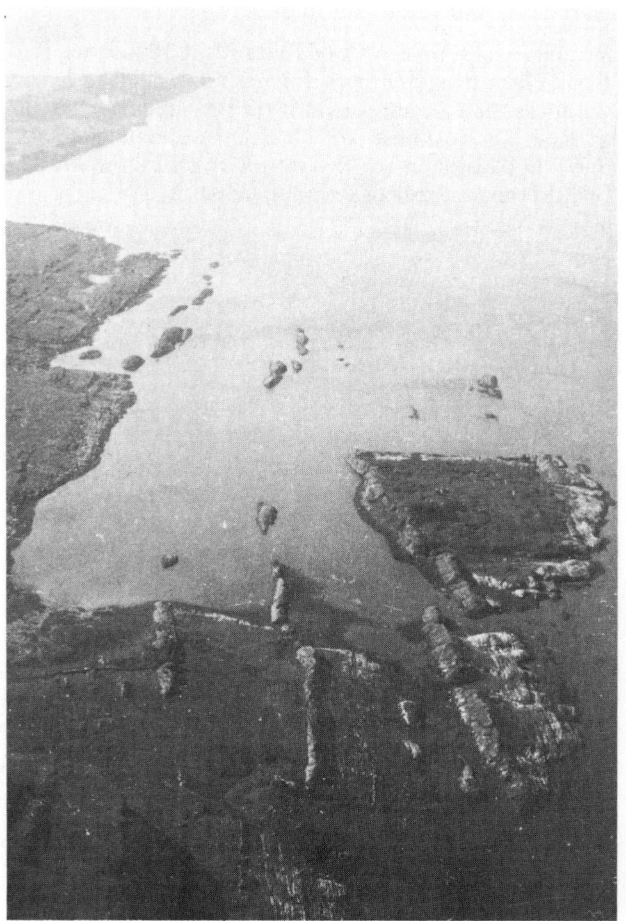

Achanarnich Bay from NNE.

Corryvreckan

56°09′N 5°43′W

The Gulf of Corryvreckan, between Scarba and the north end of Jura is one of the most notorious stretches of water anywhere around the British Isles, although it is half a mile wide, with no hazards near the surface. With one significant exception it is over 100 metres deep for the greater part of its width.

The hazardous nature of this passage is due to three factors: the strength of the current, the turbulence at the boundary of eddies on both sides (and overall whenever the tidal stream is opposed to the wind), and the presence of one rock which has a least depth over it of 29 metres.

The turbulence is not confined to the gulf itself; even in calm weather it extends several miles WNW as the flood tide meets the relatively stationary body of water further offshore. This is named on the charts as the Great Race.

Because of its width and depth, Corryvreckan takes the bulk of the tidal stream passing backwards and forwards between the north end of the Sound of Jura and the open sea. In addition to this the spring range at Loch Beag, 3 miles east of the east entrance to the gulf, is 2.1 metres, whereas at Glengarrisdale Bay, 3 miles SSW of the west entrance, it is 3.1 metres.

The turbulence is naturally greatest on the flood, particularly when the tidal stream meets a westerly wind blowing from the open sea with any accompanying swell.

The 29-metre rock rises abruptly from depths of over 60 metres two cables from the Scarba shore and it is located south of the west point of a bay a little west of halfway along the south shore of Scarba. A standing wave downstream of this rock is said to rise to 4 metres, and may combine with a westerly swell to rise to twice that height. The east face of the rock is steeper than the west, so that the standing wave is steeper and higher on the flood tide.

This rock is on the boundary of a strong eddy on the flood which runs down the west side of Scarba and into Corryvreckan. This eddy, as it rejoins the main stream abreast of the rock creates, at times, a distinct whirlpool. On the ebb an eddy of similar strength forms, also on the north side of the gulf.

Among the islands on the south side of the west entrance there are further strong currents, especially on the ebb, when an anticlockwise eddy is set up to the west of Eilean Mor; this causes severe overfalls, particularly over a submerged reef which extends a cable WNW of Eilean Mor. There are several submerged and drying rocks among these islands, and most careful chartwork is needed to avoid them.

From the above it will be obvious that the fundamental advice, especially to yachtsmen unfamiliar with the West Coast, must be to avoid Corryvreckan and to avoid being drawn accidentally into it, although under certain conditions it is passable and is often used by experienced local yachtsmen as well as by fishermen.

Tides

The flood tide runs westwards, beginning about +0430 Oban (−0100 Dover) at springs; +0515 Oban (−0015 Dover) at neaps.

The ebb runs eastwards, beginning about −0145 Oban (+0515 Dover) at springs; −0100 Oban (+0600 Dover) at neaps.

The spring rate is at least 8 knots.

Passage notes

From east to west the most favourable conditions for passing through Corryvreckan are slack water, a light to moderate fair wind, and no swell. The ebb is less violent than the flood, and it may be better to go through against the ebb, particularly near the beginning or towards the end, at the expense of having a foul tide. A further advantage is that you can beat a retreat if you find conditions uninviting at the west end; in the sheltered waters to the east of Jura it is difficult to form any idea of conditions to the west of the gulf. Bear in mind, however, that if you go through Corryvreckan on the last of the ebb, the Great Race will build up very quickly when the tide turns and you need to be clear of its track.

A passage on the flood should be considered only at neaps with a light to moderate easterly wind, and only if you are sure that there is no swell. The flood stream sets from the Sound of Jura across the gulf towards the Scarba shore and you must take care to keep within the southern half of the passage. Remember particularly the flood eddy on the north side at the west end, and keep clear of it if heading northwards.

From west to east the gulf should not be approached while the flood is running and a yacht should not be in the area at all during the flood if there is any swell. Give the northwest of Eilean Mor a wide berth especially if the ebb is well developed.

From whichever direction you are considering approaching Corryvreckan you must be sure that conditions are suitable for the passage, and unless you are certain of this, avoid it.

Anchorages

Bagh Gleann nam Muc is on the south side of the west entrance of Corryvreckan. The tidal stream provides shelter from any swell, except from northwest at slack water. Owing to the strength and uncertain direction of the currents among the islands this anchorage should only be approached or left within half an hour of slack water at springs, or within an hour at neaps.

There is a submerged rock in mid-channel east of Eilean Beag, and drying rocks near the shore on either side; there is another submerged rock 1½ cables east of Buige Rock. The head of the bay is divided by a rocky promontory; the better anchorage is on its west side.

Bagh Gleann a' Mhaoil on the southeast of Scarba provides temporary anchorage out of the main tidal stream, in which to wait for a favourable tide through the gulf.

Kinuachdrach (Kinnochtie), on the northeast corner of Jura, see page 9.

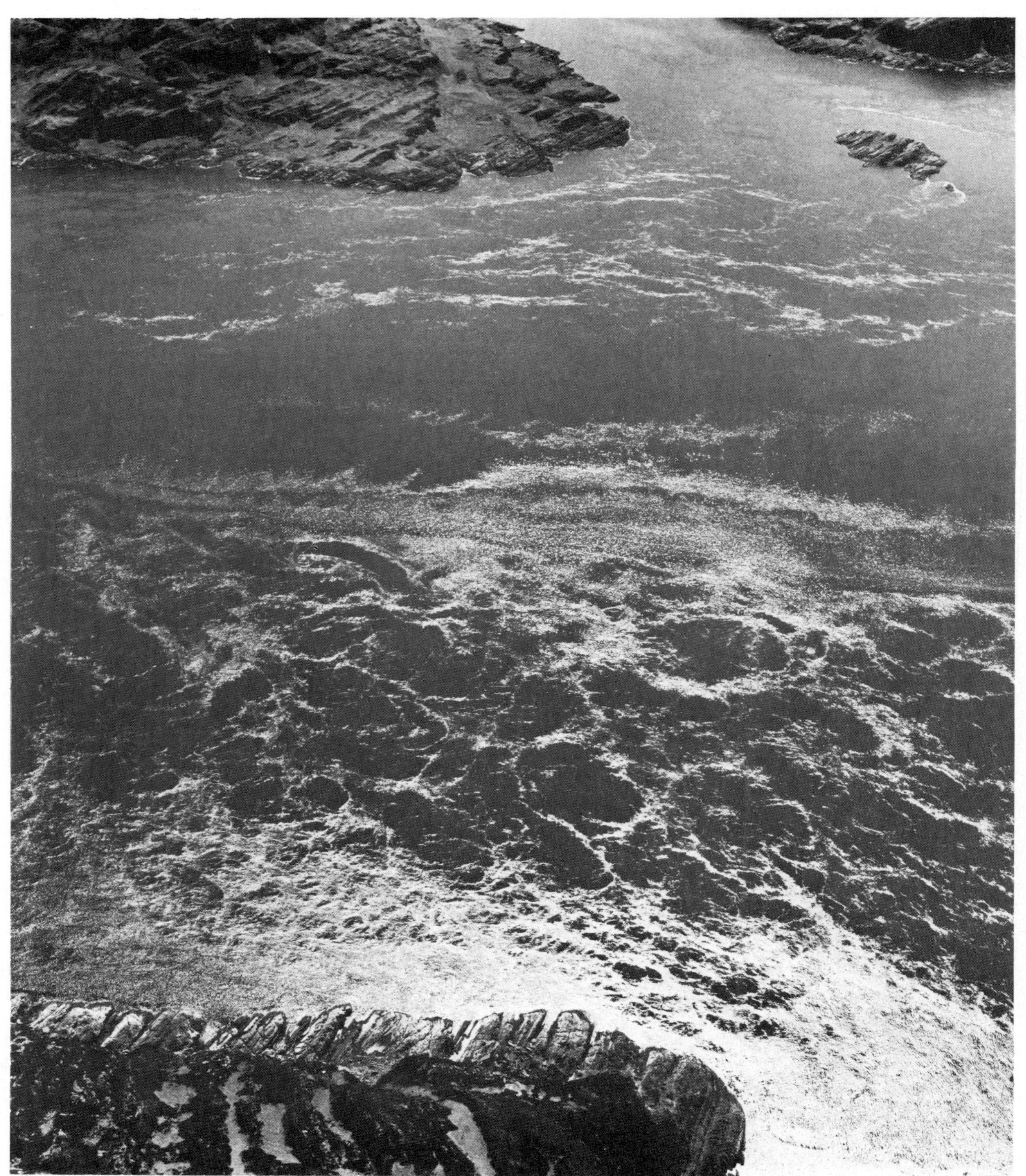

Photo: John Dewar Studios

Corryvreckan from above Scarba, looking south. Eilean Beag is top right, with the entrance to Bagh Gleann nam Muc beyond it. The tide is ebbing, so that a spring flood against a westerly wind can be imagined. The gulf is two thirds of a mile wide at this point.

Grey Dogs

56°12′N 5°43′W

Named on some charts as Bealach a' Choin Ghlais, and sometimes known as Little Corryvreckan, the passage between Lunga and the north end of Scarba is at times more hazardous than Corryvreckan itself. It is less than a cable wide at its narrowest point, with a group of islets and rocks above water in the eastern entrance. Except at slack water the eddies make it very difficult to keep a boat under control, and the ebb is more dangerous in that it tends to set a boat onto the islets. As there is less volume of water passing through, the race to the west is less extensive than at Corryvreckan.

Tides

The flood tide runs westwards, beginning about +0430 Oban (−0100 Dover) at springs; +0515 Oban (−0015 Dover) at neaps.

The ebb runs eastwards, beginning about −0145 Oban (+0515 Dover) at springs; −0100 Oban (+0600 Dover) at neaps.

The spring rate is about 8 knots.

Directions

Pass through only at slack water or with the very last of the flood. If necessary wait, on the east side just north of a jetty half a mile south of the north end of Scarba, or on the west side at Camas a' Mhor-Fhir, a deep inlet on the southwest side of Lunga.

Loch Crinan

56°06′N 5°33′W

Loch Crinan is sheltered from the open sea, but because it is shallow quite a steep chop can build up. The only good shelter outside the canal basin is in Crinan Harbour, a quarter of a mile west of the canal entrance, but this is full of moorings. In anything but heavy weather from north or west, however, good anchorage can be had near the canal entrance on a bottom of sand and clay.

Tides

Loch Beag (56°09′N 5°36′W)
Constant −0100 Oban (+0600 Dover).
Height in metres

MHWS	MHWN	MTL	MLWN	MLWS
2.4	1.7	1.4	1.1	0.3

Tidal streams east of the 10-metre contour are slight.

Landmarks

From north of west the hotel at Crinan, a large white building, is conspicuous. Duntrune Castle, on the north side of the loch, tends to merge into the background.

Approach

From southward keep at least half a cable off Ardnoe Point.

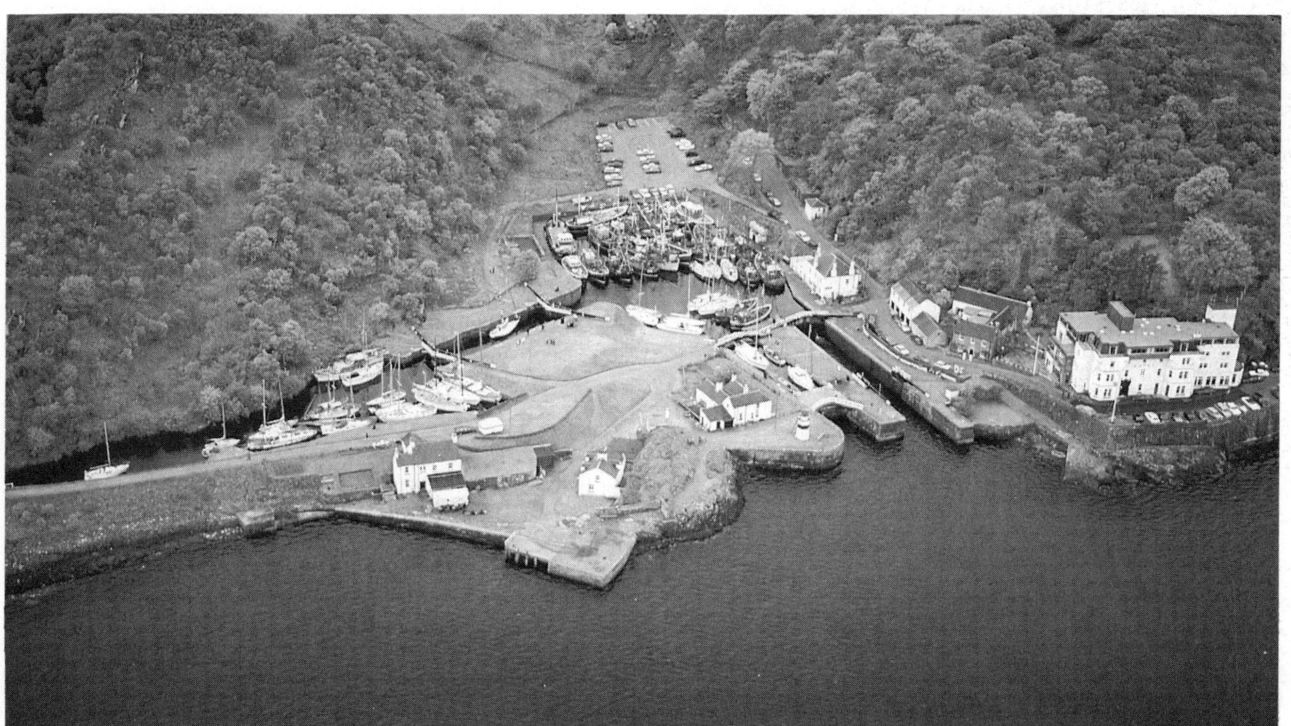

Crinan from north. The pier is on the left and the sea lock, the bottom gates of which are open, is right of centre. The hotel is on the right, with a stone slipway below its left-hand corner. The canal basin is almost completely full of fishing boats, as it is a Saturday. A yacht is in Lock 14 beyond the pier.

From the Dorus Mor make for the hotel.

From Loch Craignish either pass southwest of Eilean nan Coinean (Rabbit Island), or east of it, keeping at least a cable off Scodaig, the point of the mainland here, to avoid submerged rocks southwest of the point. A rock half a cable off the east side of Rabbit Island is normally above water but may be covered by a very high tide.

Black Rock, 2 cables north of the hotel, has a drying reef extending half a cable east of it. The head of the loch dries up to half a mile, roughly on a line joining Duntrune Castle to the two islands at the head of the loch and continuing to a point two cables east of the canal entrance.

Lights

At night the light beacon at the canal entrance shows Fl.WG.3s8m4M, white from the shore to 146° and green from 146° clockwise to the shore. The white sector leads close southwest of Rabbit Island and well southwest of Black Rock.

There are lights on either side of the sea lock entrance, 2F.R(vert) on the east side and 2F.G(vert) on the west side.

Anchorages

Crinan Harbour is full of moorings but it may be possible to arrange to use one of them; contact M. Murray before leaving a boat on any mooring (although a few belong to Crinan Boats). There is a pontoon for temporary berthing on the east side of the harbour with water laid on, and small quantities of diesel are available, but there may not be depth alongside at all states of tide.

Crinan, anchor off the hotel as convenient, keeping clear of the approach both to the canal lock and to the pier. Yachts may berth temporarily at the pier, but a fishing boat may park unceremoniously on top of you. Permission should be sought from the head lock-keeper to remain alongside. The pier is rough and it is difficult to protect a yacht without fender boards. If anchored off, the best landing is at a slip on the west side of the canal lock, but it is inconvenient at low tide.

Canal basin – often very full of fishing boats, especially at weekends and yachts may be subject to minor damage. If staying even overnight it may be best to berth above the next lock. To leave a boat for several nights or longer it is best to anchor or moor in Bellanoch Lagoon, two miles along the canal; consult the lock-keeper.

Crinan Canal

The sea lock is normally left open, day and night, and you can usually go straight in unless it is filling or emptying or you are directed to stand off. Make ready warps and fenders before approaching. There is a ladder on the west side; you can expect to go alongside to starboard, but be prepared to be directed to the other side. There is often quite a strong current out of the lock due to the runoff from the canal, so it is best to get the bow warp ashore first; however if the lock-keeper is standing by to take your warps he may insist on taking the stern warp, in which case keep some way on to stem the current and avoid being swung across the lock. There may be no-one to take ropes at all, so have a crew member ready to go up the ladder. Ropes should be led well fore and aft to keep the boat under control.

If there is a shortage of water (which, although it may seem surprising in the Scottish climate, is not uncommon) the use of the sea lock may be limited to half-tide and above.

The lock is operated by a lock-keeper. While the lock is filling keep both warps tight; the bow warp may have to be led to a winch or windlass to control the boat.

The next lock up from the basin, No. 14, has very rough sides and needs extra care with fenders. At all 'inland' locks it is usual to take the stern warp ashore first to check way on entering the lock, but during and after heavy rain there may be a strong current out of the lock.

Hours of operation for the canal are as follows, Monday to Saturday inclusive: sea locks 0600–2130; inland locks and bridges 0800–1615 with a lunch break from 1200–1230. Locking may be arranged outside these hours and on some Sundays at extra cost.

River Add in the southeast corner of the loch is only suitable for shoal-draught boats, and is only accessible in quiet weather, although well sheltered once inside. There is a bar at the river mouth between drying sands, and the position of the channel is completely invisible when there is enough water to enter. I have taken a Folkboat in here, and anyone wanting to try it with a shoal-draught boat should keep Black Rock astern in line with the 11-metre islet at the south end of Garreasar (off Craignish Point) 304°; this should lead to the north side of the channel at the bar. When you have almost run out of water turn to head for the tangent of the west side of the river bank and feel your way in. There is a pool with 2 metres off the old ferry slip on the west side.

Gallanach Bay on the north side of the loch, northwest of Duntrune Castle, is a pleasant anchorage in offshore winds.

Services and supplies at Crinan

Fully equipped boatyard, chandlery and chart agent (Crinan Boats). Diesel by hose at the west side of the canal basin; ask at the coffee shop. Water hose at corner of coffee shop. *Calor Gas* at chandlery. Refuse disposal; skip at southwest corner of basin. Petrol pumps near sea lock. Garage at Bellanoch. A diver can be arranged for. Moorings laid and serviced by M. Murray.

Limited range at chandlery and at coffee shop; greater range at Bellanoch, two miles along canal. Hotel with restaurant, and coffee shop beside canal basin for those of more modest means.

Communications Phone box beside canal basin. Post office at Bellanoch. Crinan Boats watches on VHF Ch 16 during working hours. Head lock-keeper uses CB; it is intended to have VHF R/T installed during 1987.

☎ all Crinan (054 683)
Crinan Boats 232
Crinan Hotel 235
Lock-keeper 211
M. Murray 238

Loch Craignish

56°10′N 5°33′W

This is an ideal West Coast loch, with easy access, a variety of anchorages, and splendid scenery. The drawbacks are the squalls which come with the scenery and, for those who like solitude, the popularity of the loch. The east side is wild and, in a modest way, mountainous, and the west side relatively highly populated. On each side there is a string of islands, with a navigable channel behind those on the east side but not on the west. There is a well established yacht centre at the head of the loch with pontoons, and moorings are usually available.

The two main islands on the east side are Eilean Macaskin and Eilean Righ, and those on the west side Eilean Dubh and Eilean Mhic Chrion.

There may be severe squalls in easterly and northeasterly winds, especially near the east side of the loch, and westerly winds can produce surprises at times, particularly close under the lee of islands.

Tides

Loch Beag (56°09′N 5°36′W)
Constant −0100 Oban (+0600 Dover).
Height in metres

MHWS	MHWN	MTL	MLWN	MLWS
2.4	1.7	1.4	1.1	0.3

The height of tide is very much affected by wind and barometric pressure, and a strong southwesterly may raise the tide 1 metre higher than predicted in tide tables, and a strong northeasterly depress it, although to a lesser extent. Tidal streams throughout the loch are generally no more than 1 knot.

Approach

The main fairway is almost entirely free from hazards, other than very close inshore, although if coming from Crinan, or tacking, note that a reef extends over a cable SSW of the eastern chain of islands, but the tip of the reef is normally above water. In strong southerly winds, particularly on the ebb, there are moderate overfalls abreast of Eilean Macaskin. A rock 1½ cables SSW of Eilean Dubh is normally above water, but could be covered by a high tide, and needs to be watched out for if tacking. To the east of the northeast end of Eilean Mhic Chrion, Sgeir Dubh, 0.6 metre high, has shoal water extending at least half a cable all round it.

The passage on the east side of the loch has a number of submerged rocks of unspecified depth, particularly off the southeast side of Eilean Macaskin and off the northeast end of Eilean Righ. The first are cleared by keeping east of mid-channel when approaching the narrowest part at Eilean Macaskin, and the second by standing well on towards the mainland before altering course towards Sgeir Dubh. There are many fish cages in this channel, and they are thought to be encroaching beyond the area designated for them.

Anchorages

Goat Island (Eilean nan Gabhar), between Eilean Macaskin and Eilean Righ. Approach from the eastern channel, although local boats do use the passage through the reef to the north of Goat Island. If attempting this, note a rock awash off the southwest point of Eilean Righ; there is deep water between it and the point. The passage south of Goat Island has a least depth of 0.9 metres and a bottom of clean sand. There is limited swinging room and depth between Goat Island and the skerry, but look out for a partly submerged reef extending east from Goat Island. The bottom is sand with some clay.

Goat island from the east showing the passage north of it on the right, and the submerged reef which extends northeast from the east side of Goat Island.

Eilean Righ, off the east side of the middle of the island, opposite the old farmhouse.

In easterly winds shelter may be found in bays on the east side of the channel, if space can be found clear of the fish cages. Anchor as close inshore as possible to gain some shelter from the trees.

Loch Craignish from the east side, looking northwest. Goat Island is on the left, and Eilean Dubh upper right.

Bagh na Cille, on the west side of the loch, about a mile northeast of Craignish Point is suitable for quiet weather, but there is a drying reef towards the southwest side of the bay, and a 2.4-metre submerged rock one cable off the middle of the bay.

Eilean Dubh, in an area sometimes known as *The Lagoon* between Eilean Dubh and Eilean Mhic Chrion and the Craignish peninsula. Approach between the two islands, not (for the benefit of anyone foolish enough to be cruising here without a detailed chart) through any opening facing south. There is a rock awash nearly ½ cable ESE of the 1-metre high rock in the middle of the gap; keep at least a cable offshore until the 1-metre rock is abaft the beam before turning to pass north of the rock. Anchor anywhere clear of moorings. A commercial developer is proposing to fill the lagoon with moorings.

Ardfern

A well established yacht centre at the north end of Eilean Mhic Chrion. It is well sheltered except from strong northeast winds; many yachts are left on moorings here over the winter. There is almost no space for anchoring as the whole area is taken up with moorings. An apparently inviting space towards the north end is occupied by a drying rock with a rock awash ¼ cable east of it; these rocks are ½ cable south of the smaller and more southerly of two tidal islets close to the mainland.

Approach

Note the above-water rock, Sgeir Dubh, with shoal water round it. The passage north of Eilean Inshaig, which is east of the moorings, is straightforward. In the south passage a shoal spit extends further south from Inshaig than the chart would suggest; I've helped to haul two boats off this spit. There are moorings in this passage, and if the boats on them are lying to a southerly wind it would be rash to go under their sterns. There are new pontoons at the south end of the bay and a berth can usually be found alongside, either temporarily or overnight.

Loch Craignish from the same hill, looking north. Eilean Macaskin is in the middle of the photo with the lagoon beyond it on the left, Eilean Mhic Chrion is beyond, and Ardfern above the right-hand end of Macaskin.

Ardfern from above, looking southeast. Eilean Inshaig is on the left, and the shoal spit extends perhaps halfway out to the moored yachts in the entrance. Black Rock is above the end of Eilean Mhic Chrion, upper right.

Services and supplies

Ardfern Yacht Centre provides moorings and has a mobile hoist and laying up space ashore. Trailer-sailers can be launched at the slip. Repairs under cover; engineer. Diesel and water at pontoons; chandlery and *Calor Gas* at head of pier. Petrol at the hotel ¼ mile to the south. Refuse disposal. Showers. Two small shops; hotel, restaurant, bar, all ¼ mile to the south.

Communications Phone box beside hotel. VHF Ch 16 is watched by Ardfern Yacht Centre during working hours.
☎ all Barbreck (085 25)
Ardfern Yacht Centre 247
Galley of Lorne Hotel 284

Loch Shuna

56°13′N 5°35′W

The area east of Luing is sheltered except from strong southerly winds, and the surrounding shores are rather more gentle in character than much of the rest of the coast; there is a large residential development and marina at Craobh on the east shore. The east side of Shuna island is clean except for a rock awash northeast of the landing place for Shuna House, towards the north end. There are several dangers well off the east shore of the loch, as described below. The waters to the south of the south end of Luing are described on pages 7–14.

Tides

Loch Beag (56°09′N 5°36′W)
Constant −0100 Oban (+0600 Dover).
Height in metres

MHWS	MHWN	MTL	MLWN	MLWS
2.4	1.7	1.4	1.1	0.3

Seil Sound (56°17′N 5°36′W)
Constant −0025 Oban (−0555 Dover).
Height in metres

MHWS	MHWN	MTL	MLWN	MLWS
2.7	2.0	1.6	1.1	0.4

Tidal streams are generally negligible except in Shuna Sound where they reach 1 knot on the flood and 2 knots on the ebb.

Dangers and clearing marks

At the south entrance to Loch Shuna, Culbhaie, a group of rocks ¼ mile off the east shore, dries 1.5 metres with other rocks within ½ cable of its west side. These are cleared to the west by keeping Kilchoan Farm, a conspicuous white house on the north side of Loch Melfort bearing 011°, open west of Eilean Creagach, the most westerly island in Loch Shuna, about a mile south of Asknish Point. Alternatively, the east side of Reisa an t-Sruith bearing 208°, open of the west side of Reisa Mhic Phaidean, clears the west side of Culbhaie.

The passage between Shuna and the two main islands to the east is clean except for a rock awash northeast of Shuna. East of these islands careful attention to the chart is needed, although a direct passage from southward of Eilean Creagach to Craobh Haven or to Asknish Bay is straightforward. These will be described under *Anchorages*, below.

Shuna Sound is generally clean on the Shuna side, but there are rocks off the Luing shore both submerged and drying, notably off its south end and off a drying bay a mile north of the south end; the 15-metre contour will keep you clear of these.

A mile north of Shuna, Scoul Eilean has a rock awash 1 cable south of its south end and a submerged rock close southeast of the island. Degnish Point at the south of the entrance to Seil Sound has several drying and submerged rocks off its west and south sides.

Loch Melfort is the northeast branch of Loch Shuna, north of Asknish. Campbell Rock in the middle of the loch has 1.8 metres over it, but for most boats this would rarely be a hazard. The south side of Eilean Gamhna touching the north point of Shuna 245° leads southeast of Campbell Rock. On the north side of the loch, Eilean Coltair has a drying reef extending 1 cable from its south end and a drying rock 1 cable from its east side. There is a rock 2 metres high nearly half a mile east of Eilean Coltair. Other hazards in Loch Melfort are within half a cable of the shore, or within bays and anchorages where they will be referred to separately.

Culbhaie clearing mark – Reisa an t-Sruith just open west of Eilean Mhic Phaidean leads west of Culbhaie 208°.

Approach

From south see *Passage notes* for Dorus Mor (page 9). Note clearing marks described above to avoid Culbhaie which dries 1.5 metres, ¼ mile from the east shore. Pass between Shuna and the islands to the east of it, or through Shuna Sound, to the west of Shuna.

From west keep 2 cables off Ard Luing, or outwith the 15-metre contour. To the north of Shuna and the Asknish peninsula note the various hazards described above. If waiting here for a fair tide in the Sound of Luing, there is a temporary anchorage off a bay ¼ mile north of Ard Luing – not the bay 1 mile north of the point, off which there are many rocks.

Craobh Haven

56°12′.5N 5°33′W

A new development on the east side of Loch Shuna with all conveniences. The name is pronounced 'creuve'.

Approach

From west, leaving the green conical buoy north of Eilean an Duin to starboard. If this buoy is not in place keep at least a cable north of the island. Note an extensive patch of drying and submerged rocks ¼ mile north of Eilean Buidhe. There are many drying rocks inshore and to the NNE of Eilean Buidhe. Inside the entrance a line of red can buoys marks submerged rocks on the east side. In the bay on the west side of the harbour a drying reef projecting over half the width of the bay from its north side is marked by a perch. Craobh Haven at present makes no charge for daytime use of pontoon berths.

Services and supplies

Pontoon berths, boatyard (Camus Marine) with slip and mobile hoist. Divers, refuse disposal, showers, laundrette. Water, diesel, *Calor Gas*, chandlery. Shop, pub/restaurant, coffee shop.

Communications Phone box. Bus to Oban only three times per week.
☎ Craobh Haven (085 25) 222
Camus Marine (085 25) 225

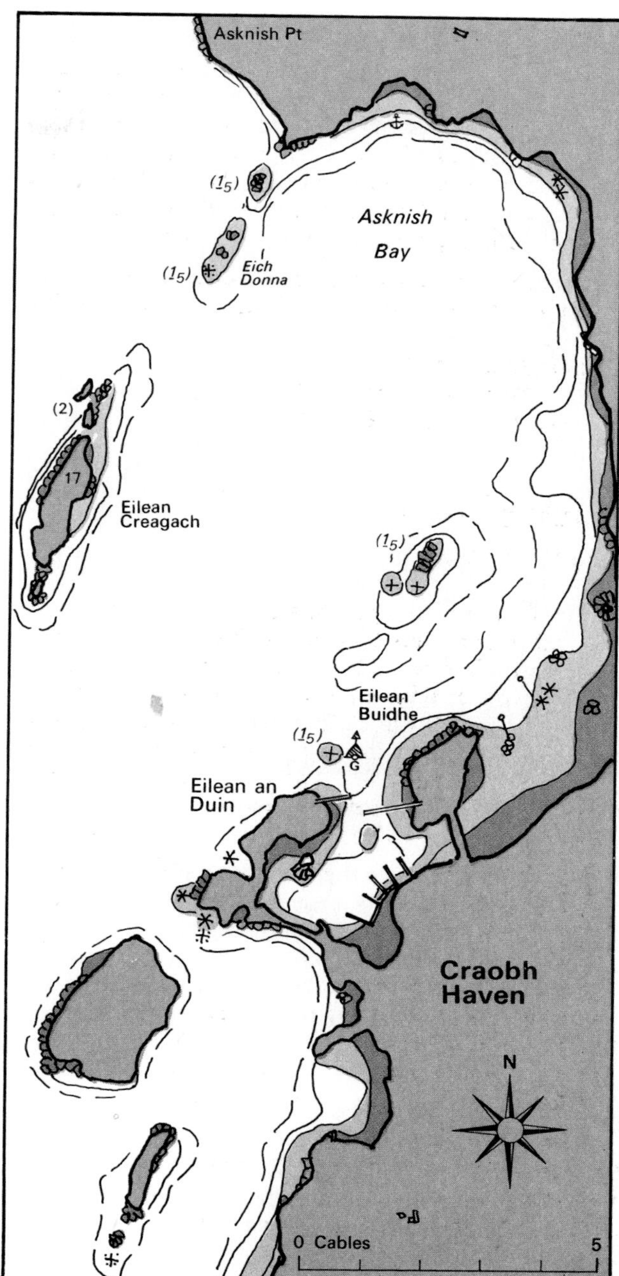

Craobh Haven

Anchorages

Asknish Bay (56°14′N 5°33′W) Approach from south, but take care to avoid the drying rocks 3 cables off the east shore. A line of drying rocks, Eich Donna, extends 3 cables SSW from the Asknish peninsula towards Eilean Creagach, and a drying reef extends over half a cable NNE from the islet at the north end of Eilean Creagach with a clear passage ¼ mile wide between the reef and Eich Donna. Some local yachtsmen use a passage between the most northerly rock, which dries 1.5 metres, and Asknish, keeping about 20 metres from the shore.

Anchor as convenient, clear of moorings in sand and weed; or, if visiting the hotel, use one of the moorings provided for visitors. The best landing is in a crack in the rocky promontory south of the hotel. An alternative anchorage north of Asknish Point is preferable in southerly winds.

The hotel has a restaurant and provides bar lunches and showers. ☎ Kilmelford (085 22) 233.

Kilchattan Bay (Toberonochy), 56°13′N 5°38′W, on the east side of Luing, nearly 2 miles north of the south point of the island. Much of the bay is shoal but it is usually possible to anchor north of the village. Several buoys in the bay mark experimental equipment and should be given a wide berth. There is a post office, but no provisions apart from an occasional van.

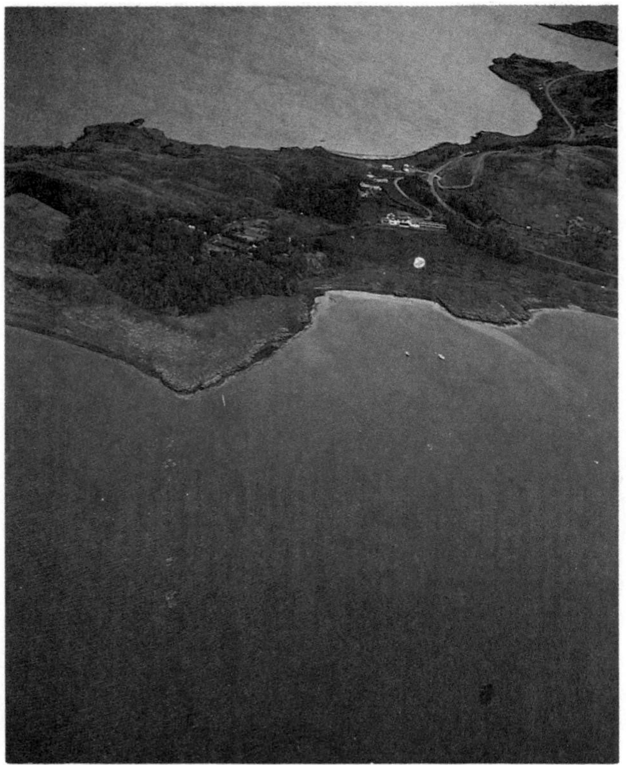

Asknish Bay from southwest – Eich Donna is on the left.

At the north end of Shuna there is a bay with the remains of a stone quay on its west side. Coming from the east, take care to avoid a submerged rock over ½ cable north of the east point of the bay. Anchor no further in than abreast of the quay, as the head of the bay is shoal with a drying reef on its southwest side.

Loch Melfort

Asknish, in a bay ½ mile ENE of the west point of Asknish. A rock in the middle of the bay, ½ cable from the high-water line, dries 1.5 metres and there are visitors' moorings for the hotel to the west of it. For hotel see page 21.

Kames Bay, on the south side of the loch, nearly 2 miles from Asknish Point behind a promontory with several bungalows on it facing west. Much of the southwest side of the bay dries and there is a group of rocks, with an area of deep water between them and the drying foreshore, but most of the best water is taken up by moorings.

On the south side of the bay is a concrete pier with a rock drying 1.8 metres northwest of it. Most of the rest of the bay is occupied by fish cages.

Fearnach Bay and Loch na Cille

56°16′N 5°30′W

In both of these bays there are moorings, some of which may be available for visitors, and limited space for anchoring.

Dangers and marks

A drying rock ½ cable off the west side of Fearnach Bay is marked by a white perch with a red triangular topmark.

At the entrance to Loch na Cille a red perch with a red can topmark stands on the end of a reef on the north side, and a green perch with a green triangular topmark stands on a rock on the south side.

Lights

At night lights on the pier in Fearnach Bay 2F.R(vert) are shown between 1 April and 31 October.

Services and supplies

The pier in Fearnach Bay has a 13-metre pontoon at the end with 2 metres depth alongside. Yachts may dry out alongside the pier for repairs (within the limitations of the tidal range); ask first at the office. Water, diesel and gas are available at the pier, and mains electricity can be provided. Showers and laundry are ¾ mile northeast of the pier. Moorings for hire.

In Loch na Cille the pier, on the south side, has a floating pontoon with diesel and water. Chandlery, *Calor Gas*, repairs to engine, hull and rigging. Moorings for hire; slipping, and winter storage ashore.

Shop, post office and hotel at Kilmelford, 1 mile from Loch na Cille, or 1½ miles from Fearnach pier.

The bay on the north side of Asknish Point. The drying rock is off a slight promontory with a fence.

Communications Phone box at Kilmelford. VHF Chs 16 and 37 answered by *Melfort Marine*.
☎ Loch Melfort Estate (Fearnach) (085 22) 257
Camus Marine (Loch na Cille) (085 22) 248, 279.

Ardinamar

56°15′N 5°37′W

A small bay between the northeast side of Luing and Torsa, west of Degnish Point. This is one of the most popular anchorages on the West Coast, with a very tricky entrance between drying rocks, although it has recently been made much easier with two steel perches erected by the CCC. There is a sill at the entrance with a depth of less than 1 metre at chart datum.

Approach

From the south keep at least ½ cable offshore to avoid drying reefs inshore and fish traps. The perches are painted green with triangular topmarks and may be difficult to pick out against the shore; take care not to go too far north before identifying them.

From the north keep a cable off the southeast side of Torsa and do not cross the 5-metre contour until the perches have been identified.

Pass 10 to 20 metres south of both perches; neither of them is on the extremity of the rock which it marks. If the perches are not seen approach very cautiously, keeping a conspicuous white paint mark on the west side of the bay just open of the south point of the entrance, bearing 290° and hold this bearing until the bay opens up.

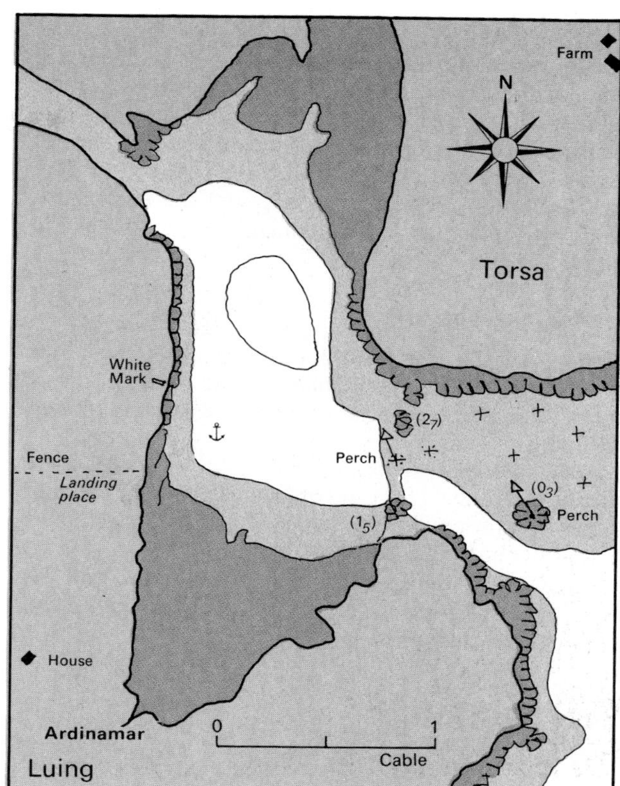

Ardinamar

Ardinamar from southeast.

Anchorage

Anchor north of a line that joins the rock off the south point of the entrance to a fence on the west shore as most of the bay dries south of this line. A strong tide runs through the gap between Luing and Torsa Beag at the northwest end of the bay for two hours after HW and the bottom between this gap and the entrance is deep, with soft mud. It is quite usual for yachts there to drag.

Services and supplies

Water tap at the house; shop, post office and phone box at Cullipool, 1½ miles. *Calor Gas* at Cuan Ferry, 2 miles. 'The Buttery' restaurant, as well as a tearoom, at Cullipool.

Irene Maclachlan has kept a visitors' book at the farmhouse since 1949, recording every yacht which comes into the anchorage, and it is customary for crews to visit her and sign the book.

There are splendid views over Cuan Sound and the Firth of Lorne from the remains of an Iron Age fort on a hill behind the house.

Seil Sound

56°17′N 5°36′W

Entered between Degnish Point and Torsa, Seil Sound runs north between Seil and the mainland, and narrows abruptly to become Clachan Sound. Towards its north end it is crossed by a single arch bridge built in the late 18th century. The bridge is being damaged by convoys of tourist coaches, and will no doubt be supplemented by a new bridge.

Beyond the bridge the passage dries completely, and a telephone cable crosses it south of the bridge, at a level slightly lower than the crown of the arch. Some years ago a Hunter 19 negotiated this passage at HW springs without lowering its mast, but it is really only passable by shoal-draught boats with masts which can be easily lowered (or motor boats with well protected propellers), and then only at HW springs. For such boats it may be a welcome alternative to a lively passage in the Firth of Lorne. The shallowest part of the channel is at the north entrance where it had become blocked with waste from a small slate quarry there. Details of that end of the channel are discussed on page 37.

Tides

Constant −0025 Oban (−0555 Dover).

Height in metres

MHWS	MHWN	MTL	MLWN	MLWS
2.7	2.0	1.6	1.1	0.4

Dangers

At the north end of Torsa there are rocks awash and submerged, 1 and 2 cables respectively NNE of the point.

Drying rocks extend a cable SSW of Ardmaddy Point on the east side of the sound.

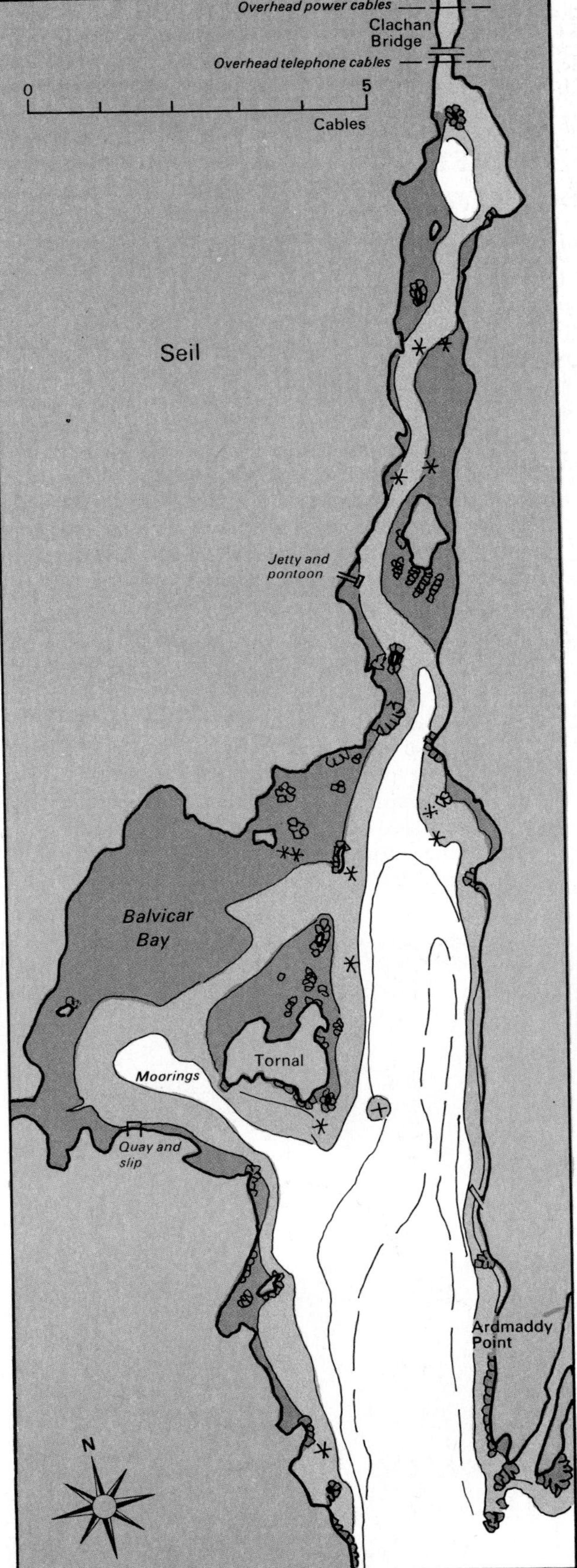

Seil Sound

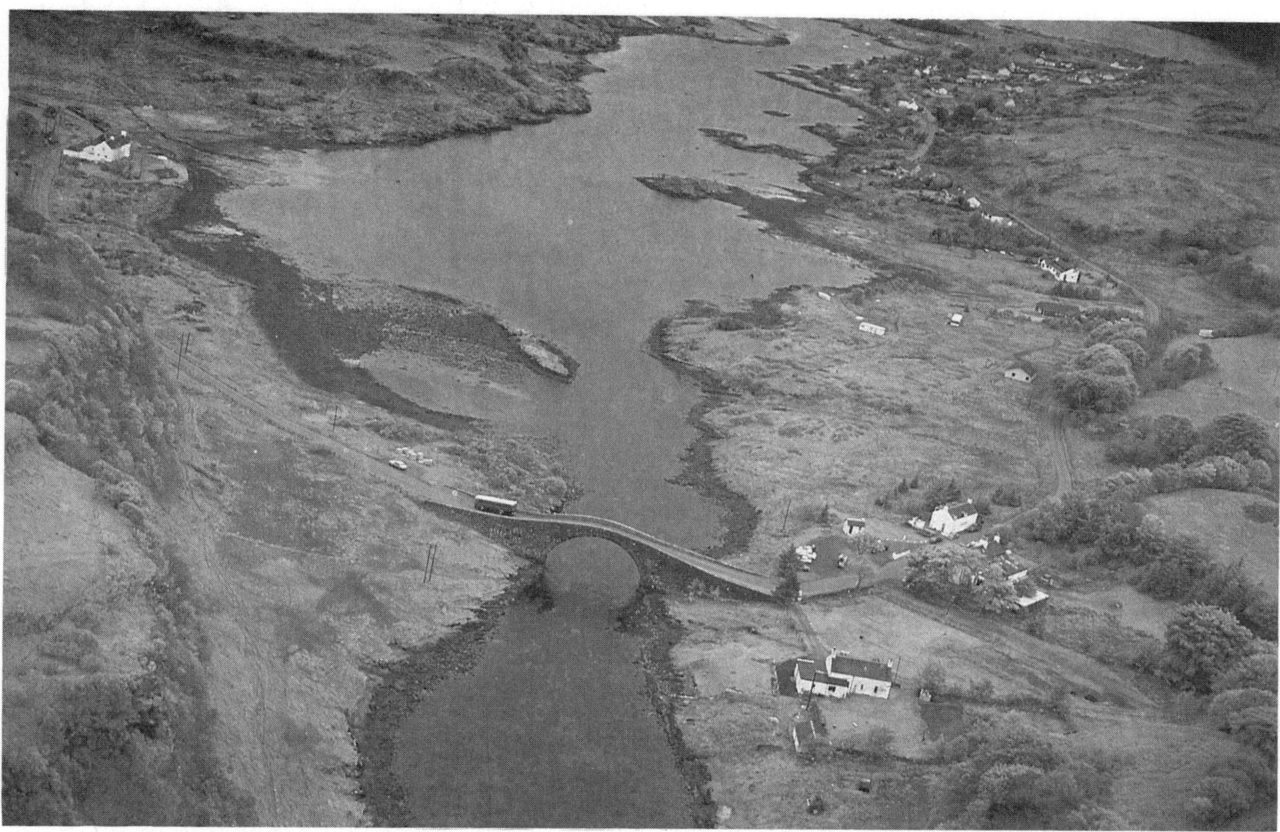

Clachan Sound from northeast.

Balvicar Bay at the north end of Seil Sound is completely sheltered but much of it dries out. Most of the area west of Eilean Tornal is occupied by moorings. The channel east of Eilean Tornal is clean except for a submerged rock nearly a cable ESE of the south end of the island. Two cables beyond the north end of the island there are drying and above-water rocks on both sides.

Services and supplies

Boatyard (Fairhurst and Raymond Ltd) has moorings, diesel, *Calor Gas*, water, repairs, pier for drying out, 10-ton crane. ☎ Balvicar (085 23) 412.

Diesel and water at Clachan-Seil Marine pontoon, on the west side of Clachan Sound, ½ mile north of Balvicar Bay. Petrol at Clachan Bridge. Shop at Balvicar. Pub at Clachan Bridge, 2 miles.

Communications Post office, phone box. Bus to Oban.

Cuan Sound

56°16′N 5°38′W

The dogleg passage between Seil and Luing provides a convenient passage between Lochs Shuna and Melfort and the Firth of Lorne, but it has some dangers and needs much greater care than the Sound of Luing. Tides run strongly with eddies on both sides, and overfalls at the west entrance with a west wind against the flood tide. The sound is crossed by overhead power cables which have clear headroom of 35 metres.

From the west the entrance is most easily identified by the pylons of the overhead cable, but they are pale in colour and not always easy to see.

Tides

The flood tide runs westwards, beginning about +0430 Oban (−0100 Dover) at springs, +0515 Oban (−0015 Dover) at neaps.

The ebb runs eastwards, beginning about −0145 Oban (+0515 Dover) at springs, −0100 Oban (+0600 Dover) at neaps.

The spring rate in both directions is 7 knots.

Seil Sound
Constant −0025 Oban (−0555 Dover).
Height in metres

MHWS	MHWN	MTL	MLWN	MLWS
2.7	2.0	1.6	1.1	0.4

Firth of Lorne (as Carsaig, Mull)
Constant −0010 Oban (−0540 Dover).
Height in metres

MHWS	MHWN	MTL	MLWN	MLWS
4.1	3.1	2.4	1.8	0.6

Dangers and marks

North of Torsa there are rocks awash and submerged, 1 and 2 cables respectively NNE of the point. In the east reach there are many submerged and drying rocks up to ¾ cable off each shore.

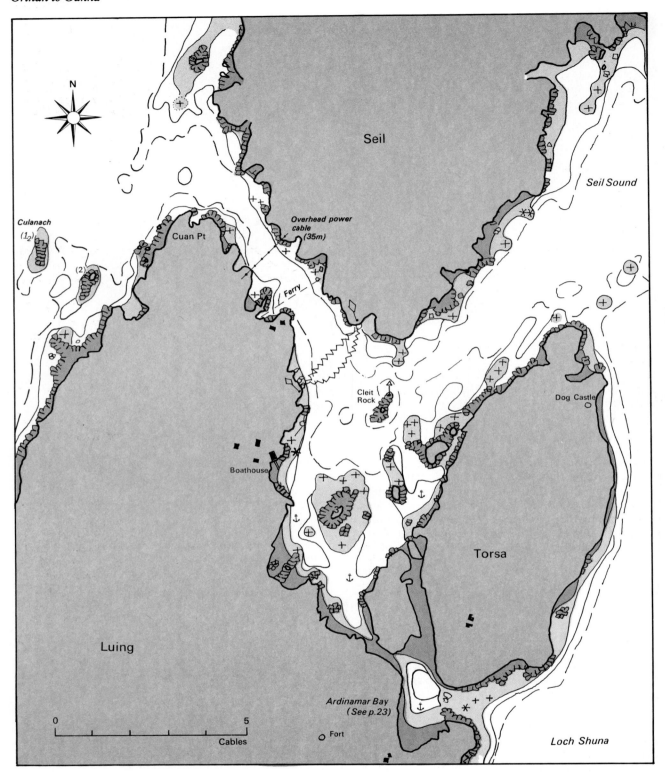

Cuan Sound

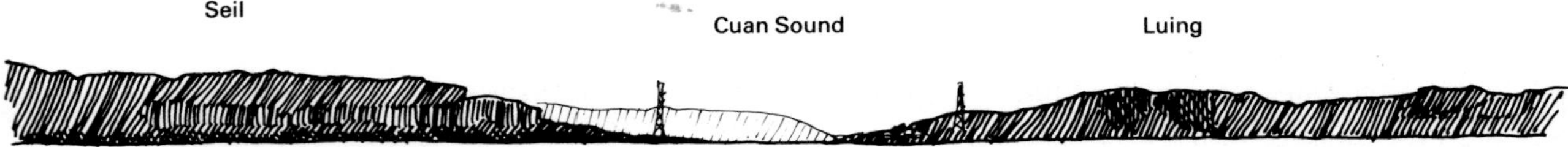

Cuan Sound from westward. The pylons are pale in colour and often not easy to see.

Cuan Sound – Cleit Rock from ENE. The perch is not at its outer end.

At the bend in the sound Cleit Rock (An Cleiteadh), 1½ cables south of the south point of Seil, has a yellow perch with a triangular topmark, maintained by the CCC. The perch is not easy to see when approaching from the east, but should be in line with the south end of a group of houses on the Luing shore ahead. Cleit Rock shows as two separate rocks at HW, and a drying reef extends a few metres north of the perch.

Between the perch and Seil there is a rock awash (a little nearer to Seil than to the perch) and a submerged rock between the awash rock and Seil. The clear passage between Cleit Rock and the awash rock is, at the most, ¾ cable, and the currents will make it difficult to hold a steady course.

At the west entrance there is a submerged rock with a depth of 1.1 metres, 1 cable west of the north point of the entrance. WSW of the west entrance Culanach, a large rock drying 1.2 metres is about ¼ mile from the shore.

Directions

From east, going westwards keep ¼ cable northeast of the north point of Torsa to pass inshore of the rock awash 1 cable off the point, or alternatively at least ¼ mile off the point to pass outside both rocks. If taking the inshore passage keep on a course north of west from the point to avoid a submerged rock 1.8 metres, a cable west of the point.

Thereafter keep mid-channel in the east reach of the sound. Cleit Rock beacon must be identified approximately in line with the south end of a group of houses on the shore of Luing, ahead. Pass ¼ to ½ cable north of the beacon, where eddies will make steering particularly difficult, and keep heading for the Luing shore until the west reach is well open.

Keep in mid-channel in the west reach and at the west entrance head about 280° for half a mile towards a point midway between the south end of Easdale Island and the islet Dubh fheith, before altering course. Be ready for overfalls at the west entrance if there is much westerly wind.

From west identify the entrance by the electricity cable pylons and approach with the entrance bearing about 100°. If approaching from Easdale Sound, keep west of a line joining Easdale Sound to the south pylon, to clear the submerged rock north of the entrance.

Cleit Rock beacon is easier to identify from this direction. Steer towards it and alter course to pass north of the rock; however because of the orientation of the rock the ebb tide is deflected to set strongly across the north end of Cleit Rock.

Keep in mid-channel in the east reach and, if heading south after leaving the sound, you can take the passage inside the rocks off the north end of Torsa as described above.

In either direction you can pass south of Cleit Rock. There are submerged rocks half a cable southeast of the rock, so keep within ¼ cable of Cleit Rock on that side.

Anchorages

There are temporary anchorages at both entrances in which to wait for a fair tide through the sound.

At the east end the anchorage is off the ruins of Dog Castle on the east shore of Torsa, 2 cables from the north end.

At the west end Port Mary, 3 cables south of the south point of the entrance of the sound, in a bay inshore of a 2-metre skerry.

In Cuan Sound, in the bight south of Cleit Rock there are several well protected anchorages clear of the tidal stream. The most straightforward approach is along the Luing shore keeping over half a cable off the shore to clear a drying rock off the boathouse. South of this, close the shore to ¼ cable to clear submerged rocks off the 3-metre islet and pass west of the ferry mooring, a spar buoy. There is an uncharted submerged rock, 1.3 metres, half a cable southwest of the islet. If anchoring south of the islet use a tripping line to avoid fouling old moorings.

Other anchorages in this bight are between the two islets off the west side of Torsa, and northwest of Torsa Beag.

Services

Phone box and *Calor Gas* at Cuan Ferry.

Cullipool

56°15′N 5°39′W

The former slate-mining village on the west coast of Luing to the east of Fladda lighthouse has an occasional anchorage from which to visit the Garvellachs, begin a passage to Iona, or to wait for the tide in the Sound of Luing.

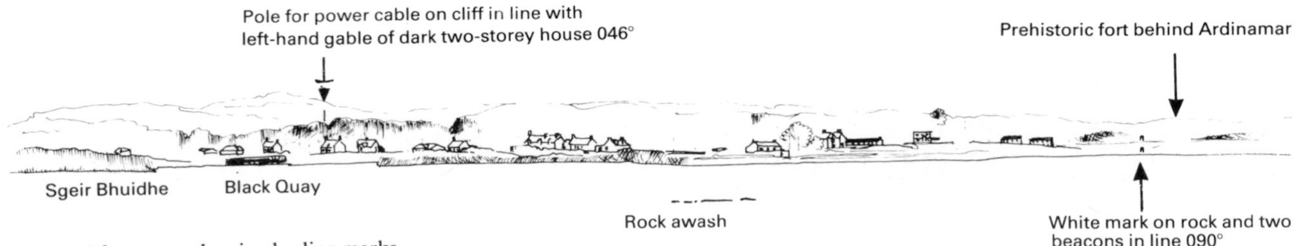

Cullipool from west showing leading marks.

Tides

Firth of Lorne (as Carsaig, Mull)
Constant −0010 Oban (−0540 Dover).
Height in metres

MHWS	MHWN	MTL	MLWN	MLWS
4.1	3.1	2.4	1.8	0.6

Approach

From west, with Fladda lighthouse bearing 270° astern in line with the highest point of Garbh Eileach, identify and keep in line ahead two beacons on shore with triangular topmarks 090°. Do not anchor on this line around HW, to avoid obstructing the passage of fishing boats to their moorings east of Fraoch Eilean, which they can only approach at that time.

From north keep very close (about 10 metres) to Rubha Buidhe, heading for the skerries 1½ cables south of the point; increase the distance off to about 20 metres at the south end of the point. Do not attempt to pass between Sgeir Bhuidhe and the rocks on its east side.

Anchorages

Black Quay southeast of Rubha Buidhe. From south hold onto the leading line described above until the passage west of Rubha Buidhe is clearly open, to avoid the rock awash a cable south of Sgeir Bhuidhe. Steer with Rubha Buidhe bearing about 011° to pass close west of the skerries south of the point and anchor between the quay and the skerries southwest of it in about 4 metres, black mud. The tide runs through this anchorage at about 1 knot. There are rings on the skerries to which to take a warp, but take care not to obstruct the passage.

Fraoch Eilean in the mouth of an inlet between Fraoch Eilean and the islet northeast of it. Access to the pool east of Fraoch Eilean is impracticable for anyone without intimate local knowledge; it can only be entered close to HW and the tides are very unpredictable.

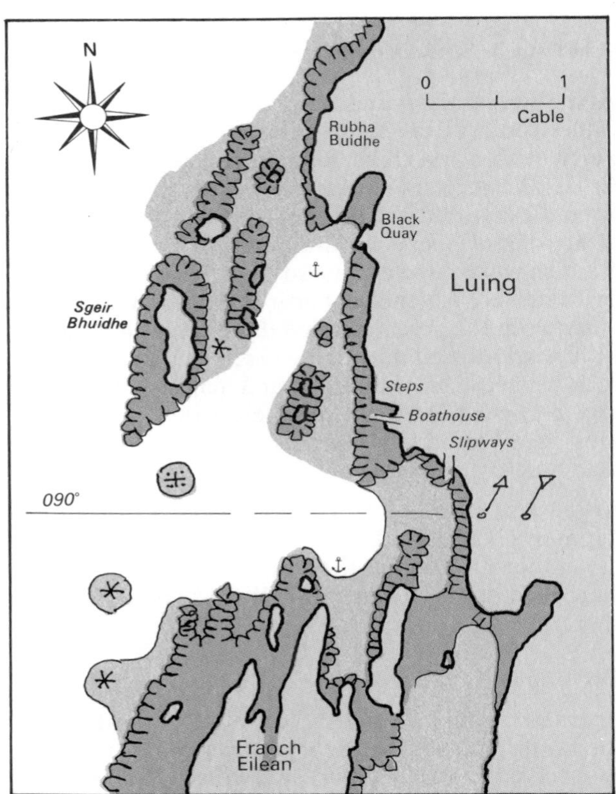

Cullipool

Supplies

Shop (with post office) ¼ mile along road to southeast. Restaurant, 'The Buttery', and separate tearoom. Water at standpipe in Cullipool old village, ½ mile north.

II. Firth of Lorne

The Firth of Lorne is open to the Atlantic to the WSW and any sea from that direction becomes higher and steeper as the shores of the firth close in. If the ebb tide is running against an onshore wind conditions may be very unpleasant, particularly in contrast to the protected passages of the Sound of Luing and southward.

The main fairway of the firth is clean and it is only to the east and southeast of the Garvellachs that there are any significant unmarked rocks.

Slate for the roofs of Glasgow, Edinburgh, Dundee, Belfast and even America came from a small group of islands in this area during the 18th and 19th centuries. At first, of course, it was all carried in fairly unhandy sailing vessels, loading at islands in the tideway such as Belnahua. Building stone was also quarried, for example at Carsaig on Mull; there was no wharf and vessels were loaded at the base of the cliff where the stone was quarried. It's worth remembering these earlier seamen when we find it difficult making our way around in our handy modern cruiser-racers.

Charts

2386 and *2387* respectively cover the south and north parts of the Firth of Lorne at 1:25,000. The south part of the firth is also covered, together with waters further south and west on *2169* at 1:75,000.

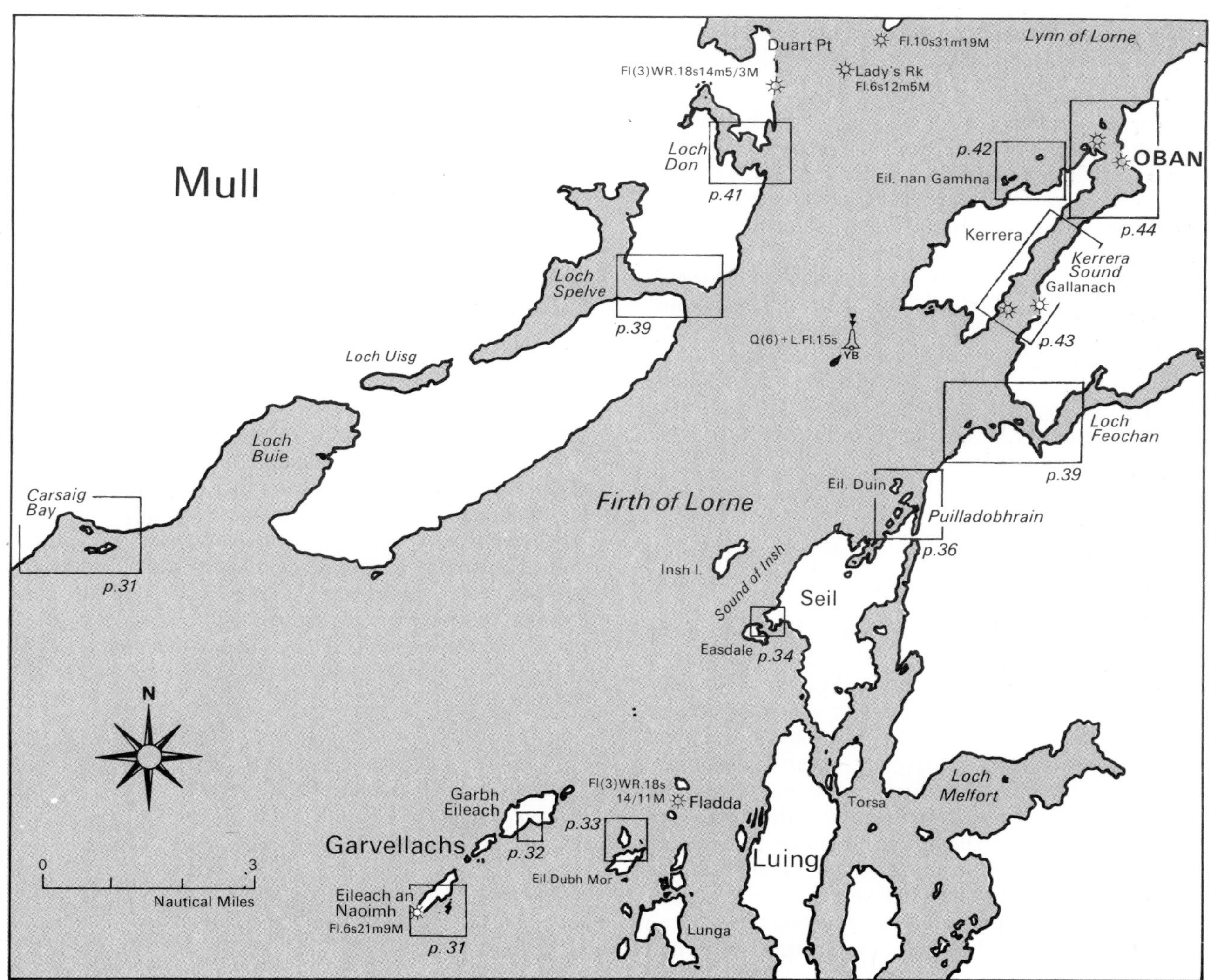

Tides

In the fairway of the firth the stream turns progressively clockwise, setting northeastwards about +0430 Oban (−0100 Dover); southwestwards about −0155 Oban (+0500 Dover).

Tidal streams generally run at 1 to 1½ knots but southeast of the Garvellachs the spring rate is 2 to 3 knots with an eddy setting southwestwards after half-flood. Between Fladda and Easdale the spring rate is 3 knots.

Constant averages −0010 Oban (−0540 Dover).

Height in metres at Carsaig (Mull)

MHWS	MHWN	MTL	MLWN	MLWS
4.1	3.1	2.4	1.8	0.6

Dangers and marks

The two main dangers are separate submerged rocks, six miles apart, both named Bogha Nuadh, and both marked by buoys. One, halfway between Fladda and Easdale has a red can buoy to the east of it, and swell usually breaks on the rock. To distinguish it from the other its buoy is named on the chart as Bono Rock. Another rock, Bogha Ghair ¼ mile NNE of the buoy, with 4 metres over it should also be avoided if there is any sea running.

The second Bogha Nuadh, nearly two miles southwest of Kerrera, is marked by a south cardinal light buoy.

Conspicuous marks are: Scarba, at 446m the highest land to the south of the Firth of Lorne; the Garvellachs; Insh Island (Sheep Island) west of Seil; and Lismore lighthouse at the north end of the firth. Dubh fheith, an isolated rock 12-metres high, 1½ miles northeast of the Garvellachs, is a useful reference point.

Southeast of the Garvellachs there are several dangerous rocks, of which the worst is Bogha ant Sagart which dries 0.3m, approximately halfway between Lunga and the Garvellachs. It is cleared to the ESE by keeping the west side of Eilean Dubh Beag touching the east side of Insh Island 025°, and to the WNW by keeping Dubh Fheith in line with the west side of Insh Island 026°.

Directions

The passage northwest of the Garvellachs and Dubh fheith presents no problem other than from steep seas when the wind is against the tide.

On a passage from or to the west side of Jura the Great Race which extends several miles to the west of Corryvreckan should not be crossed on the flood, particularly at springs or in strong west winds. Southeast of the Garvellachs use the clearing marks described above to avoid Bogha ant Sagart. Other drying rocks are out of the way of a direct passage, but careful chartwork is needed if exploring within this area.

Passing from or to the Sound of Luing pass east of Bono Rock red buoy. From the north identify Scarba and then Fladda lighthouse to find the right passage.

North of Insh Island look out for drying rocks over a cable northeast of Dubh Sgeir (a rock above water half a mile northeast of the island), which would be a hazard if tacking, or if heading from the Sound of Insh to the Sound of Mull. Note also Bogha Nuadh, 2 miles southwest of Kerrera.

Directions for Loch Linnhe, the Lynn of Lorne, and Loch Etive are given in the following chapter; and in Chapter 4 for the passage between Lismore and Mull as well as for the Sound of Mull.

Lights

At night you will need to keep fixing your position by bearings on the following lights.

Garvellachs Fl.6s21m9M (not visible from NE between 215° and 240°).

Fladda lighthouse Fl(3)WR.18s13m14/11M, showing red over Bono Rock bearing 169°–186°, white from eastward, and not visible from west of the red sector. To avoid the southwest tip of Easdale Island you have to keep on the boundary between the red and white sectors.

Dubh Sgeir Fl.6s7m6M, less than half a mile ESE of Fladda is visible all round except where obscured by Belnahua. Until the Garvellachs light becomes visible north of the islands, and Lismore lighthouse is visible west of Insh Island you are mainly dependent on a bearing of this (Dubh Sgeir) light.

Bogha Nuadh light buoy, 2 miles SW of Kerrera, Q(6)+LFl.15s.

Lismore lighthouse Fl.10s31m19M is very distinctive.

Lady's Rock Fl.6s12m5M ½ mile SW of Lismore.

Black's Memorial Fl(3)WR.18s14m5/3M, on Mull, 1 mile west of Lady's Rock, showing red over Lady's Rock and west of 353°, and white elsewhere; not very bright.

Carsaig

56°19′N 5°59′W

An occasional anchorage on the south coast of Mull a couple of miles west of Loch Buie, providing some shelter behind Gamhnach Mhor, a low islet off the southeast of the bay and suitable for overnight anchorage in settled weather or to wait during the day for better visibility. There is a fine masonry quay on the northeast side of the bay, but there appears to be less than 1.5 metres alongside it at half-tide. Two iron perches mark reefs on the northeast side of the approach to the pier. A phone box is ¾ mile along the road. In quiet weather an alternative temporary anchorage is off the beach in the northwest corner of the bay.

Tides

Constant −0010 Oban (−0540 Dover).

Height in metres

MHWS	MHWN	MTL	MLWN	MLWS
4.1	3.1	2.4	1.8	0.6

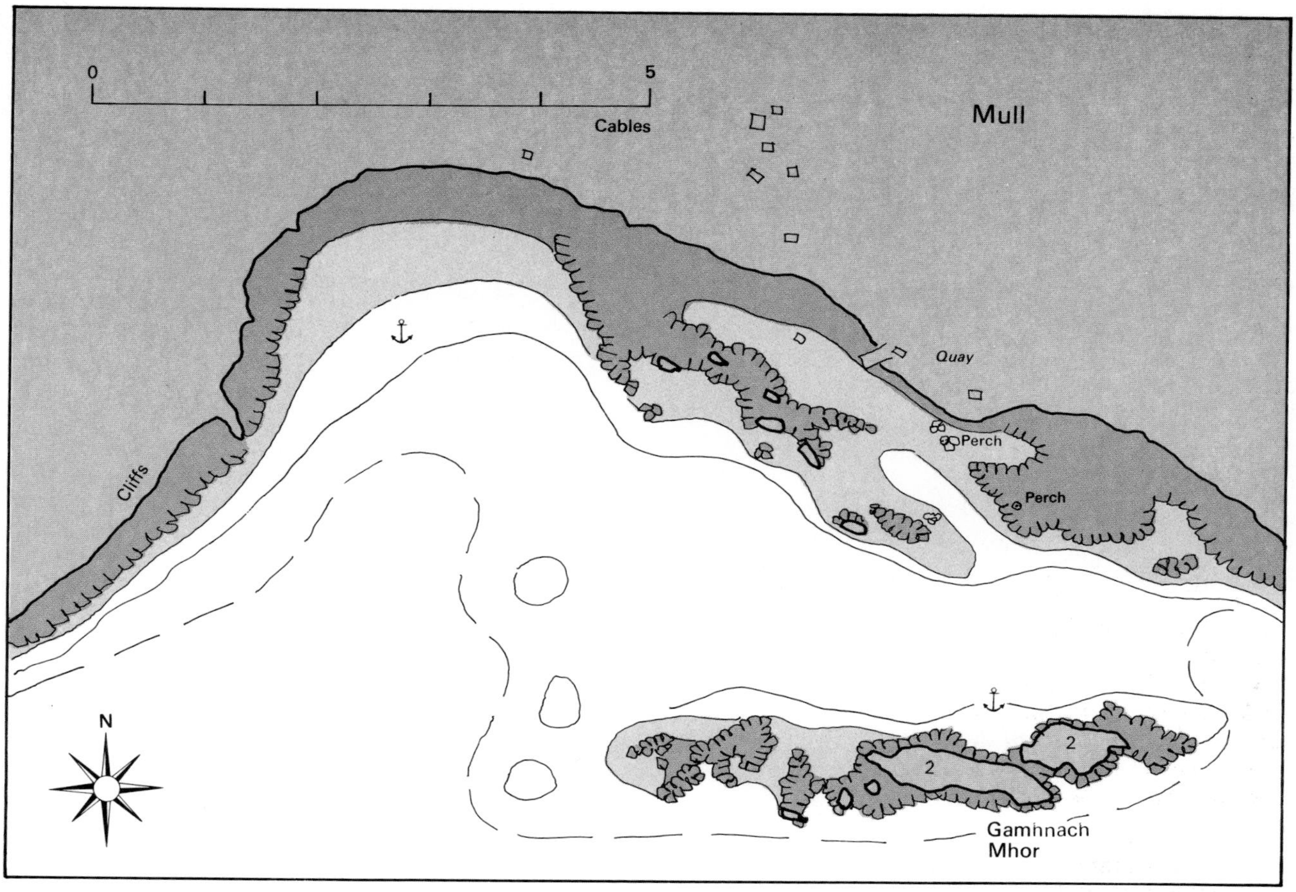

Carsaig Bay

Loch Buie has no shelter from seaward and only very occasional anchorage at the head, east of Eilean Mor. Note the drying rocks a cable east of the islet on the east side of the island; there are several moorings used by small working boats.

Garvellachs or Isles of the Sea

56°13′N 5°48′W

The Garvellachs are well worth visiting in settled weather but the anchorages are too exposed to be often suitable for staying overnight. On Eileach an Naoimh (Neave) there are extensive remains of 9th-century monastic buildings, and a grave reputed to be that of St Columba's mother.

Tides

Constant −0010 Oban (−0540 Dover).

Height in metres at Carsaig, Mull

MHWS	MHWN	MTL	MLWN	MLWS
4.1	3.1	2.4	1.8	0.6

On the southeast side of the Garvellachs, an eddy on the flood runs southwestwards from about +0130 Oban.

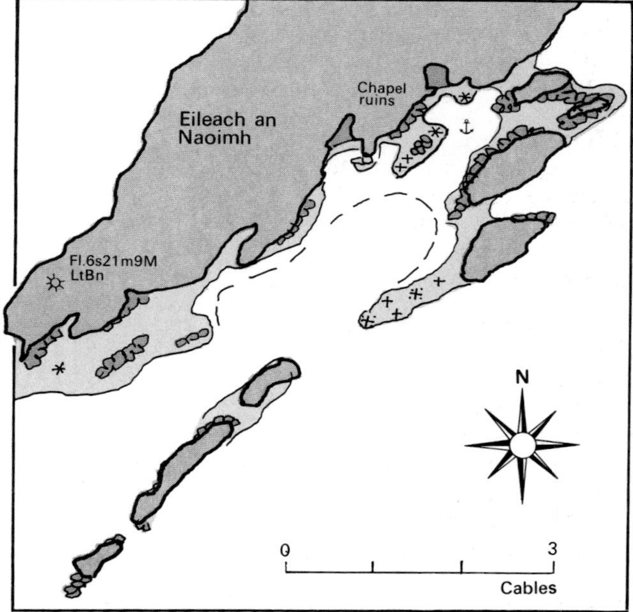

Eileach an Naoimh

Eileach an Naoimh anchorage.

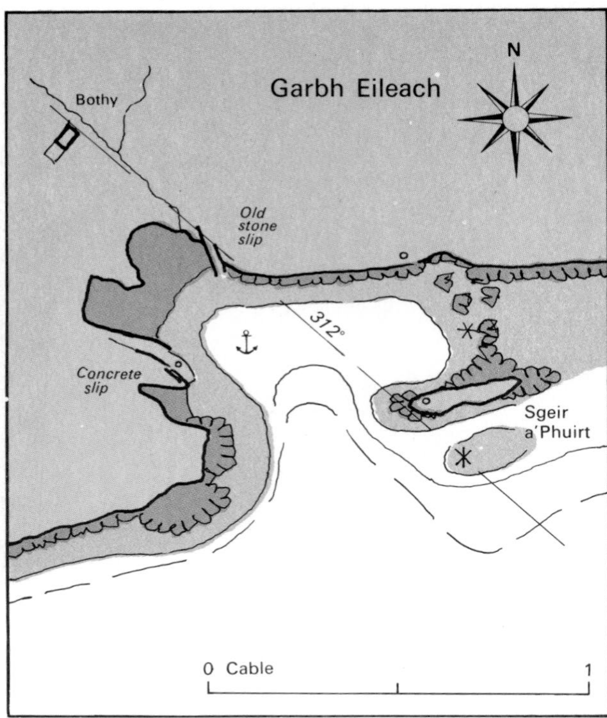

Garbh Eileach

Eileach an Naoimh (Neave)

The most southwesterly of the group.

Approach

From east or southeast make for the southwest side of a gap in the skerries, keeping nearer to that side to avoid a reef, part of which is awash, on the northeast side of the gap.

From southwest it is possible to pass between the skerries and the island, but keep closer to the skerries to avoid submerged rocks on the island side.

The northeast end of the channel between the skerries and the island is awash at chart datum, with dense weed, but there do not appear to be any individual rocks at a higher level, so that if there is no swell it is passable by a boat of moderate draught above half-tide.

Anchor off the old landing place, or behind the drying rock at the northeast end of the inlet. When the rock is covered it can usually be seen showing white underwater, but note the submerged rocks at both ends of it.

Garbh Eileach landing place – the concrete slip is on the right; the old stone slip at the bottom of the photo.

Garbh Eileach

The largest of the group, towards their northeast end. The landing place in the middle of the southeast side of the island provides an occasional anchorage. Keep the cottage open west of the west end of Sgeir a' Phuirt; the line shown on the plan runs through the position of the submerged rock south of the islet, it is not a clearing mark. There are mooring points on the west end of Sgeir a' Phuirt and on the shore to the north of it, and at the concrete slip.

The Black Isles

56°14′N 5°43′W

Eilean Dubh Mor and Eilean Dubh Beag, a mile and a half southwest of Fladda provide reasonable and very secluded anchorage on the east side of the narrows between the two islands. It is doubtful if this channel ever dries right across, but a large rock a little south of mid-channel dries at least 3 metres. Local fishermen say the basin east of the narrows is sheltered from swell; I have only anchored there in completely calm conditions.

Approach

From north keep only half a cable off Eilean Dubh Beag to avoid a drying rock a cable off its east side.

From east pass either close south of the islet off the north end of Eilean Dubh Mor or not less than half a cable north of it. If taking the southern passage keep to the north of the east end of the channel to avoid a submerged rock half a cable northeast of the point of Eilean Dubh Mor.

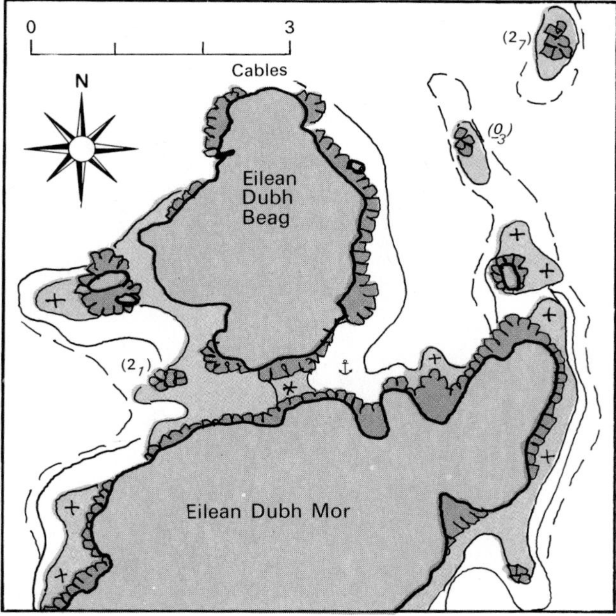

The Black Isles

Anchorages

Anchor between the two islands as near the narrows as will give you swinging room between the reefs, or off the east side of Eilean Dubh Beag.

Both of the bays on the north side of Eilean Dubh Mor are foul with submerged and drying rocks, but it is possible to anchor off the promontory between them.

Fishermen use the passage through the narrows, north of the drying rock. If you want to try it for the first time do so from east to west, but only if there is no swell and you are sure of the position of the rock. Note another rock drying 2.1 metres, 1½ cables west of the narrows.

Fladda (56°15′N 5°41′W) provides a temporary anchorage NNE of the island during flood tide.

Belnahua 4 cables WNW of Fladda has the remains of very extensive slate quarries, which penetrated far below sea level. Over a hundred people, including the families of the quarrymen, lived on this island which is less than ¼ mile across. It makes an interesting visit on a quiet day, but anchoring there needs care as the tide runs at 5 knots at springs. On the ebb, anchor in the tidal lee at the south end of the island. On the flood anchor as close inshore as possible off the jetty on the east side. Keep an eye on your boat all the time; the bottom is mostly slate waste.

Easdale from cliffs on its north side. The two northern beacons are on the right; the southwest beacon is just to the left of a moored fishing boat close to Easdale Island. A bank dries out at least to the line between the two most westerly beacons.

Easdale

56°17′.5N 5°39′.5W

For at least two centuries Easdale was one of the two main centres of the Scotch slate industry, so that its character is that of derelict industry, with miners' rows converted to holiday homes. It also has what must be one of the largest tourist shops on the West Coast, fed by a steady flow of coaches from Oban.

Easdale Island has more industrial archaeology and fewer visitors, and a small shipping company operates a couple of 'puffers' from its drying harbour. A museum on Easdale Island has an excellent collection of photographs and exhibits showing the industrial and social life of the place when it was a working community.

For the last 60 years it has been said that Easdale Sound was silting up, but a recent survey by a resident yachtsman shows that for the most part it is as deep as ever, except in the southwest corner. Ellanbeich was originally separated from Seil by a channel, later filled in by waste from the quarries, which themselves are now flooded. A proposal to form a small marina in one of these quarries was refused planning permission, so that a derelict piece of wasteland lies in place of a potentially useful facility.

Identification from the west

A mile southeast of the south end of Insh Island, the hill at the west point of Seil falls as an almost sheer cliff to Easdale Sound.

Tides

Constant −0010 Oban (−0540 Dover).

Height in metres at Carsaig, Mull

MHWS	MHWN	MTL	MLWN	MLWS
4.1	3.1	2.4	1.8	0.6

Dangers and marks

The sound is very narrow (note the large scale of the plan) and the shoals and rocks too numerous to describe. The old beacons survive and are being repainted to conform to current IALA practice, but in September 1986 the repainting had not been completed; the northeast beacon was red and the northwest one black. The remains of the pier are conspicuous. At HW springs the southwest beacon almost covers.

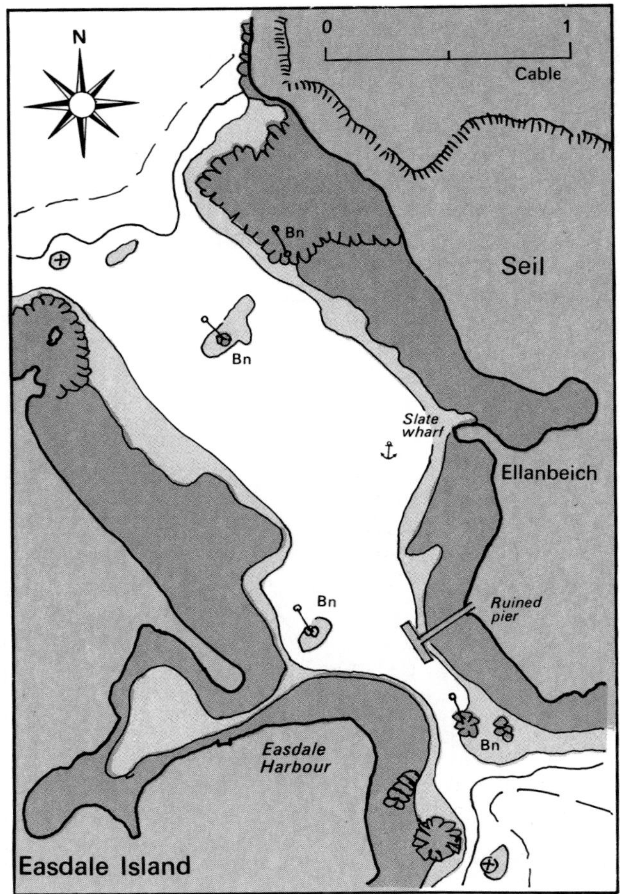

Easdale Sound

Approach

From southeast keep the south end of Insh Island just open south of the head of the ruined pier 320°. This entrance is very narrow, the clear passage at low tide being no more than 20 metres wide. After passing the pier alter course to the north.

From northwest don't cut the corner, but when you have identified the first two beacons approach with the south point of Insh Island astern, rather closer to the northeast beacon. Steer first for the slate wharf 130° and, after passing the beacons, towards the head of the ruined pier 155°.

Easdale Sound, southeast entrance – the southeast beacon is to the right of the pier; the northwest beacon left of the pier head, and Insh Island beyond. The southwest beacon is beyond the spit in the left foreground.

Easdale northwest entrance at LW – note how the rocks on the left extend well beyond the north beacon which is half hidden behind them. The pier is conspicuous and the northwest beacon right of centre. The high cliffs are out of the photo to the left.

Anchorage

Anchor off the slate wharf, well east of a line between the two most westerly beacons. The drying bank on the west side of the sound probably extends beyond this line, and the bight west of the southwest beacon is occupied by fishing-boat moorings.

Shoal-draught boats may find a berth in Easdale Harbour, especially if able to take the ground, but might have to move at short notice if a puffer were to come into the harbour near HW. The bottom is stony in places.

Supplies and services

Shops and restaurant at Ellanbeich.

Communications Post office, phone box. Bus to Oban.

Ardencaple Bay

56°19′N 5°36′W

There is an occasional anchorage close east of Rubha Garbh Airde, the northeast point of Seil, but it may be obstructed by fixed fishing equipment.

Shelter in settled weather or moderate southerly winds may be found in the south corner of the bay, off Ardfad Point.

Puilladobhrain

56°19′.5N 5°35′W

The name, pronounced approximately 'puldohran',

Puilladobhrain from northeast.

Puilladobhrain

translates as 'the pool of the otter', although, no doubt, any otters have long since been frightened away by the yachts. Almost as sheltered as any anchorage on the West Coast and only 7 miles from Oban, this is one of the West Coast's most popular anchorages and you will be lucky to find less than a dozen and a half yachts there on any evening in July. Double that number is about the limit and it does sometimes overflow. However, at the end of the summer of 1986 several moorings were laid in the pool; if these are allowed to remain the value of this anchorage as a refuge will be dangerously reduced.

As in many other anchorages, a shoal-draught boat able to take the ground will be at an advantage in being able to use the areas at the head of the pool which other yachts cannot reach. The islets on the west side of the pool are low enough to let you watch the sun (if any) set over Mull.

Identification

Puilladobhrain is not named on charts, but is 3 cables southeast of Eilean Duin at the northeast end of Seil. Eilean Duin itself, which looks like a ruined castle 18 metres high although it is in fact a natural rock formation, is the key to identification from any direction. An orange drum marks the northeast end of Eilean nam Beathach.

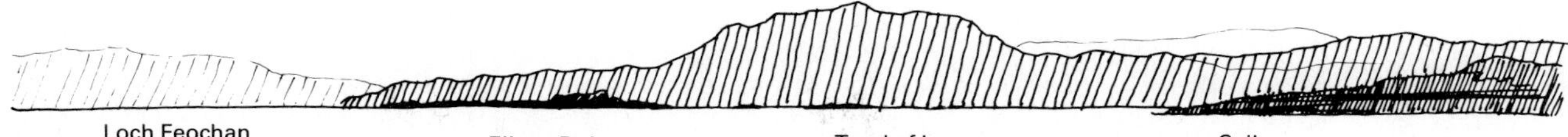

Approaching Puilladobhrain from southwest. The distinctive skyline is the Toad of Lorne; Eilean Duin is below it.

Tides

Constant as Oban (−0530 Dover).

Height in metres

MHWS	MHWN	MTL	MLWN	MLWS
4.0	2.9	2.4	1.8	0.7

Approach

From south pass the northwest point of Seil and identify Eilean Duin, the outermost island about a mile to the northeast. Keep at least a cable NNE of the island to avoid a submerged rock (whose position will usually be obvious from lobster pot buoys), and round the end of Eilean nam Beathach, 3 cables further SSE, about half a cable off (but no more) to avoid the Dun Horses which dry 2.7 metres, near the mainland shore.

From north Eilean Duin is less easy to identify against Seil, but when you have picked it out, steer for it until you can see the bridge through Clachan Sound. After the sound is shut in it is safe to alter course to port avoiding the Dun Horses.

Dangers and marks

A drying rock close to the east shore of Eilean nam Beathach is easily avoided by keeping in mid-channel. Two cairns in line below the high-water line of Eilean nam Freumha lead clear of this rock, but over a spit at the west end of the islet southeast of Eilean nam Beathach. The cairns are difficult to see unless they have been freshly painted, and almost cover at HW.

Another drying rock, on the leading line, close to the shore of Eilean nam Freumha is marked by a painted cross on the shore. Other rocks at the head of the pool are shown on the plan, which is based on a detailed survey by Ian Wallace.

Supplies

Pub at Clachan Bridge, half a mile by footpath from a signpost on the shore near the head of the pool; the ground to the east is boggy – land as near to the head as possible. Petrol at the pub; post office and phone box at Clachan Seil, a mile further south. The nearest shop is at Balvicar, 3 miles south.

The 18th-century Clachan Bridge, popularly known as 'The Bridge over the Atlantic' and incorrectly attributed to Telford, is well worth a visit even for those for whom the pub holds no interest. There is a variety of curious geological formations on Eilean Duin, and a herd of wild goats.

Clachan Sound

56°19′N 5°35′W

The usefulness of the passage between Seil and the mainland, even to shoal-draught boats, is limited by overhead cables, as well as by the bridge, and by the extent to which the north end of the sound dries. It is charted as drying 1.5 metres, but Ian Wallace puts it at 2.4 metres, which is about mean tide level at Oban.

The only figure given relating to clearance at the bridge is that the crown of the arch is 12 metres above the bed of the channel. An electricity supply cable crosses the sound north of the bridge, and a telephone cable, apparently below the level of the arch, south of the bridge.

Some years ago a Hunter 19 passed through this channel without lowering its mast, and in 1986 a Wayfarer dinghy did so. A shoal-draught boat able to lower her mast easily would find this a painless alternative to the Firth of Lorne on a blowy day, given enough rise of tide to get over the bar at the north end.

Tides

Tidal streams run strongly between Clachan Bridge and the north end of the sound, turning at HW and LW Oban. Heights and constant are as Oban.

Barrnacarry Bay

56°21′N 5°33′W

An occasional anchorage on the south side of the entrance to Loch Feochan for settled weather or moderate southerly winds.

Puilladobhrain leading line – the white painted cairns. A white cross on the shore to the right marks the position of a drying rock.

Barrnacarry from north.

Approach

From south and west keep ¼ mile offshore to avoid a 1.5-metre shoal, and drying rocks to northwest of the bay. Approach the bay with the farm buildings in line with the west side of the largest above-water rock in the bay 182° to pass E of the drying rocks. Anchor towards the southwest side of the bay.

Loch Feochan

56°21′N 5°31′W

A mile and a half southeast of the south end of Kerrera, this loch has until now been rarely visited because of the drying banks at the narrowest part of the entrance which cause very strong tidal streams and restrict access. In 1986 Bill Robertson established Ardoran Marine and buoyed the entrance so that it is now fairly straightforward.

Tides

HW as Oban. The ebb continues until two hours after LW Oban at springs, but rather earlier at neaps. Bill Robertson says the maximum rate of the stream is 3½ knots.

Approach

There is a shallow sand bar across the entrance to the west of Ardentallen point. Southeast of the point the channel is almost blocked by banks and drying rocks, but a channel close southeast of the point has been marked with five pairs of buoys of which the first are south of the point. It is best to approach at slack LW which is about two hours after LW Oban. Note the tortuous course of the buoyed channel, particularly at the third pair of marks.

Beyond the buoyed channel the loch is clean as far as Ardoran Marine, about a mile northeast of Ardentallen Point, except for a rock drying 0.5 metres more than a cable SSW of the promontory at Ardentallen House.

Beyond Ardoran, Eilean an Ruisg in the middle of the loch has rocks all round it. The north side is cleaner, but ¾ cable NNW of the island a rock dries 0.6 metres, and the best passage is closer to the island.

Services and supplies

Moorings, pontoons, slip and crane; diesel, *Calor Gas*, water, repairs. Hotel and stores nearby.

Loch Feochan from the south side of the entrance, looking northeast. Ardentallen Point is on the left, and the first pair of buoys is southeast of it. The second and third port-hand marks are beacons on shore; the third starboard-hand buoy is well in to a bay on the northeast side of Ardentallen Point, marking the west side of a drying patch of rock which is just showing.

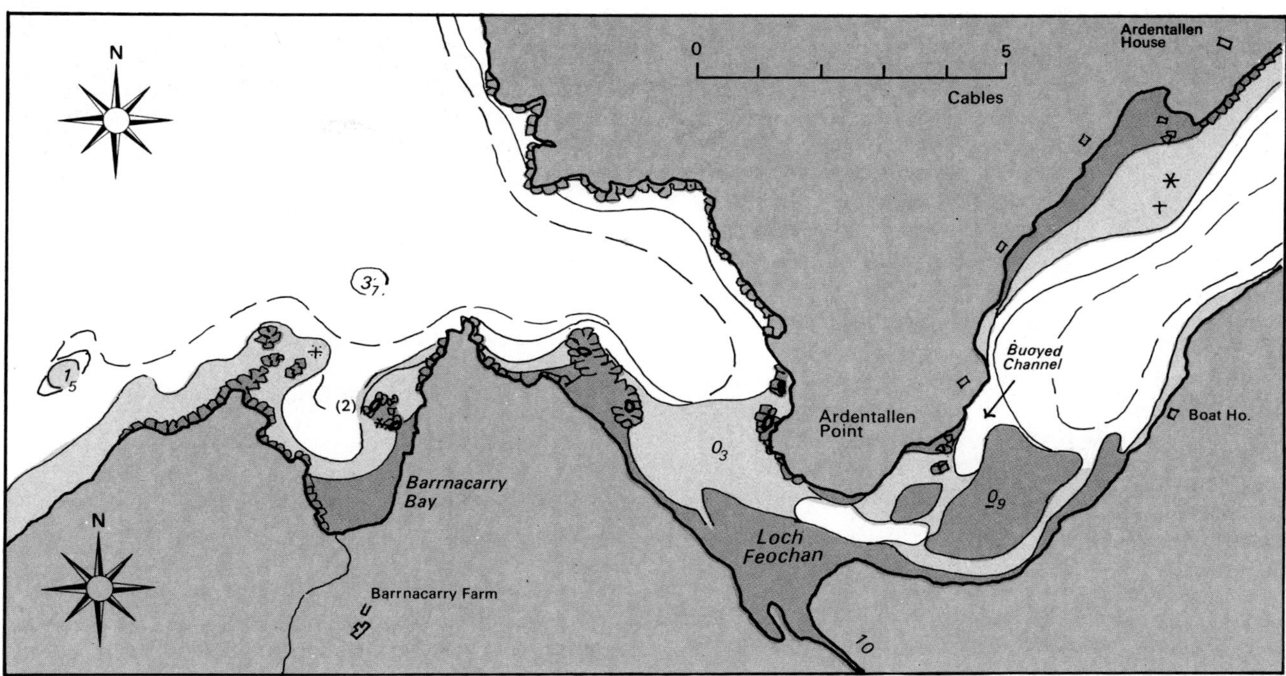

Loch Feochan and Barrnacarry Bay

Loch Spelve

56°23′N 5°42′W

On the west side of the Firth of Lorne, Loch Spelve is completely landlocked and surrounded by an impressive range of hills, which sometimes produce correspondingly impressive squalls.

The narrow entrance is quite tricky, with shoals extending three quarters of the way across the channel from the south side and a rock drying about 0.5 metre, half a cable off the north side. Two pairs of cairns kept in line at different stages of the passage are intended to keep you off the rock, but several visitors have found that the cairns have a tendency to get up and walk away at a critical moment, being easy to mistake for sheep unless freshly painted. A white paint mark on the shore is supposed to show the position of the rock, but some other confusing marks have recently been added.

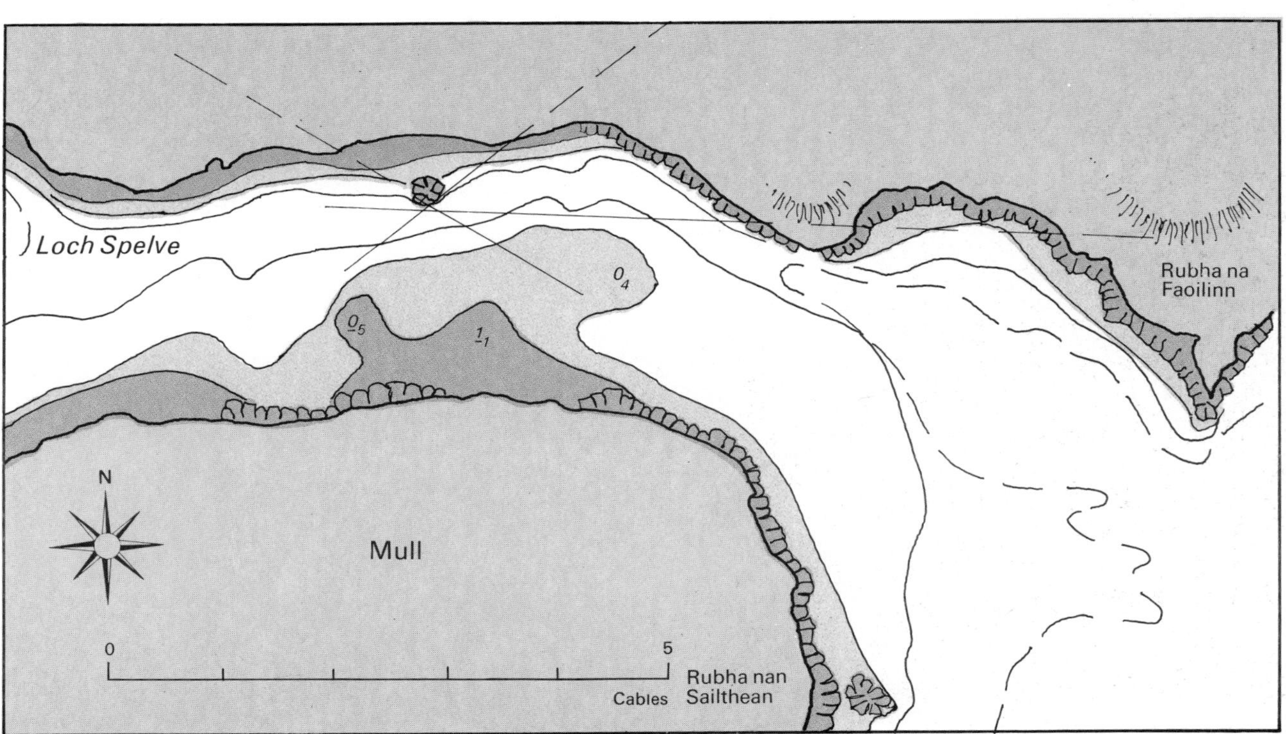

Loch Spelve

Tides

Constant as Oban (−0530 Dover).

Height in metres

MHWS	MHWN	MTL	MLWN	MLWS
4.0	2.9	2.4	1.8	0.7

Streams run at 3½ knots at springs.

Marks

The first leading line, ahead on entering, consists of white or off-white cairns, the back one being on the skyline. The second line, astern, has a white painted cross for a front mark, and a white painted stone among trees for a back mark. Both of these lines cut the outer edge of the drying rock.

A clearing line is the vertical cliff on Rubha na Faoilinn (astern) just open of the dark shoulder of the next (second) point to the west.

Approach

Make for the second point on the north side (note reefs drying about ¼ cable off Rubha na Faoilinn) and identify and keep open the line astern described above, and the cairns in line ahead if they can be picked up. When you have passed the worst of the shoal on the south side (indicated by a patch of shingle at the high-water line), head for Croggan pier on the south side of the loch.

Above half-tide yachts of moderate draught can go through in mid-channel.

Anchorages

Head of southwest arm of the loch provides reasonable shelter. The bottom rises abruptly from 12 metres to a foreshore which dries over ½ cable on the south and southwest sides.

Ardura at the west side of the north arm, as far into its southwest corner as depth permits. Extensive drying foreshore, and fierce gusts in westerly winds.

Northeast bay, on the east side of a promontory clear of fishing floats and a rock just above MHWS in the middle of the head of the bay.

There is a phone box at Croggan, southwest of entrance.

Loch Don

56°25′N 5°40′W

A curious place of shoals and drying banks, rather like a river from the east coast of England set down among mountains. The entrance is identified by a conspicuous white house at Grass Point, about two miles south of Black's Memorial light beacon.

Approach

There are no marks to guide you round the twists of the channel, and the best you can do is to feel your way in

Loch Don, looking northwest over Grass Point at about half-tide.

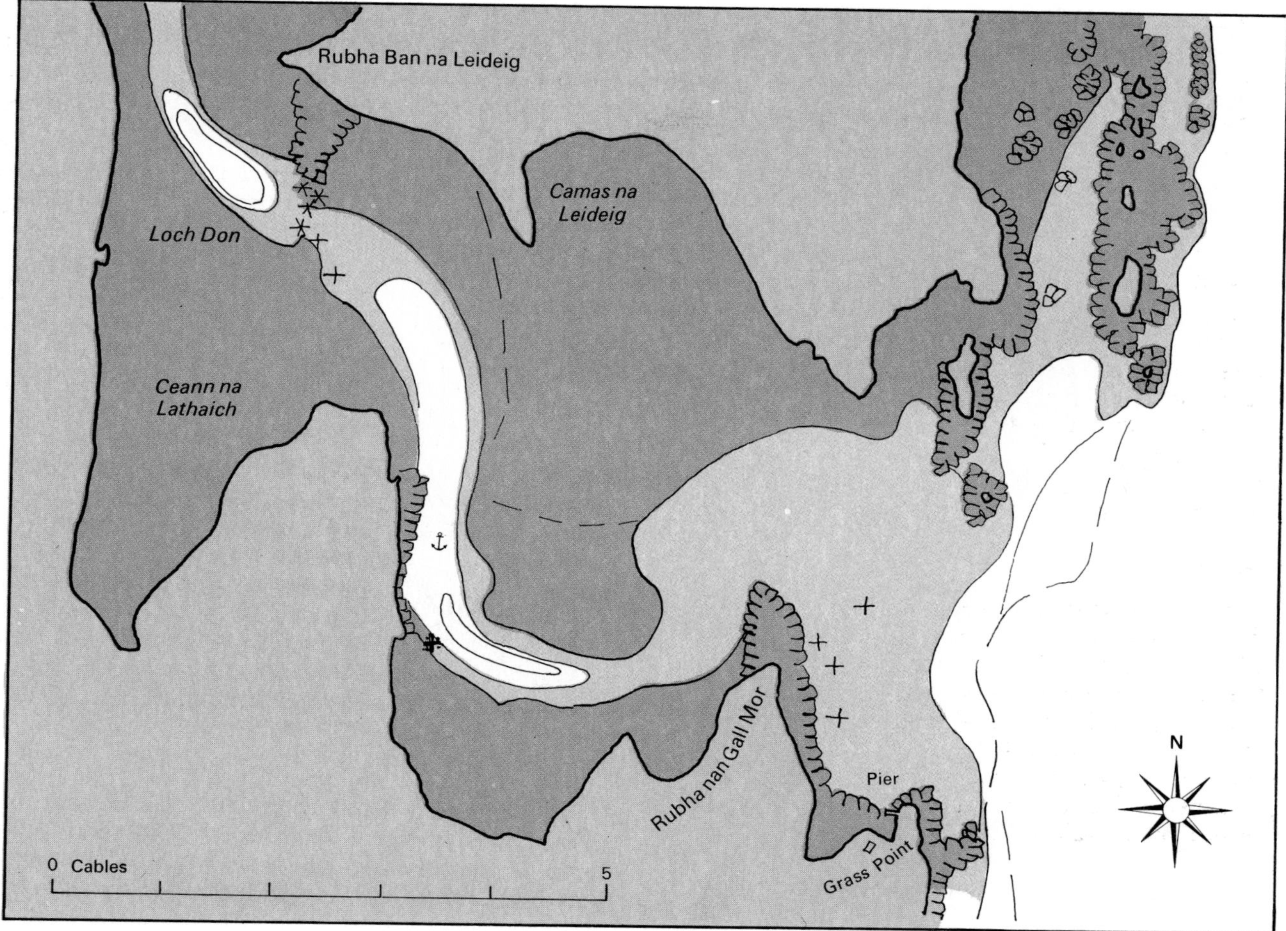

Loch Don

on a rising tide, watching the echo sounder as you approach the edges of the channel. Don't try to cut across the bank in the middle of the loch, which extends east further than it would appear to do, and has large boulders scattered over it; pass well north of Rubha nan Gall Mor and hold towards its west side (the east side of the channel). Anchor close to the east side of the next promontory to the west.

Anchorage

There is a useful temporary anchorage off the pier at Grass Point (which was originally the main ferry pier for Mull). Leave room for tourist launches to approach the pier.

There is a phone box at Grass Point.

Kerrera

Oitir Mhor Bay (Otter More), 56°25′N 5°31′W, on the northwest side of Kerrera, a mile from its north end, provides reasonable shelter in moderate summer weather, away from the disturbance of passing traffic in Oban Bay. The approach is straightforward, except from southwest between Eilean nan Gamhna and Kerrera where drying rocks reduce the navigable channel to a width of about 30 metres on its north side; drying areas on either side make it necessary to take an indirect course to the east of the narrows. The southwest side of the bay dries off 1 cable, allow for this when anchoring.

Kerrera Sound

56°24′N 5°31′W

A sheltered approach to Oban from the south, with most, but not all, of the hazards well marked and lit. There are some reasonable anchorages in the sound, but all of them are likely to be disturbed by passing traffic. Gylen Castle at the south end of Kerrera is worth a visit; in quiet weather you can anchor in the bay south of it.

Tides

Tidal streams run at 1 to 2 knots turning about 1½ hours before HW and LW Oban.

Height in metres at Oban

MHWS	MHWN	MTL	MLWN	MLWS
4.0	2.9	2.4	1.8	0.7

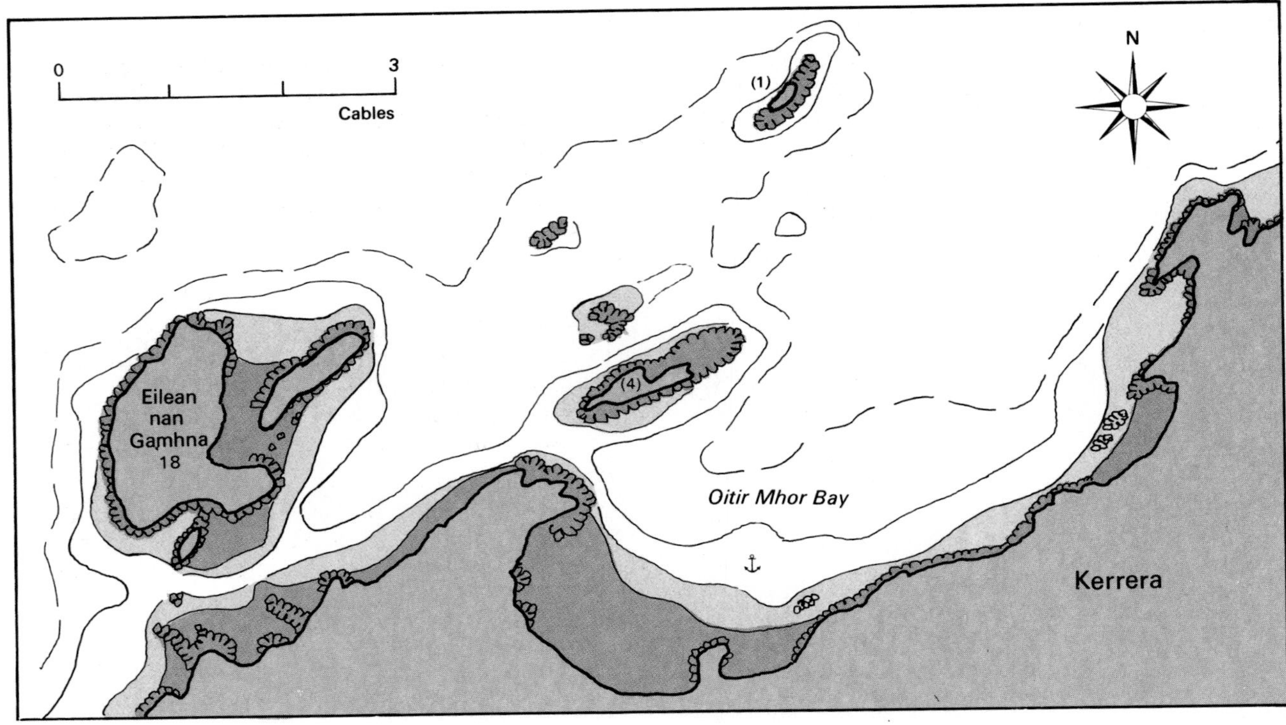

Dangers and marks – from south

Sgeirean Dubha and Cutter Rock, drying 1 cable off the Kerrera shore, ¾ mile northeast of the south end of the island, are marked by a white light beacon. Cutter Rock, which covers at half-tide, is over 1½ cables SSW of the beacon.

An unmarked reef drying 0.9 metres is ½ cable from the mainland opposite the light beacon.

Little Horseshoe Shoal ½ mile NNE of Sgeirean Dubha is marked on its south side by an unlit port-hand buoy.

An unmarked rock drying 0.3 metres ½ cable off Gallanach Boatyard on the mainland, ½ mile northeast of Little Horseshoe Shoal, is in line with the north gable of a house at the outer end of the quay, above the pontoon.

Ferry Rocks more than ½ mile further northeast are in mid-channel, some of them drying and some submerged. The northwest side is marked by a starboard-hand light buoy, and the southeast side by an unlit port-hand buoy. A separate rock 2 cables further northeast is marked by an unlit starboard-hand buoy.

Further north there is an unmarked shoal west of the south point of Heather Island, but the main passage is southeast of the island.

Underwater cables cross the sound from the south end of Horseshoe Bay, as well as immediately northeast of the ferry. Long-distance telephone cables are landed in Port Lathaich on the mainland to the east of Sgeirean Dubha, at the south end of the sound.

South entrance to Oban Bay. Two of the Ferry Rocks buoys are in the foreground; the third is out of the photo to the left. Heather island is left of centre. Sgeirraid buoys are beyond the promontory on the right.

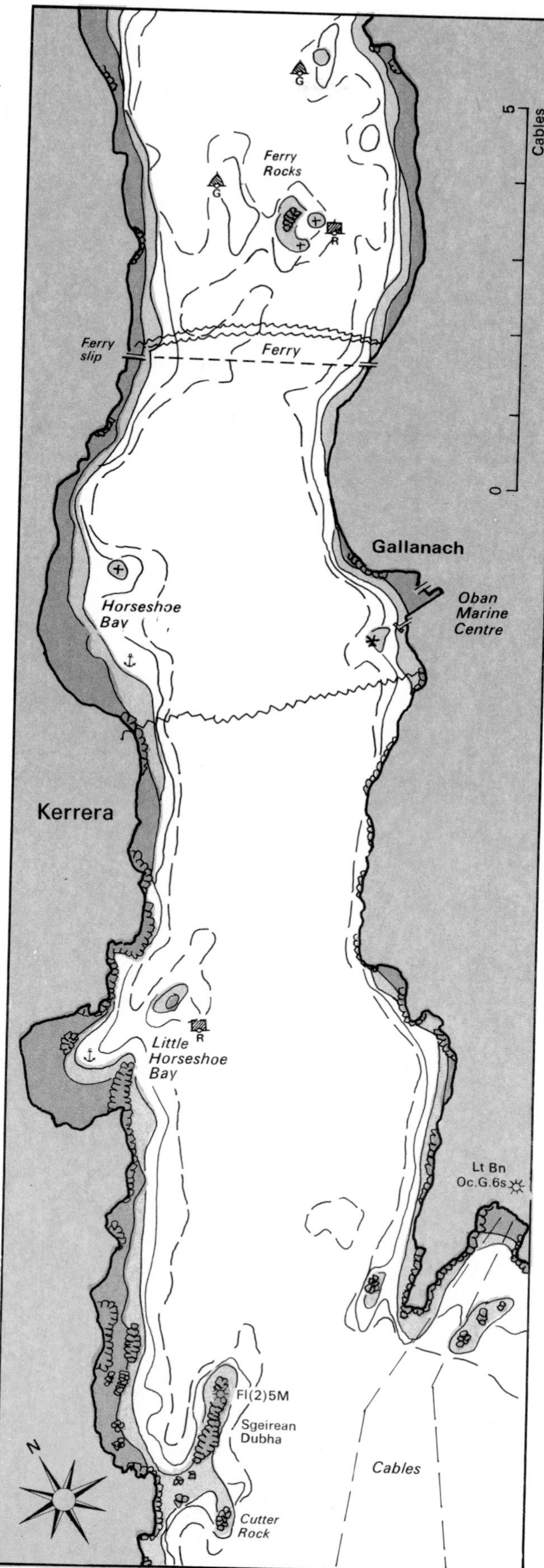

Kerrera Sound

Directions

There is little to add to the above except to emphasise that you must not pass between the first two buoys at Ferry Rocks, or west of Heather Island unless you have a large-scale chart. There is considerable traffic in the sound; observe the rules of the road, but look out for other vessels which may not do so. Oban Bay is described on page 45.

Lights

At night the following lights give you just enough guidance, but you will need to take bearings or use the echo sounder to keep clear of unlit dangers. The 15 or 20-metre contours generally clear all dangers but a 7-metre shoal ¼ mile northeast of Sgeirean Dubha may cause some anxiety.

Port Lathaich light beacon on the mainland, Oc.G.6s6M, visible 037°–072°, gives some guidance in the approach. It is obscured just south of Cutter Rock.

Sgeirean Dubha light beacon Fl(2)12s7m5M.

Ferry Rocks west buoy Q.G.

For lights further north see *Oban Bay*, page 45.

Anchorages

Little Horseshoe Bay Note the position of the shoal in relation to the buoy and the drying reef which extends nearly a cable from the south point. The bay dries out fairly level, but it would be risky to dry out there because of possible damage from wash.

Gallanach Boatyard Most of the space is taken up by moorings but the boatyard may have one to spare, or in Horseshoe Bay on the other side of the sound. Go alongside the pontoon to enquire (watch out for the drying rock). The quay dries alongside but has about 1.2 metres at LW neaps.

Horseshoe Bay is partly occupied by moorings. Inshore of them is drying foreshore; to the north is a 1.8-metre submerged rock, and beyond that the bay is mostly very deep, but you might find a place close inshore towards the ferry slip.

Heather Island Most of the space west of the island is occupied by fish cages, but it should be possible to anchor off the bight on Kerrera north of the island. There is some risk of fouling old moorings.

Services and supplies

Gallanach Boatyard (Oban Marine Centre) has moorings, slipway, hull and engine repairs, some chandlery, winter storage. *Calor Gas*, diesel, water at pontoon, showers. ☎ Oban (0631) 63388.

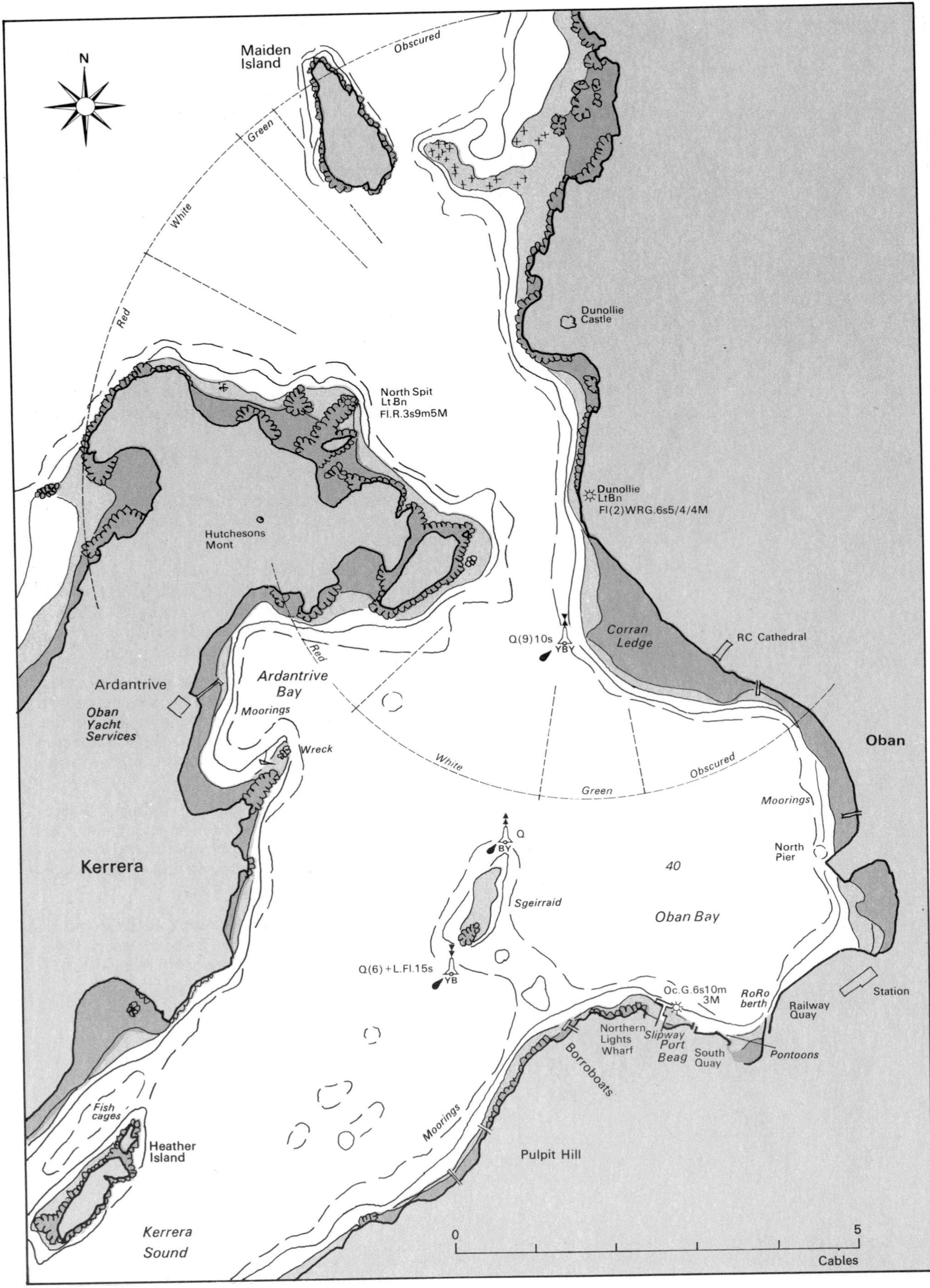
N
Maiden Island
Obscured
Green
White
Red
Dunollie Castle
North Spit Lt Bn Fl.R.3s9m5M
Dunollie Lt Bn Fl(2)WRG.6s5/4/4M
Hutchesons Mont
Q(9)10s
YBY
Corran Ledge
RC Cathedral
Red
Ardantrive
Ardantrive Bay
Oban Yacht Services
Moorings
Wreck
White
Green
Obscured
Oban
Moorings
Q
BY
North Pier
40
Kerrera
Sgeirraid
Oban Bay
Q(6)+L.Fl.15s
YB
Oc.G.6s10m 3M
RoRo berth
Station
Railway Quay
Northern Lights Wharf
Slipway
Port Beag
South Quay
Pontoons
Borroboats
Fish cages
Heather Island
Moorings
Pulpit Hill
Kerrera Sound
0
5
Cables

Oban Bay

Oban Bay

56°25′N 5°29′W

This is the most convenient place on the West Coast for stores, changing crews, and for launching trailer-sailers, with pontoons at South Quay for visiting yachts, but it has little attraction for an overnight stay, with the urban surroundings and wash from passing traffic. There have been various proposals for marinas including one by the HIDB which involved blocking Kerrera Sound with a causeway.

Tides

Oban is a standard port (−0530 Dover).

Height in metres

MHWS	MHWN	MTL	MLWN	MLWS
4.0	2.9	2.4	1.8	0.7

In the north entrance tidal streams run at 2½ knots springs, turning about 1½ hours before HW and LW Oban. The flood stream runs northwards.

Charts

2387 (1:25,000), *1790* (1:10,000); *2171* (1:75,000).

Identification

In poor visibility the town may not be easily seen from seaward. Conspicuous features are a radio mast close south of the town, and Hutchesons Monument, a stone obelisk at the north end of Kerrera.

Dangers and marks

Sgeirraid (Sgeir Rathaid – locally known as the Scrat), a reef at the south entrance to Oban Bay, is marked at its south end by a south cardinal light buoy, and at its north end by a north cardinal light buoy.

Corran Ledge towards the north entrance on the mainland side is marked at its outer end by a west cardinal light buoy.

Kerrera North Spit on the south side of the north entrance, is marked by a cylindrical light beacon with red and white bands.

Approach

From south pass either side of Sgeirraid, preferably to the east if making for Oban.

From north the main passage is south of Maiden Island; you can pass east of the island, but keep about ¼ cable off it as submerged rocks extend from the mainland to within half a cable.

Keep a particularly good lookout, especially if you are under sail, for large commercial vessels, car ferries in particular, moving fast. They will have limited scope to manoeuvre.

Keep at least ¼ cable off the east point of Kerrera at the narrowest part of the entrance as unmarked drying reefs extend from the shore here, and pass west of Corran Ledge buoy.

This buoy is so far out from the mainland that even since it was changed to a west cardinal buoy yachts and fishing boats have beached themselves on the ledge. Until 1986 there was a starboard-hand buoy here and it was common for vessels of all kinds to leave it to starboard coming in from the north; over two dozen stuck on the ledge in 1985. Officially, the change is experimental.

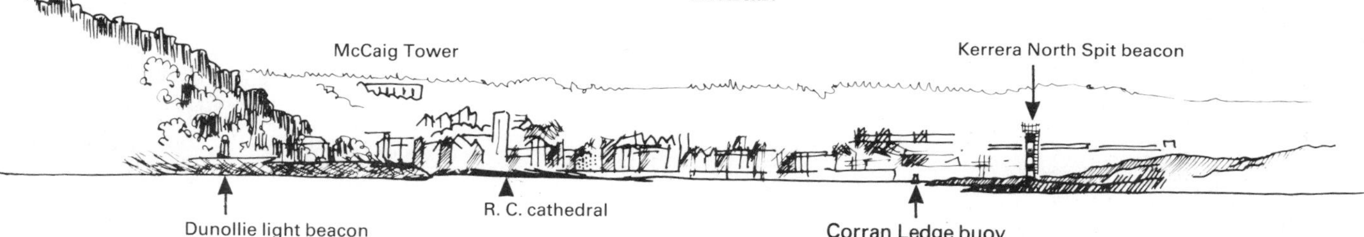

Oban Bay north entrance. Kerrera North Spit beacon is on the right, with the northeast point of Kerrera beyond and the Corran Ledge buoy, which must be left on its west side, just showing beyond again. From the left, Dunollie light beacon is low down on the wooded shore and the Roman Catholic Cathedral shows over Corran Ledge, with MacCaig's Tower above and left of it.

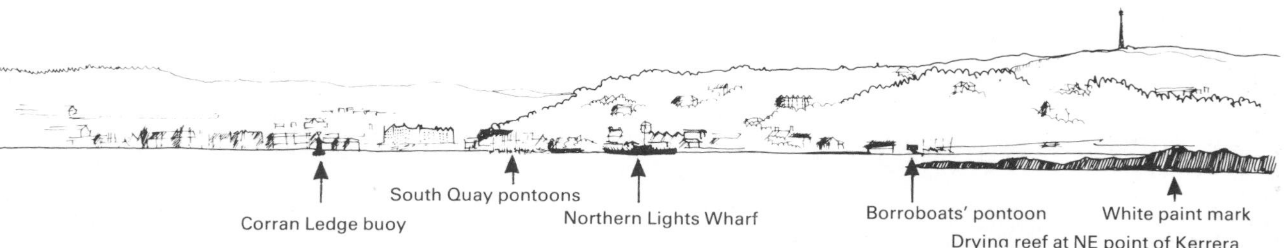

Oban Bay from north, with Corran Ledge buoy on the left, in line with the Railway Quay. The ship in the centre is the lighthouse tender *Fingal* at the Northern Lights Wharf; the South Quay pontoons are to the left of it, and Borroboats' pontoon to the right above the end of the reef in the foreground. The reef, at the northeast point of Kerrera, dries for about 20 metres, with a white painted rock inshore of the end.

Lights

At night lights may not be easy to make out against those of the town; also, for the same reason, keep a particularly good lookout for other vessels.

Sgeirraid buoys show the usual lights for cardinal buoys, Q(6)+LFl.15s to the south and Q at the north.

Corran Ledge buoy shows Q(9)10s.

Dunollie light beacon, 2 cables north of Corran Ledge shows a sectored light, Fl(2)WRG.6s7m5–4M, white over the fairways to SSW and NW, red over Kerrera and green to the mainland side, obscured from the east side of the bay.

Kerrera North Spit light beacon shows Fl.R.3s9m5M.

North Pier and South Quay both show 2F.G(vert).

Northern Lights Wharf shows Oc.G.6s10m3M.

From south pass either side of Sgeirraid.

From north approach in the white sector of Dunollie light; Corran Ledge light buoy should appear before Kerrera North Spit is abeam. After passing the beacon come round gradually to starboard but don't get closer to Kerrera than the 10-metre contour. Corran Ledge Buoy in line with the Oc.G light on Northern Lights Wharf gives a fair clearing line for this point. Pass west of Corran Ledge buoy and make for the berth chosen.

Anchorages, moorings, berths alongside

The piermaster's office is often unmanned, and the Railway Quay and South Quay are controlled by separate organisations, so that R/T calls to 'harbourmaster' or 'harbour control' are unlikely to be answered.

South Quay Pontoons are provided but berths are normally limited to yachts less than 10.5 metres. The berth nearest the shore is reserved for the lifeboat. The stone slip at the west end of the pier is frequently used by working boats, and nearly dries. The pontoons may become untenable in strong northwest winds.

Railway Quay Yachts may berth alongside but you take your chance with fishing boats, and may not be able to get near a ladder. The quay is constructed of timber piles so that fender boards are essential. It is best to approach a boat larger than your own and ask permission to lie alongside. You can usually lie here overnight on Saturday. If you want to check before berthing at the Railway Quay, call *Calmac Oban*.

Keep out of the way of car ferries approaching or leaving the RoRo berth at the south end of the Railway Quay.

Owing to developments at Railway Quay there are likely to be no berths for yachts at either South Quay or Railway Quay after 1987.

Oban South Quay. The RoRo berth at the south end of the Railway Quay, on the right, is now being rebuilt. The North Pier is beyond, and the Roman Catholic Cathedral is at the top left.

North Pier Large yachts sometimes berth here if the space is not otherwise needed.

North of North Pier it is possible to anchor but there are many moorings, and an obstruction on the bottom about 1 cable NNW of North Pier. Watch the depth carefully, allowing for swinging room as the foreshore dries off about 60 metres, beyond which the bottom quickly drops away. There is sometimes space in the northeast corner of the bay, off a concrete slip southeast of the Roman Catholic cathedral.

Ardantrive Bay is mostly occupied by moorings and it may be possible to arrange with Oban Yacht Services to use one of these. If approaching from the south take care to avoid the drying spit which extends a cable NNE from the south point of the bay, with a wreck on it which rarely covers.

Cardingmill Bay (Brandystone), ¼ mile southwest of Northern Lights Wharf, is completely occupied by private moorings.

Services and supplies

Diesel (Railway Pier and Ardantrive). Water (South Pier, Railway Pier and Ardantrive). Moderate-sized boats may be able to take on diesel and water at Borroboats' pontoon a cable west of Northern Lights Wharf.

Petrol in town. *Calor Gas* at Ardantrive, or in town, ½ mile from piers.

Slipping, moorings, winter storage, hull and engine repairs; drying out on concrete slip alongside pier by arrangement with Oban Yacht Services at Ardantrive. General repairs at Port Beag, by South Quay (D. Currie). Vale Engineering at South Quay. Divers.

Chandlery and chart agent (Nancy Black) in Argyll Square near the Railway Quay; chandlery at Ardantrive.

Supermarkets and shops in Oban.

Communications Train and bus to Glasgow. Car ferries to Mull, Lismore, Coll, Tiree and Colonsay. Post office, phone boxes at railway station and elsewhere. Car hire. Tourist information office. Car parking at station.

☎ all Oban (0631)
Caledonian MacBrayne 62285
Coastguard 63720
D. Currie, boatbuilder 62102
Nancy Black (chandlery) 62550
Oban Divers 62755
Oban Yacht Services 63666
Piermaster (North Pier) 62892
Tourist information 63122
Vale Engineering 64513

Oban, Port Beag slip; if you want to launch a boat there, check before arriving that there will be space.

III. Loch Etive and Loch Linnhe

These lochs together with the branches of Loch Linnhe are set in some of the most dramatic scenery on the West Coast including, of course, Britain's highest mountain, and many others which drop sheer into the sea. Parts of the shore have no access by road and this is an ideal area for cooperative ventures between yachtsmen and climbers. By contrast, Lismore in the middle of the mouth of Loch Linnhe is green and fertile, consisting mainly of limestone. A further contrast is the new mammoth granite quarry on the west side of Loch Linnhe, feeding 65,000-ton bulk carriers.

Charts

Admiralty *2378*, *2379*, *2380* cover the whole of Loch Linnhe and its branches at 1:25,000, except for the upper part of Loch Etive for which *5076* (which is an old chart with depths in fathoms, but still currently available) is needed. Ordnance Survey maps *41* and *49* also cover this area. For a short visit (although it sounds like heresy) these two maps together with Imray chart *C65* may be found sufficient.

Dunstaffnage Bay and Connel Sound

56°27′N 5°25′W

Much of Dunstaffnage Bay dries out and towards the west side there are moorings, and fish cages belonging to the Scottish Marine Biological Association laboratory. Dunstaffnage Yacht Haven has pontoons and swinging moorings on the southeast side of the bay. Shoal-draught yachts may find a space to anchor inshore of the moorings. The pontoon pier on the northwest side of the bay has a gate which is normally locked. There is an extensive housing development at the head of the bay, with the SMBA laboratory on the west side. Dunstaffnage Castle (which is well worth visiting) is on Rubha Garbh, the northwest point of the bay.

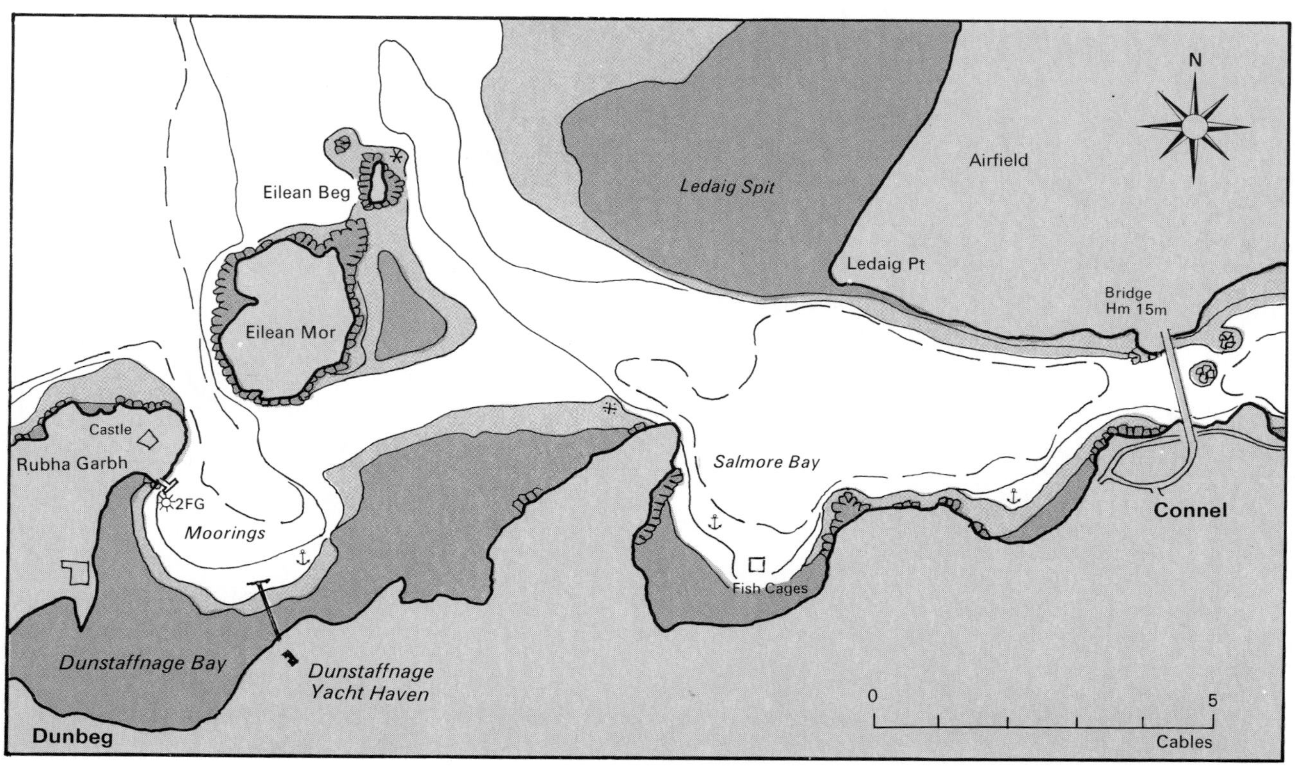

Dunstaffnage and Connel

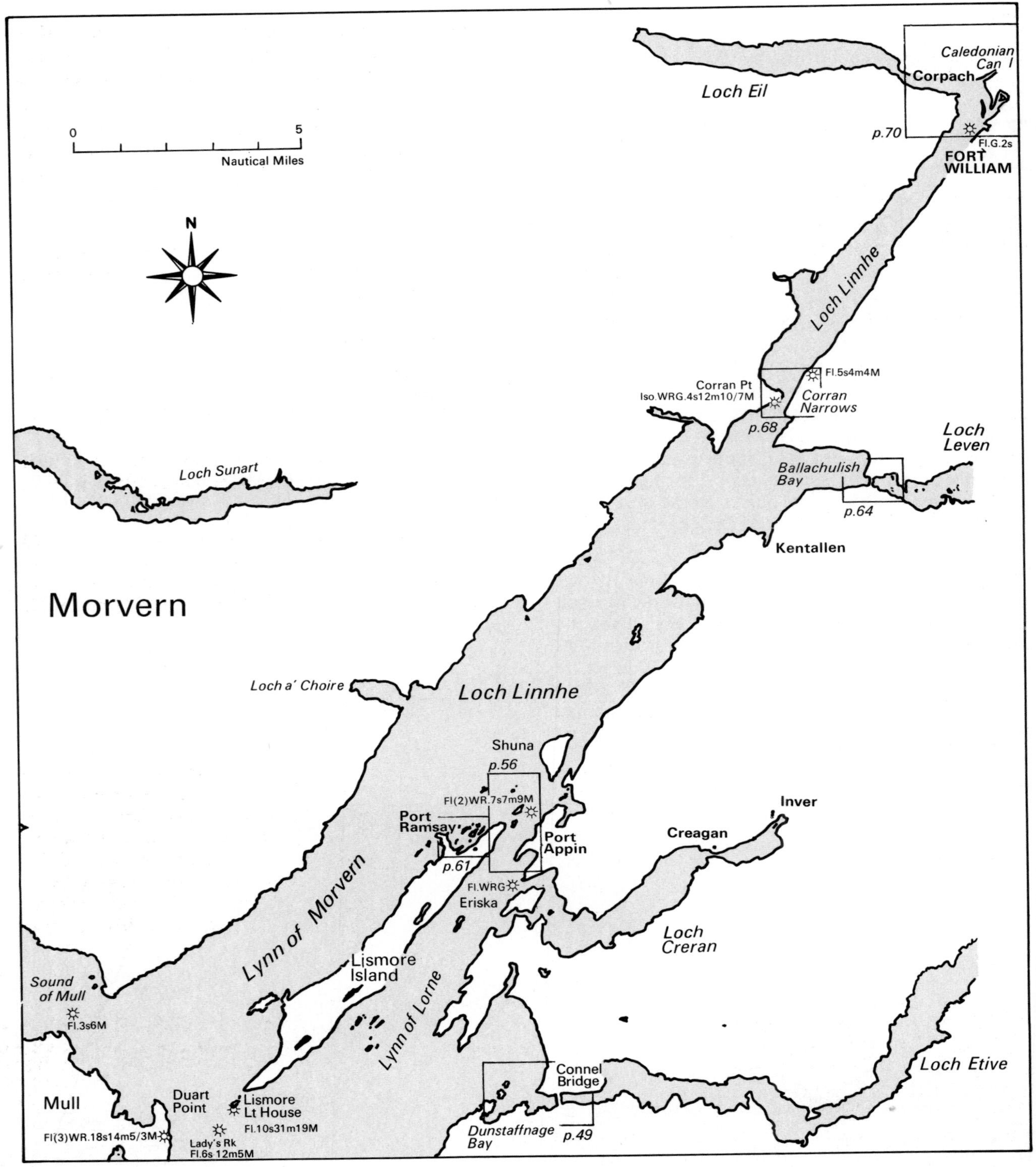
Caledonian Can l
Corpach
Loch Eil
p.70
Fl.G.2s
FORT WILLIAM
0
5
Nautical Miles
N
Loch Linnhe
Fl.5s4m4M
Corran Pt
Iso.WRG.4s12m10/7M
Corran Narrows
p.68
Loch Leven
Ballachulish Bay
p.64
Loch Sunart
Kentallen
Morvern
Loch a' Choire
Loch Linnhe
Shuna
p.56
Fl(2)WR.7s7m9M
Inver
Port Ramsay
Port Appin
Creagan
p.61
Fl.WRG
Eriska
Loch Creran
Lynn of Morvern
Lismore Island
Sound of Mull
Fl.3s6M
Lynn of Lorne
Loch Etive
Connel Bridge
Mull
Duart Point
Lismore Lt House
Fl.10s31m19M
Fl(3)WR.18s14m5/3M
Lady's Rk
Fl.6s 12m5M
Dunstaffnage Bay
p.49

Tides

At Dunstaffnage Bay the constant is as Oban (−0530 Dover).

Height in metres

MHWS	MHWN	MTL	MLWN	MLWS
4.1	3.0	2.4	1.9	0.8

Identification and approach

The entrance can be identified by Connel Bridge when the entrance opens up from north of west. The approach from southward is clean, but if coming from the Lynn of Lorne keep at least ¼ mile off Garbh Ard, the point immediately west of Ardmucknish Bay, 1¼ miles northwest of the entrance. Pass south of Eilean Mor, but keep clear of shoal water on the south side of the entrance.

At night (or dusk) do not mistake Dunbeg village, which can be seen over low ground south of Dunstaffnage Castle, for the entrance.

To continue further east keep towards Eilean Mor at first to avoid drying banks extending over halfway between the mainland and the island. Steer 075° for the low-lying Ledaig Point on the north side of Connel Sound to avoid drying banks east of the island as well as a rock awash half a cable northwest of Rubha Ard nan Leum. From here onwards there are eddies all over the place and steering needs close attention.

It is possible to enter Connel Sound by the north side of Eilean Beag, but keep clear of a half-tide rock half a cable northwest of the island. A drying spit off Ledaig Point extends three quarters of the way across the channel, so pass about a cable east of Eilean Beag and come round gradually to head for the bridge. A post on the south side of the spit is well to the east of its outer end.

Anchorages

Dunstaffnage Bay There is unlikely to be space to anchor except for shoal-draught boats, or larger boats at neaps, inshore of moorings and only after taking careful soundings. Moorings or pontoon berths are available at Dunstaffnage Yacht Haven.

Salmore Bay (Camas Bruaich Ruaidhe), east of Dunstaffnage Bay. The foreshore dries off up to a cable and the bay quickly becomes deep; part of the bay is occupied by fish cages. The bottom is stony with weed, so take particular care that your anchor is holding.

South Connel Bay east of Salmore Bay has several moorings in it and is more affected by the tide, but is more convenient for stores.

Services and supplies

Dunstaffnage Yacht Haven on the southeast side of Dunstaffnage Bay has slip with mobile hoist, water, diesel, *Calor Gas*. Mechanical and hull repairs. Showers.

General store at Dunbeg. Shop and hotels at Connel. Small shop, and restaurant, at Dunstaffnage Yacht Haven.

Communications Post office and phone box at Dunbeg and Connel. Phone box also at yacht haven. Local bus service to Oban from Dunbeg. Train and bus at Connel. Dunstaffnage Yacht Haven, ☎ Oban (0631) 66555.

Loch Etive

56°27′N 5°20′W

Apart from the usual crop of unmarked rocks there are three specific obstacles which discourage visitors from entering Loch Etive. The first in order of appearance is the bridge at Connel, with a charted clearance at MHWS of 15 metres. Next, immediately east of the bridge a drying reef extending more than halfway across the channel from the north side holds back the water and causes a tidal fall, known as the Falls of Lora.

Dunstaffnage Yacht Haven; Eilean More on the right, Dunstaffnage Castle in the trees on the left. A fishing boat is at the pier below the castle.

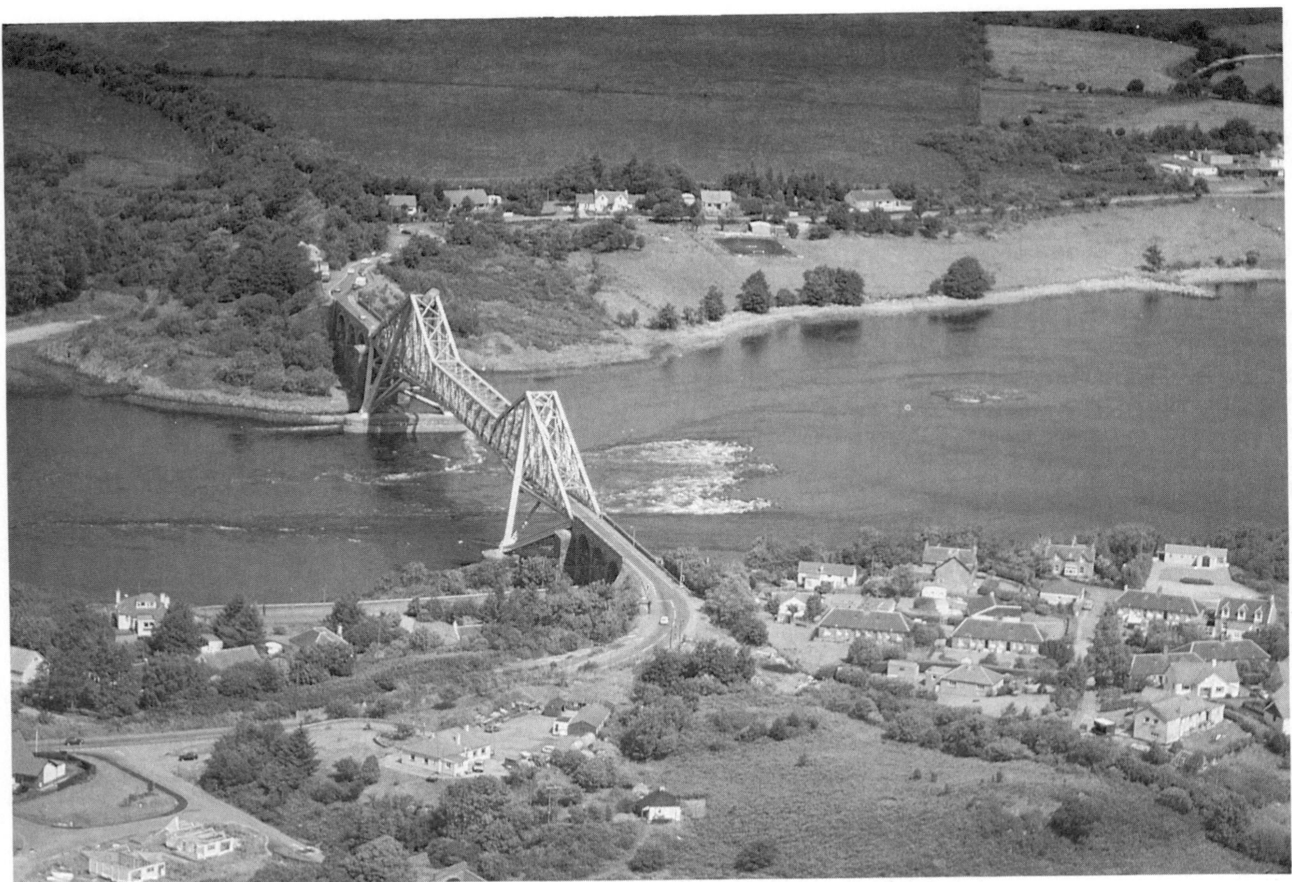

Connel Bridge, from the south. The ebb tide is pouring over the reef close east of the bridge.

Lastly, at Bonawe, five miles east of the bridge, a very high-voltage electricity cable crosses the loch, with a safe clearance at its lowest point of 12 metres.

The shores of the lower part of the loch are pastoral and well wooded. Beyond Bonawe the loch is over-shadowed by high mountains with no road except at its head, and the few farms are supplied by mail boat. Fish farming is developing rapidly. On the north side of Bonawe narrows there is a quarry from which granite is taken away by sea. On the south shore at Bonawe the buildings of a late 18th-century iron foundry have been restored; all the iron ore was brought from Wales and Cumbria by sailing coasters which had to negotiate the falls under sail or with sweeps.

Tides

Tidal streams run at up to 6 knots in the narrows at Connel. The east-going stream begins about −0345 Oban (+0310 Dover); west-going stream begins about +0200 Oban (−0330 Dover).

Meteorological conditions may cause these figures to vary by up to 1½ hours with a tendency to be early rather than late, owing to the greater frequency of, and exposure to, westerly winds. There is almost no slack water. This information is based on recent research by the SMBA laboratory at Dunstaffnage.

The reefs to the east of Connel Bridge hold back the water so that at HW springs the level is 0.5 metre higher outside the loch than inside, and at LW springs it is 1.2 metres higher inside than outside. Again, there is virtually no slack water, and the stream runs very strongly through the channel south of the reef with eddies on either side. Recommendations as to the time to pass the falls vary from half an hour either side of the turn of the tide to 2 hours, one figure being given by the owner of a sailing yacht with a small engine, the other by the skipper of a fishing boat.

At Kilmaronag Narrows, 1½ miles east of Connel Bridge, the tides turn about ten minutes later than at Connel. There are strong eddies along the south shore east of the narrows on the flood, flowing west, and west of the narrows on the ebb, flowing east.

Falls of Lora and Lower Loch Etive

56°27′.5N 5°23′W

Approach

From the west the best approach is to be at the narrows a little before the tide turns eastwards so as to go through at fairly slack water. Read the notes about tides above, and allow for the tide turning up to 1½ hours early in strong southwesterly winds or if the barometer is low, or up to 1½ hours late in the opposite conditions. If you are early anchor off the Dunstaffnage Arms Hotel on the south shore. If you appear to be late, don't push your luck – the tide sets strongly towards rocks on the south shore at the east end of the channel.

Steer for the space between the bottom of the first and second oblique struts of the bridge from its south tower. There is no satisfactory mark for clearing the south end of the reef, but at low tide it is uncovered. Turn to steer diagonally across to the north shore; there is a submerged rock a little south of mid-channel nearly half a mile east of the bridge. There are rocks off the end of Dunfiunary, a point on the south shore on which there is a house with a round tower, and violent eddies beyond it.

At Kilmaronag Narrows, a mile east of the bridge, the tide runs at nearly the same rate as at the falls. Rocks, of which the outermost is submerged, extend more than halfway across the channel from islets on the southeast shore, and the foreshore on the northwest side dries off 50 metres southwest of the narrowest part of the passage.

Kilmaronag Shoal, 0.6 metres, is 1 cable northwest of Kilmaronag Point. There are several rocks and banks drying up to a cable from the shore between these narrows and Bonawe, about 4 miles further east. Ardchattan Shoal, 2¼ miles east of Kilmaronag Narrows, with a charted depth of 2 metres, is rather north of mid-channel off the jetty at Ardchattan House on the north shore.

Connel Bridge from the west.

Flood tide pouring past the promontory east of Connel Bridge.

Kilmaronag Narrows looking northeast; there are submerged rocks northwest of the line of rocks running out from the right.

Anchorages

Achnacreemore Bay North of the narrows. Except in onshore winds anchor at the north end of the west shore, but keep clear of a rock which dries 0.6 metres, a cable south of the mouth of a burn.

Stonefield Bay (Linne na Craige), 56°27′.5N 5°19′W is on the south shore a mile west of the narrows. Anchor east of Eilean Traighe, towards the head of the bay. Alternatively, east of Abbot's Isles on the east side of the bay. The channel there is rather deep and an eddy sets through with the flood; anchor in the bight close to the islands. There may be lost moorings here.

Auchnacloich Bay, the next bay east of Stonefield, provides some shelter. Leave clear access to the pier which is used by workboats from the SMBA laboratory.

Sailean Rubha, west of Airds Point, 3 miles from Kilmaronag Narrows, provides good shelter in 4 metres, but there are rocks towards the head of the inlet.

Airds Bay, southwest of Bonawe Narrows has a foreshore drying out for over half a cable beyond which the depth increases very quickly. At the concrete jetty east of the river mouth in the southeast corner of the bay there are underwater cables running WNW from the head of the pier and northwest from a point on shore north of the pier. The best anchorage is west of the pierhead, with the pierhead bearing 090°; north of this line there is a danger of fouling the cable and south of it is close to the low-water line.

Several moorings here are provided by Polfearn Hotel for the use of customers. The hotel has a VHF radio shore station, working on Ch M.

Supplies

Shop, post office, phone box, hotels; petrol at Taynuilt, ¾ mile from Bonawe Pier.

The 18th-century ironworks at Bonawe are an outstanding example of the industrial archaeology of the period (near Airds Bay). Gardens at Ardchattan Priory on the north shore of the loch are open to the public.

Bonawe and Upper Loch Etive

56°27′N 5°13′W

Overhead power cables cross Bonawe Narrows with a safe clearance of 12 metres at their lowest point, but more than this towards the north side. In case any shoal-draught boats should enter the mouth of River Awe on the south side of the narrows, note that there are power cables crossing the river, ¼ mile from its mouth, with a safe clearance of 4 metres.

Charts

The head of the loch, beyond Bonawe is only covered by Admiralty chart *5076* which is a reproduction of an obsolete chart with depths in fathoms.

Tides

Bonawe constant is +0200 Oban (−0330 Dover).

Height in metres

MHWS	MHWN	MTL	MLWN	MLWS
2.0	1.2	1.0	0.5	0.2

Tidal streams at these narrows run at 2½ knots springs on the flood, 1½ knots on the ebb.

Head of Loch Etive – the ruined pier.

Dangers

A drying bank extends up to a cable northeast of the old ferry slip on the south shore.

The upper loch is mostly clean except for drying rocks extending over ¼ mile from the north point of Inverliever Bay on the southeast shore, 3½ miles from Bonawe Narrows. Winds tend to be erratic unless the true wind is straight along the loch.

Anchorages

Most bays are very deep and there are many fish cages. The best anchorage is at the head of the loch between the ruined pier on the west shore and a tidal islet northeast of it, but this is exposed to southerly fetch.

Lynn of Lorne

56°30′N 5°28′W

The passage from Oban to Loch Linnhe by the east of Lismore is sheltered from the west but tides run strongly and careful pilotage is needed at the north end.

Charts

The passage can be negotiated with these directions and chart *C65*, but *2378* at 1:25,000 will be needed for exploring inshore.

Tides

Port Appin constant is −0005 Oban (−0535 Dover).

Height in metres

MHWS	MHWN	MTL	MLWN	MLWS
4.2	3.1	2.5	1.9	0.8

At the south end of the Lynn of Lorne the tidal stream turns NNE at +0445 Oban (−0045 Dover); SSW at −0140 Oban (+0515 Dover).

Southwest of the group of islets off the southeast side of Lismore an eddy on the flood sets southwestwards.

At the north end of the Lynn of Lorne, the tidal stream turns NNE at +0600 Oban (−0030 Dover); SSW at −0015 Oban (−0545 Dover).

The rate of tidal streams in the Lynn of Lorne varies from 1 knot at the south end to 2½ knots at the north end at springs.

Dangers and marks

Drying rocks extend 1 cable WSW of Rubha Fion-aird, the east point of the south entrance. Over a mile west of this point is a group of islands, the shores of which are generally clean, but with a rock drying 4 metres between the most easterly islands of the group.

2 cables west of Eilean Dubh, 2½ miles NNE of this group, there are rocks above water with extensive drying rocks SSW and NNE of them, and with shoal water between them and the island. There is a submerged rock 1 cable NNE of its north end.

Branra Rock, which dries 2.7 metres, 6 cables NNE of the island, has an iron beacon with a barrel topmark.

A light beacon stands on Dearg Sgeir, 1¾ cables southwest of Airds Point at the north side of the entrance to Loch Creran.

Appin Rocks, which dry at half-tide, extend 2 cables southwest of the next point to the north, in which there is a natural arch. A starboard-hand buoy is moored 4 cables WSW of the point. The flood tide sets NNW across these rocks which might affect a yacht tacking, or entering Airds Bay. The Lobster Stone dries 0.9 metres, 1½ cables off Lismore, WNW of the buoy.

Inn Island lies in the channel between the mainland and the north end of Lismore, with Sgeir Bhuidhe, on which is a light beacon, on the mainland side of the channel. Drying rocks extend over 1½ cables SSW of Inn Island, with a perch with a radar reflector near their south end, and another perch on the south side of a gap between the rocks and the island. Drying rocks also extend over 1½ cables southwest of Sgeir Bhuidhe

In the passage west of Inn Island a drying spit on the Lismore side is marked at its outer end by another perch with a radar reflector, and further north the ferry slip has a red perch with a spherical topmark on it. There is a submerged rock ¾ cable east of the north point of Lismore.

Directions

From south keep beyond a cable off Rubha Fion-aird on the east side of the entrance and pass east of Eilean Dubh, and at least ¼ mile off the mainland shore here; pass either side of Branra Rock beacon. Pass within a cable to the west of Appin Rocks starboard-hand buoy, to avoid the Lobster Stone. Pass in mid-channel between Inn Island and Sgeir Bhuidhe light beacon.

There is a clean passage between Lismore and both the first group of islands and the rocks west of Eilean Dubh.

To continue the passage north, and for the north and west of Lismore, see page 63.

From north keep at least a cable off the shore of Shuna and outwith the 5-metre contour to avoid submerged rocks there, but keep closer to Shuna than to rocks above water between Shuna and Lismore as drying rocks extend 1½ cables from them towards Shuna. Keep to the middle of the channel between Inn Island and Sgeir Bhuidhe.

Lights

At night, given enough visibility to see the outline of islands and Branra Rock beacon it should be possible to negotiate this passage with the help of the following lights, but the large-scale chart would be needed, with the bearings over which each light is obscured by islands carefully plotted.

Lismore lighthouse Fl.10s31m19M; obscured NW of 237°
Sgeir Bhuidhe light beacon Fl(2)WR.7s7m9M

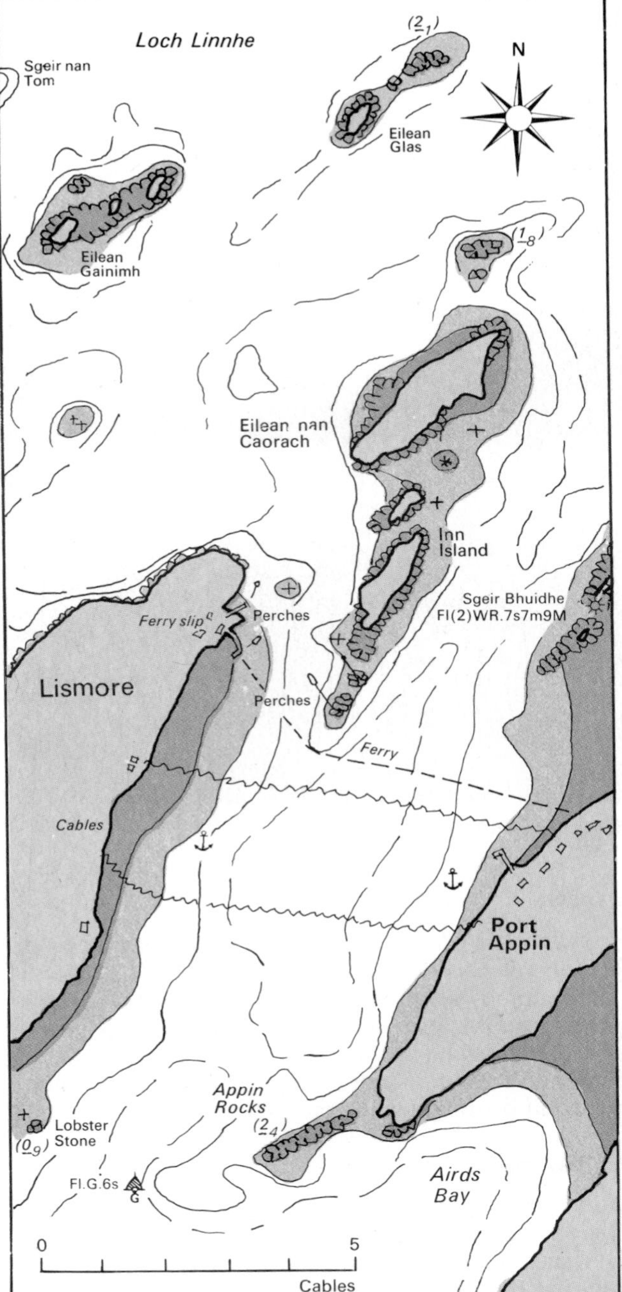

Appin Narrows

Airds Point light beacon Fl.WRG.2s2m3–1M
Appin Rocks buoy Fl.G.6s

Anchorages

Apart from Port Appin there are no regular anchorages within this sound but chart *2378* will show several possible occasional anchorages.

Achnacroish, Lismore (56°31′N 5°29′W), temporary anchorage clear of the pier which is used by a car ferry from Oban.

Port Appin – the perch on rocks at the south end of Inn Island is about 20 metres from their south end. Sgeir Bhuidhe light beacon to the right.

Port Appin from northwest. Lismore ferry slip and beacon on the right; rocks south of Inn Island in the centre.

Airds Bay, north of the entrance to Loch Creran. The head of the bay dries off for ¼ mile. Exposed to southwest, and the flood tide sets strongly across Appin Rocks.

Port Appin (56°33′N 5°25′W), off the pier, or not more than a cable to the southwest, as there are cables crossing the channel both north and south of this. Alternatively, off the Lismore shore, also clear of the cables.

Supplies

Shop, post office, phone box, hotel, *Calor Gas*. Water tap 200 metres northeast of pier.

Loch Creran

56°31′N 5°24′W

The entrance, through which the tide runs at 4 knots at springs, needs to be taken with care. Tidal streams turn as at the north end of the Lynn of Lorne (page 55). Look out for commercial traffic to the Alginate Industries factory at Barcaldine.

Tides

Barcaldine constant is +0015 Oban (−0515 Dover).

Height in metres

MHWS	MHWN	MTL	MLWN	MLWS
4.1	3.0	2.4	1.8	0.8

Dangers and marks

Glas Eilean, 4 cables WSW of the entrance, has a submerged reef off its southwest end. Dearg Sgeir which dries 3.7 metres, on the northwest side of the entrance, is marked by a red light beacon. On the southeast shore opposite this beacon, a submerged reef runs obliquely out from the shore, ending in a drying rock almost in mid-channel, ESE of the beacon.

On the northeast point of Eriska is a green light beacon. Opposite this point is an unmarked drying rock, about a third of the width of the channel from the east shore. Two cables SSE of this rock is a rock above water with an extensive drying reef round it.

Sgeir Caillich, a long ridge of rock above water, extends northeast from the south shore of the loch 4 cables southeast of Eriska, ending in a drying reef marked by a green conical light buoy. Two cables east of the buoy submerged rocks extend over half a cable from the northeast shore.

Beyond Sgeir Caillich the foreshore dries off up to 2 cables in several places. West of Caolas Creagan, 4 miles further up the loch, Black Rocks dry 3.7 metres, off a promontory 4 cables WSW of the narrows.

Caolas Creagan (56°33′N 5°17′W) is crossed by a disused railway bridge with a headroom of 12 metres, and a power cable with the same clearance. The bridge has two spans, of which the north one is obstructed by rocks. Tidal streams in Caolas Creagan run at up to 5 knots and turn about 45 minutes later than at the entrance.

Two cables east of the bridge, as the narrows begin to open out, the foreshore on the south side dries off 50 metres. A drying shingle spit extends from the north shore 3 cables east of the bridge; its position is indicated by a prominent white house. The north side of the head of the loch dries for half a mile.

Creagan Narrows bridge from the shore on the north side.

Creagan Narrows from the bridge showing the spits on either side.

Directions

In the entrance keep closer to Dearg Sgeir red beacon than to the shore of Eriska, and after passing a cable beyond the beacon keep in mid-channel. A clearing mark for the rocks on the southeast side of the entrance is Branra Rock beacon in line with the north high-water mark of Glas Eilean.

On rounding the north end of Eriska the tide will tend to carry you north of the channel; keep closer to the northwest point of Eriska than to the mainland opposite to avoid the drying rock there. Pass northeast of the buoy off Sgeir Caillich, but keep at least a cable off the northeast shore beyond it. In the main part of the loch keep outwith the 10-metre contour.

At Caolas Creagan pass more than a cable off the promontory 4 cables WSW of the bridge and approach the middle of the south span with the extremity of the south shore beyond under the middle of the span, bearing 100°. Clear of the bridge keep north of mid-channel until after the loch has opened out, and then keep south of mid-channel to clear the end of the spit on the north side.

Lights

Dearg Sgeir light beacon Fl.WRG.2s2m3–1M, shows white over the fairway in both directions, green over Eriska and Eriska Shoal, and red over Glas Eilean and over dangers on the NW side. It is obscured between 093° and 196°.

Eriska NE Point light beacon shows Q.G.2m2M between 128° and 329°

Sgeir Caillich buoy Fl.G.3s

Approach in the white sector of Dearg Sgeir light. Appin Rocks buoy (Fl.G.6s) on the port beam will give some indication of how near to the beacon you are; the echo sounder will not be much help. Pass close southeast of the beacon until in the white sector again, and when Eriska beacon appears steer to pass close northeast of it with the Fl.G light buoy ahead. There are no lights further up the loch.

Anchorages

South Shian between Eriska and Sgeir Caillich. The southwest side of the bay dries off for 2 cables. Anchor off the stone slip at the south end of Sgeir Caillich, or off the east side of Eriska outwith the 5-metre contour (there are shoal patches close to it), and clear of moorings and fish cages. The bay half a mile SSE of Sgeir Caillich provides reasonable anchorage, but the foreshore dries off 1 cable.

Barcaldine (56°32′N 5°19′W) on the south side of the loch close west of the pier and Alginate Industries' factory. Moorings available from Creran Moorings.

Creagan provides temporary anchorage, except in fresh to strong westerlies, off Creagan Inn on the north shore, west of the bridge. Pub, bar meals.

Head of the loch near the southeast shore.

Supplies

At Barcaldine, a post office (early closing Wednesday and Saturday), phone box, shop and *Calor Gas* at caravan site, all within ½ mile. Boathouse Grill. Creran Moorings can arrange for mechanical repairs.
☎ Ledaig (063 172) 265.
Sea Life Centre nearby.

Lynn of Morvern

56°31′N 5°33′W

This is the main entrance to Loch Linnhe, between Lismore and Morvern, and it is generally clean and deep. There are only occasional anchorages until the north end of Lismore. Coming from southward the strong tidal streams between Lismore and Mull have to be taken into account, but otherwise there are neither the pilotage problems nor the interest of the Lynn of Lorne.

Dangers and marks

Liath Sgeir, drying 3 metres, is just over a mile north of Lismore lighthouse halfway between the lighthouse and the southwest end of Bernera Island, and slightly to the west of a line joining these two points. This is a hazard if tacking, or making direct for the Lynn of Morvern from south of Lismore.

The new granite quarry at Glensanda on Morvern, west of the north end of Lismore, is a landmark on an otherwise featureless shore.

At the northwest point of Lismore there is a white beacon on the promontory west of Port Ramsay.

Tides

Constant as Oban (−0530 Dover).

Height in metres

MHWS	MHWN	MTL	MLWN	MLWS
4.3	3.2	2.5	1.8	0.7

The north-going stream begins −0545 Oban (+0110 Dover); the south-going stream begins +0025 Oban (−0505 Dover).

In the Lynn of Morvern the main body of the tidal stream runs at 1 knot, but on the flood a narrow stream runs northwards from Lismore lighthouse across to the Morvern shore and then northeast towards Shuna island, at 2½ knots.

On the ebb an eddy sets into Bernera Bay. Also on the ebb, at springs only, there is a strong eddy off the Morvern shore northeast of Bernera, running at 4 knots to the southeast, with overfalls.

Directions

Except for Liath Sgeir there are no specific hazards and the main consideration is to carry a fair tide. With wind against tide there may be steep overfalls between Lismore and Mull, and on a passage from the Firth of Lorne to Loch Linnhe, the Lynn of Lorne may be a more comfortable choice.

Lights

Lismore lighthouse Fl.10s31m19M is obscured NW of 237°.

Glensanda jetty Fl.R.3s4m4M.

Sgeir Bhuidhe light beacon at Appin, Fl(2)WR.7s7m9M, provides a cross bearing when bearing more than 100°.

Corran Narrows lighthouse, Iso.WRG.4s12m10–7M, shows red to the west of 030°.

Anchorages

Achadun Bay, Lismore (56°30′N 5°34′W), east of a promontory northeast of Bernera Island. Occasional anchorage on the west side of the bay. Alternatively in the bay at the northeast end of Bernera.

Bernera Bay, southeast of Bernera is a further alternative in northerly winds. There is a submerged rock 1 cable east of the rocks above water on the west side. Achadun Castle ruins are a short distance from each of these bays.

An Sailean (56°31′N 5°31′W), about the middle of the northwest side of Lismore is a shallow inlet, suitable as an overnight anchorage only for shoal-draught boats or for those of moderate draught at neaps.

Achadun Bay from the castle.

Achadun from the north. The castle is on the left, Bernera on the right. The anchorage is just left of the promontory in the centre of the photo.

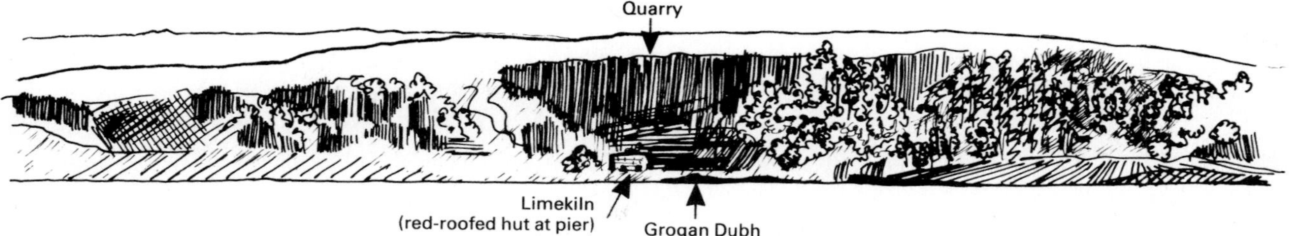

An Sailean from seaward. The broad face of the old quarry with the limekiln below are the most conspicuous features.

There are remains of extensive limestone quarries and limekilns from which lime was shipped out in the first half of the last century.

Grogan Dubh, a rock just above HW springs with a perch on it in the middle of the entrance, is near the north end of a drying reef extending from the southwest point of the entrance. The deepest part of the pool is abreast of the high-water mark of this point.

Port na Moralachd (56°33′N 5°28′W) south of the northwest point of Lismore provides reasonable shelter close inshore at the south side of the bay. There is no clear passage between the offlying islands, and the only approach is from the southwest. If coming from northward, note that submerged rocks extend over half a cable southwest of the most southerly islet.

Port Ramsay

56°33′N 5°27′W

A good anchorage at the north end of Lismore, with many rocks in the approaches; two of them have been marked for the benefit of workboats from the Glensanda quarry. Perches with white encapsulated radar reflectors stand on the rock which dries 3 metres on the west side of the entrance, and on the rock which dries 2.4 metres, 2 cables northeast of Eilean Ramsay. Neither of these perches is at the extreme edge of the rock. There are ruins of several limekilns, and the lime-burners' cottages on the east side of the bay are now nearly all used as holiday cottages.

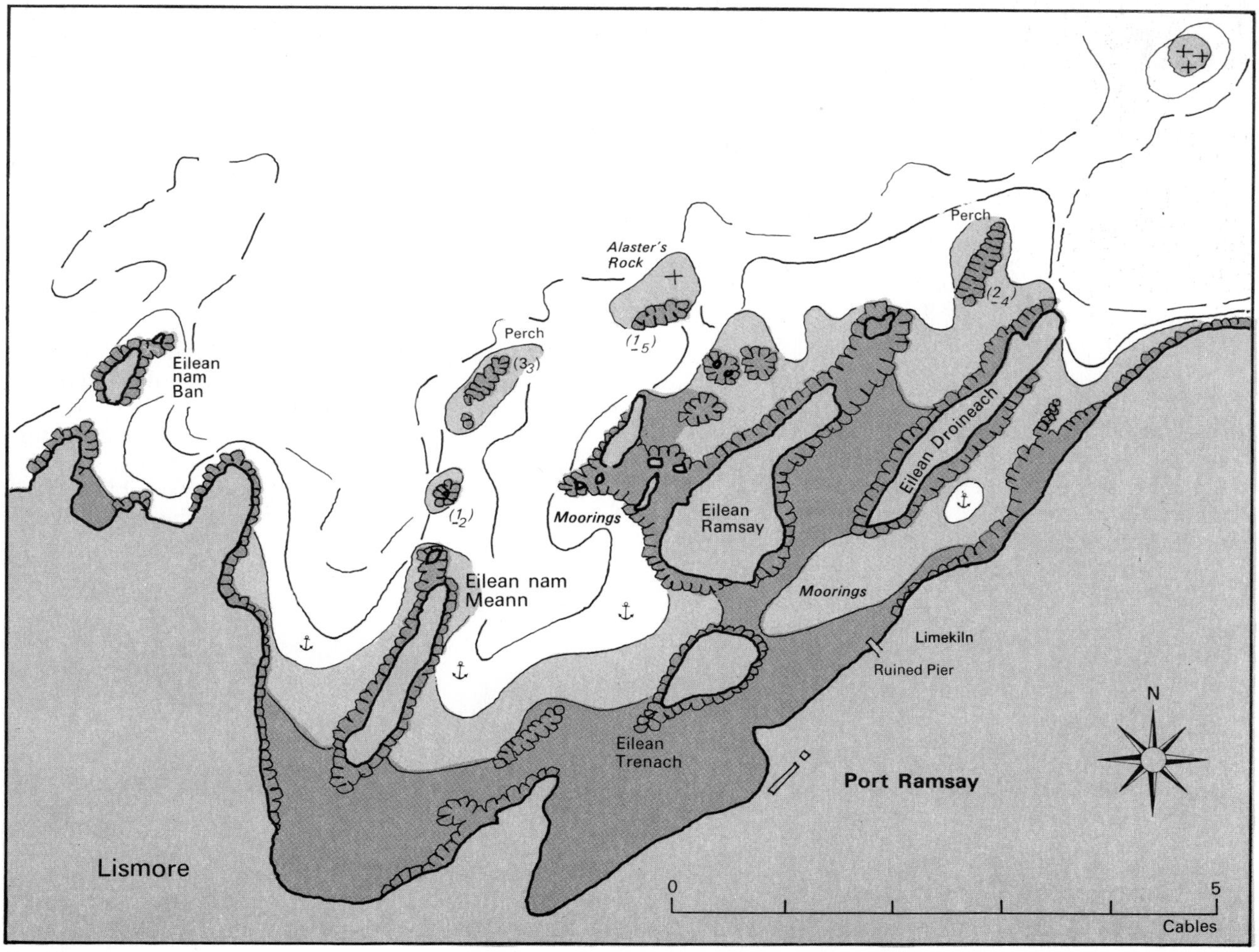

Perch
Alaster's Rock
Perch
Eilean nam Ban
Eilean Droineach
Moorings
Eilean Ramsay
Eilean nam Meann
Moorings
Limekiln
Ruined Pier
Eilean Trenach
Port Ramsay
Lismore
N
0 5 Cables

Port Ramsay

Port Ramsay from the west.

Tides

Constant as at Port Appin −0005 Oban (−0535 Dover).

Height in metres, as at Port Appin

MHWS	MHWN	MTL	MLWN	MLWS
4.2	3.1	2.5	1.9	0.8

Approach

From west the rock 1 cable north of Eilean nam Meann probably only covers at HW springs. If it is showing, pass either side of it, but not more than ½ cable from its north side, to avoid a rock which dries 1.2 metres. If it is covered pass 30 metres north of the islet north of Eilean nam Meann, then rather further off the northeast point if coming round to the east side of that island.

From north there are many rocks and islets up to a mile north of the anchorage, of which the furthest northwest is Sgeir nan Tom with drying rocks 1½ cables southwest of it. Pass over ¼ mile southwest of Sgeir nan Tom or not more than a cable east of it and identify the perch on the drying rock on the west side of the entrance. Approach with the perch bearing not more than 200° to avoid Alaster's Rock, a cable northeast of the perch, and pass half a cable east of the perch, heading to pass down the east side of Eilean nam Meann.

Port Ramsay approach from NNE. Alaster's Rock is showing on the left and the white perch is on the rock on the west side of the entrance. The rock drying 1.2 metres is showing between the higher rocks.

From east pass a cable north of the perch on the rock which dries 2.4 metres northeast of Eilean Ramsay, but no further off to avoid a submerged rock further northeast. Keep Sgeir Bhuidhe light beacon just open of the northeast point of Lismore 100° to pass between these two rocks. Steer to pass well north of the next perch, keeping north of the 10-metre contour until the perch bears 200°, before turning to pass east of it as above.

Anchorages

The best is off the east side of Eilean nam Meann, but no further south than the middle of the island as the head of the bay dries off nearly 2 cables. Alternatively, anchor between the west end of Eilean Ramsay and Eilean Trenach. The bay west of Eilean nam Meann is also suitable.

With sufficient rise of tide it is possible to enter by the southeast of Eilean Droineach, but there is a sand bar with a depth of only 0.3 metres, and a stony spit roughly parallel to and near the centre of the channel. The course to take is about a quarter of the width of the channel away from Eilean Droineach. Anchor in a pool abreast of the south part of the island; further southwest it is shoal with some moorings.

Water at standpipe behind cottages; phone box.

Shuna Sound

56°35′N 5°23′W

A shoal passage between the island of Shuna and the mainland, 1½ miles NNE of Sgeir Bhuidhe light beacon. A shoal spit extends three quarters of the width of the channel from Shuna, and there are shoals south of the spit on the mainland side. The traditional line to lead through is to keep the left-hand side of Appin House above Knap Point, although the deepest water is to the east of this line. It is best avoided within two hours of LW.

Anchorages

Dallens Bay, on the east side of Knap Point dries out at the head for nearly 2 cables and there are several private moorings. The east shore dries off for a cable further north.

Alternatively, in Shuna Sound, towards the island, southwest of Knap Point.

Loch Linnhe – central part

56°38′N 5°24′W

Off the northwest shore of the loch there are several drying and submerged rocks, of which the most southerly is about 4 miles northeast of the entrance to Loch Corrie (Loch a' Choire). The furthest offshore of these is Sanda Shoal, marked by an unlit port-hand buoy, about 2 miles southwest of Sallachan Point, which is marked by an unlit red beacon.

Tides

As in the Lynn of Morvern.

The north-going stream begins −0545 Oban (+0110 Dover); the south-going stream begins +0025 Oban (−0505 Dover).

Constant as Oban (−0530 Dover).

Height in metres

MHWS	MHWN	MTL	MLWN	MLWS
4.3	3.2	2.5	1.8	0.7

Directions

No specific directions are needed except to keep clear of the rocks and shoals on the northwest side of the loch. These are all avoided by keeping ½ mile offshore or outwith the 30-metre contour.

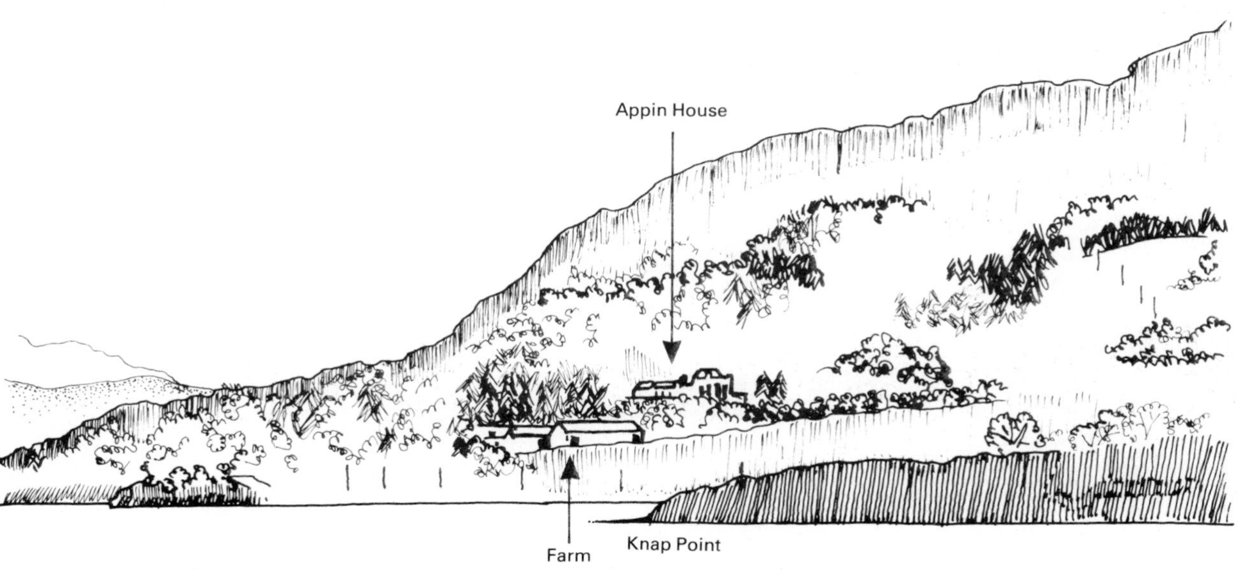

Shuna Sound leading line.

Loch Corrie

56°37′N 5°30′W

The name of this inlet on the northwest shore (Loch a' Choire on the charts) may be translated as 'a cauldron', which probably derives from the squalls which drop into the loch from the splendid ring of mountains surrounding it. Like several other potential anchorages most of it is either too deep or too shallow, and there are many fish cages on its north side. The head of the loch dries out for over ¼ mile. It is worth visiting for the scenery, preferably in settled weather.

The best anchorage is off a stone slip on the north side at the head of the loch, ½ cable offshore and ½ cable to the east of the slip. An alternative anchorage is off a cottage on the south side of the loch.

Eilean Balnagowan on the east side of Loch Linnhe, about 3 miles northeast of Shuna, provides some shelter on its east side, to the north of a reef which shows above water at MHWS. There is a drying rock 1 cable northeast of the north point of the island.

Ballachulish Bay and Loch Leven

56°40′N 5°10′W

Loch Leven is one of the most spectacular of West Coast lochs with hills over 800 metres crowding in on both sides. The upper five miles of the loch average less than ¼ mile wide but, apart from the scenery, would hold little attraction for a sailing yacht's crew.

The narrows, between Ballachulish Bay and Loch Leven, are crossed by a road bridge of bold or brutal design, depending on your point of view. Two miles east of the bridge on the south shore are Ballachulish slate quarries, which continued in operation until about 30 years ago, being easier to work than those at Easdale, and having rail transport. The area between the quarries and the shore has now been cosmetically landscaped. One of the earliest aluminium smelters powered by hydroelectricity was established in 1908 at Kinlochleven, at the head of the loch.

Chart

2380 (1:25,000)

Tides

In the main body of the loch the tidal streams run at up to 1 knot, but at the narrows, and at Caolas nan Con, five miles further east, they run at over 5 knots.

At the narrows the in-going stream begins at −0515 Oban (+0115 Dover) and the out-going stream begins at +0100 Oban (−0430 Dover).

At Caolas nan Con the in-going stream begins ¾ hour later, but the out-going stream begins at the same time as at the narrows.

The tidal constant at Corran, just north of the entrance to Loch Leven is +0005 Oban (−0525 Dover), and at the head of Loch Leven it is +0045 Oban (−0445 Dover).

Height in metres at Corran

MHWS	MHWN	MTL	MLWN	MLWS
4.4	3.3	2.5	1.7	0.7

There are no official figures for heights within Loch Leven, but the range is likely to be substantially less than outside the narrows.

There are moderate overfalls west of the narrows on the ebb with a westerly wind.

Dangers and marks

Cuil-cheanna Spit shoals very gradually to a starboard-hand light buoy, over a mile SSW of the north point of the entrance to Ballachulish Bay.

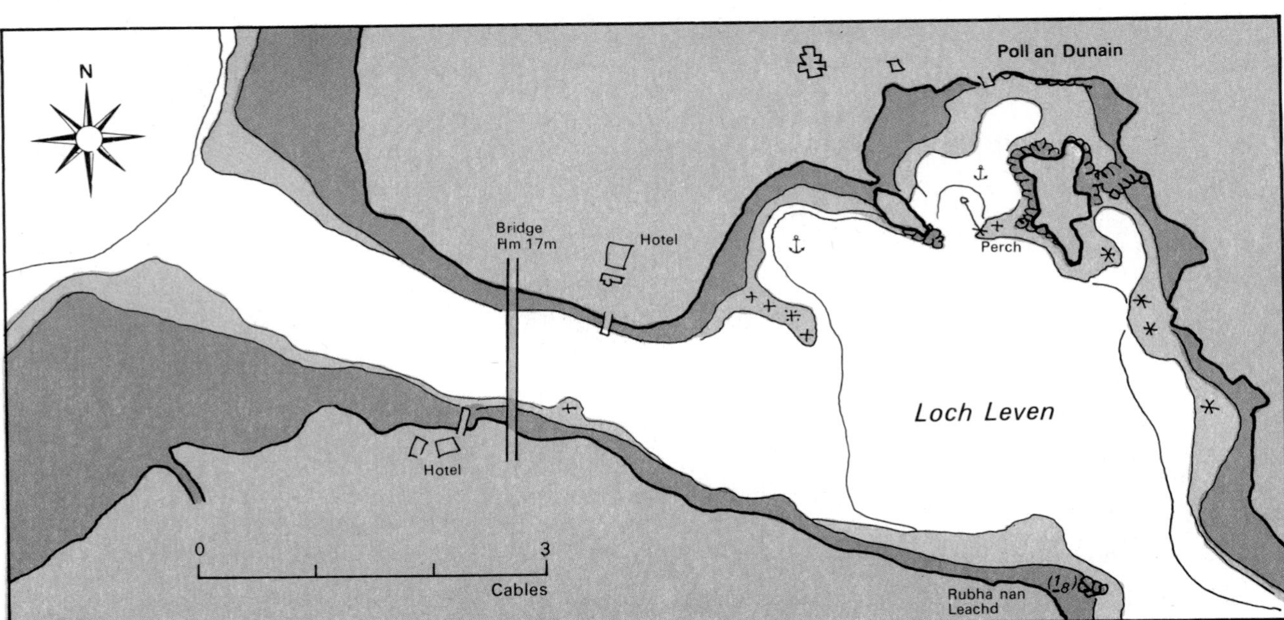

Loch Leven

On the south side of the bay there are rocks close inshore, and 1½ miles west of the bridge, a drying rock ½ cable offshore is marked by an unlit starboard-hand buoy. Unlit Admiralty mooring buoys are laid in Ballachulish Bay but their numbers and location seem to change every few years.

West of the narrows there are drying banks of stones on both sides of the channel with a bar between them on which the greatest depth is only 3 metres.

Ballachulish Bridge, at the narrows, has a charted headroom of 17 metres.

Half a cable east of the bridge there is a submerged rock 50 metres off the south shore. East of the narrows both shores dry out up to ½ cable, and there are rocks in the bay northeast of the narrows.

At Eilean Choinneich, a mile east of the bridge there are drying and submerged rocks up to 3 cables east of the island, and in the bay to the north of it. There are rocks southeast of the next group, St Mungo's Islands, but their north side is clean.

At Caolas nan Con, which is about 5 miles from the bridge there are drying banks on the south side of the channel marked by decaying timber beacons at each end.

Directions

Pass south of Cuil-cheanna Spit buoy, which is slightly south of the middle of the entrance to Ballachulish Bay.

Approach the narrows from north of west, with Rubha nan Leachd, the south point beyond the bridge, under its midpoint, bearing about 110°.

A mile east of the bridge pass south of Eilean Choinneich, and continue east for half a mile to avoid the rocks east of the island; the 20-metre contour should keep you clear of these rocks. Pass north of St Mungo's Islands (Eilean Munde), ¾ mile further east. At Caolas nan Con, 5 miles east of the bridge, keep within a quarter of the apparent width of the channel from the north side.

Lights

At night Cuil-cheanna Spit buoy is lit Fl.G.6s, and there are street lights on Ballachulish Bridge.

Anchorages

Kentallen Bay, on the south side of the entrance to Ballachulish Bay, is very deep almost to the low-water line and there are several moorings. The rocky promontory at the head of the bay is on the low-water line.

In Ballachulish Bay there are only occasional anchorages for use in settled weather or to go ashore for stores. All of them are exposed to onshore winds, and the best is probably at Onich on the north side, to the east of the ruined pier. The broken stumps of a timber extension remain around the head of the pier, which dries.

Diesel, petrol, *Calor Gas*, some chandlery, and mechanical and electrical repairs at Cameron's garage, ☎ Onich (085 53) 224. Shop, post office, phone box.

Kentallen – the low water line is between the rocky promontory at the head of the bay on the left and the small white building on the right.

Poll an Dunain. The ebb is sweeping out of the bay over a submerged reef in the foreground. The rock in the entrance to the inner anchorage shows in the background, with the drying reef off the west point.

Ballachulish – two inlets in the foreground provide some shelter.

St Mungo's Islands from the south; Anchor in the bight southeast of Eilean Munde, or further east but note the drying rock.

Poll an Dunain (Bishop's Bay) east of the narrows on the north shore. A reef, part of which dries, extends a cable from the west shore of the bay, and the ebb tide, which runs anticlockwise round the bay, sets across this reef.

Much of the inner pool is shallow and most of it is occupied by moorings, but it is usually possible to find space to anchor. A drying rock in the middle of the entrance to the pool is marked by a thin steel perch which almost covers at HW. A drying reef extends almost ¼ cable off the west point of the entrance.

The hotel at Ballachulish Bridge is reached by a shore path.

Ballachulish Two rather bleak rectangular inlets have been formed in the landscaping works at the quarries on the south shore, both with a concrete quay at the head. The more easterly inlet, which faces Eilean Munde, is more sheltered.

At Ballachulish (south) there are shops, bank, post office, phone box, fish-and-chips.

Eilean Munde Occasional anchorage south of the islands, between the largest and most westerly (St Mungo's Island, on which is a graveyard and ruined chapel) and an islet on its east side. Further east there is a large drying rock southeast of the next islet, with a submerged rock ½ cable further southeast.

Kinlochleven off the wharf on the south side towards the head of the loch. Beyond this the loch is shoal and drying for ¼ mile.

Shops, garage, post office, phone box in Kinlochleven.

Loch Linnhe – upper part

56°47′N 5°10′W

The upper part of Loch Linnhe is impressive, with high mountains on each side, but offers little interest to the crew of a sailing yacht unless going to or from the Caledonian Canal, which leads to the east coast of Scotland, but the lochs along the canal itself are worth visiting on their own account. The wind is normally funnelled along Loch Linnhe, one way or the other. The longer a loch and the higher the mountains at its head, the greater, generally, is the rainfall. Loch Linnhe is one of the longest, with the highest mountain.

Fort William has nothing to offer the yachtsman except the convenience of shops and some services. There are two adequate anchorages at the head of the loch, and an expedition to the top of Ben Nevis, the highest mountain in Britain, can be made, although its head is not often clear of cloud. The continuous staircase of locks on the canal, Neptune's Staircase, is worth seeing. Another expedition which might take you out of the rain is the railway journey to Mallaig, and the coast on the way – particularly if you haven't time to go there by sea. Steam trains are being run on this line as an additional tourist attraction.

Loch Eil, to the west of the head of Loch Linnhe, is more open and unusually featureless.

Owing to the distance between them, Corran Narrows and the head of the loch will be described separately.

Charts

2380 (1:25,000). *2372* shows both Corran Narrows and the head of the loch at 1:10,000 and 1:6,250 respectively, but is hardly necessary for yachts.

Corran Narrows

56°43′N 5°14′W

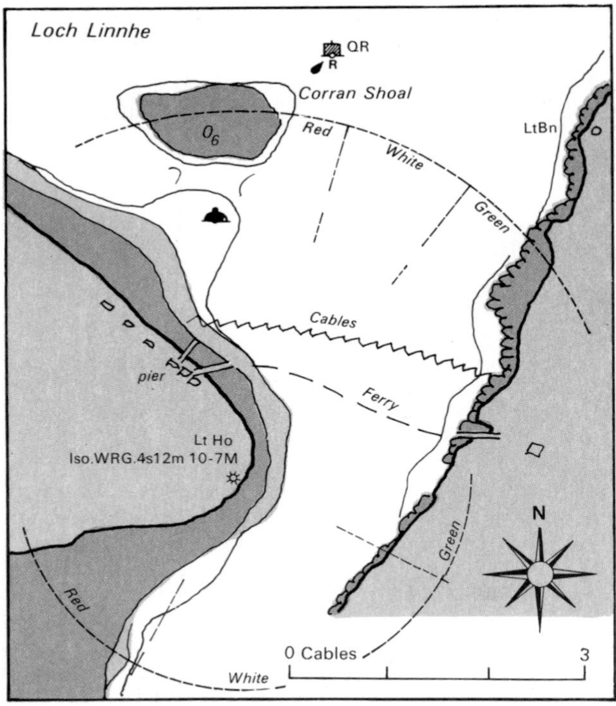

Corran Narrows

Dangers and marks

Shoals on both sides up to 2 miles SSW of the narrows are marked, on the east side by a green conical light buoy at the south end of Cuil-cheanna Spit, and on the west side by red can buoys, one lit and one unlit. On Sallachan Point, 2 miles southwest of the narrows, there is an unlit red beacon.

At Corran Point, on the west side of the narrows there is a white lighthouse. Corran Shoal, north of the lighthouse, is marked by a red can light buoy, northeast of the shoal and nearly ½ mile north of the lighthouse. On the east shore, ½ mile northeast of the lighthouse there is a white rectangular light beacon.

Tides

The tidal stream in the narrows runs at over 5 knots at springs, with eddies on both sides, mainly north of the narrows on the flood and south of them on the ebb.

The in-going stream begins −0600 Oban (+0055 Dover); the out-going stream begins +0005 Oban (−0525 Dover).
The constant is +0005 Oban (−0525 Dover).

Height in metres

MHWS	MHWN	MTL	MLWN	MLWS
4.4	3.3	2.5	1.7	0.7

Directions

Between the more southerly port-hand buoy and the east point of the entrance keep towards the buoy as the east shore dries off for 1½ cables. With chart *2380* and carefully watching the echo sounder it is feasible to sail inshore of the buoys.

Lights

Corran Point lighthouse, Iso.WRG.4s12m10–7M, shows red to west of the fairway, white over the fairway and the shore to SE of the fairway, and green between 215° and 305°.
Pier NNW of Corran Point Fl.R.5s7m3M
Cuil-cheanna buoy Fl.G.6s
Red buoy Fl(2)R.15s
Corran Shoal buoy Q.R
Corran north beacon, on east shore, Fl.5s4m4M

Anchorages

Corran Point, north of the pier, clear of ferry moorings, and avoiding both the shoal and very deep water on either side. Avoid also the underwater power cables crossing the narrows.

Camas Aiseig There are many fish cages, but the best anchorage is ½ mile northwest of the pier, about halfway between a stone slip and a group of houses at the mouth of a burn 3 cables further north. Don't go closer in than the 5-metre line, as there are drying rocks on the low-water line.

There is a shop, and petrol, at Clovulin, 1 mile south from the pier.

Camas Aiseig – the ferry slip on the left, with the pier left of centre.

Upper Loch Linnhe

56°49′N 5°07′W

The loch north of Corran Narrows is generally clean except for drying banks at the mouths of burns on either side. Underwater tests are carried out in this part of the loch and there may be buoys, usually yellow, of no navigational significance.

Fort William is on the east side of the loch towards the head. North of the town a long pier extends from the east shore. North of the pier, Lochy Flats dry out half a mile from the east shore. Their outer edge is marked by a green conical light buoy.

3 cables north of Lochy Flats buoy, a red can light buoy marks McLean Rock which dries 0.3 metre. North and west of this buoy are several low islands with drying areas up to ½ cable round them. Beyond Rubha Dearg the pulp mill is very conspicuous.

The most westerly island has a loading jetty on its east side and is connected to the mainland by a transporter structure. South of this island is a submerged rock ¾ cable off the south shore.

North of Eilean na Creich the entrance to the Caledonian Canal is marked by a cylindrical white tower with a conical slate roof. Between Eilean na Creich and the canal entrance is a red can light buoy.

Tides

The constant is +0022 Oban (−0508 Dover).

Height in metres

MHWS	MHWN	MTL	MLWN	MLWS
4.1	3.1	2.5	1.9	0.9

Directions

After passing the long pier at Fort William the two light buoys must be identified and passed on the appropriate hand. After passing the island off Rubha Dearg, if heading for Loch Eil, keep midway between the south shore and the islands to the north, to avoid the submerged rock off the south shore.

If making for the canal entrance, pass at least ½ cable northeast of Eilean na Creich and either side of the red buoy.

Lights

Fort William (long) pier shows Fl.G.2s6m4M.
Lochy Flats buoy Q.G
McLean Rock buoy Fl(2)R.12s
Buoy south of canal Fl.R.3s
Light tower at canal entrance Iso.WRG.4s6m5M; white over fairway 310°–335°, green to east, red to southwest. Obscured from west of 030°.

Anchorages

Fort William Very temporary, only for a brief visit ashore, do not leave a yacht unattended; alongside sheet piling at the car park at the southwest end of town there are ladders but nowhere to make fast.

Also temporary, between the small town pier and the long pier to the north. Shoal and drying inshore of a line between the heads of these piers.

Camas nan Gall, nearly a mile northwest of Fort William on the west shore. Keep clear of McLean Rock, ½ cable northwest of the red buoy, as well as a sub-

Fort William from northwest. Lochy Flats buoy is well out from the east shore off the mouth of the Lochy River. Ben Nevis is hidden in cloud as usual.

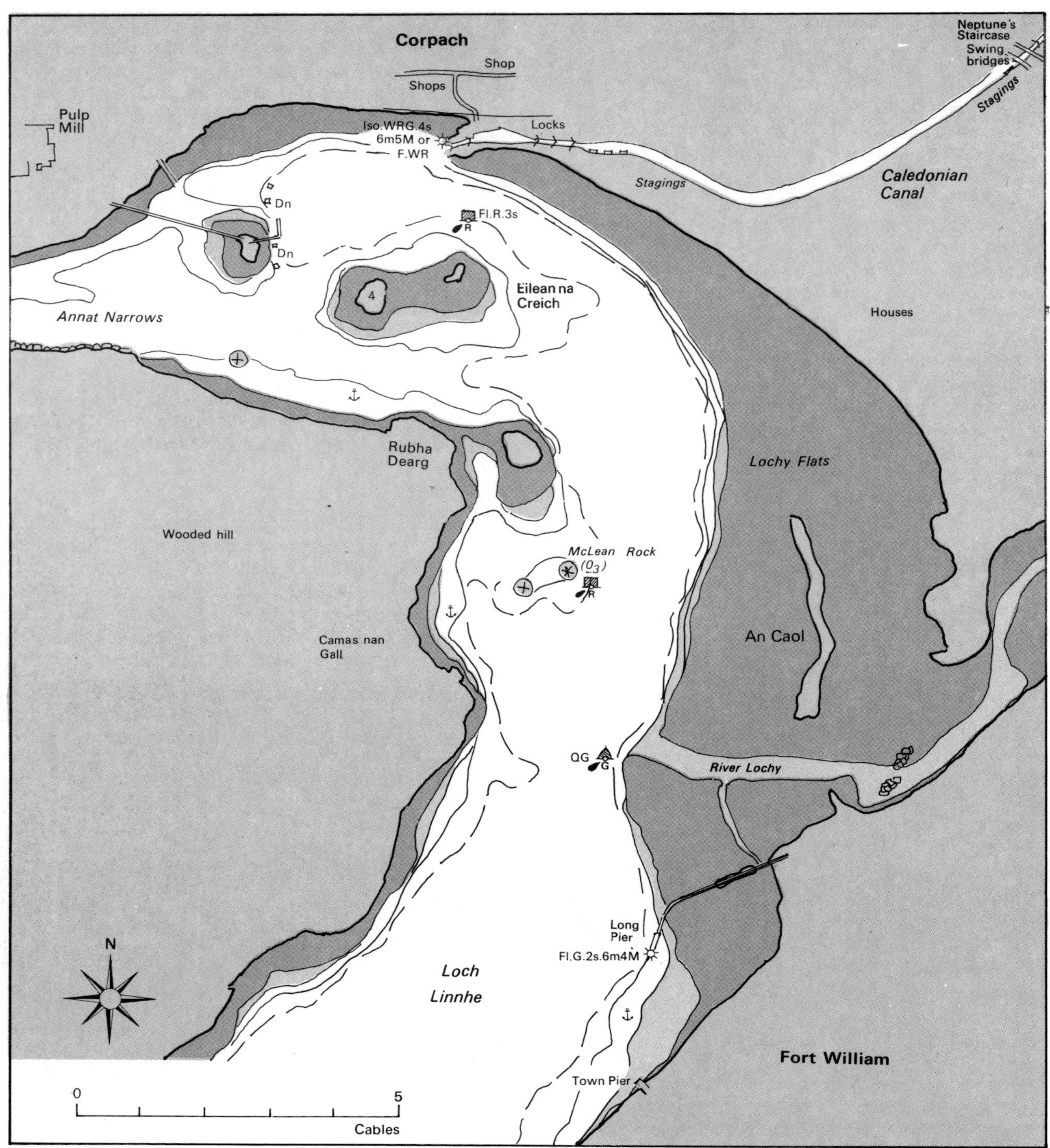

Fort William and Corpach

merged rock halfway between the buoy and the shore to the west. There are many moorings in the bay. Ferry to Fort William.

Rubha Dearg Anchor along the shore west of the point, avoiding the submerged rock noted above. Trees on shore provide some shelter from southerly winds.

Corpach, west of canal entrance, anchor clear of moorings and the approach to the canal.

Canal Make fast at a staging on the north side of the entrance and seek out the lock-keeper in his office beside the lock. Yachts are not usually allowed to stay in the basin above the sea lock, and have to go through two further locks and lie at stagings above the upper lock. There is a risk of interference, vandalism and theft. If you are allowed to stay in the basin, note that the water level is likely to rise and fall, and fenders may be pushed over the concrete dockside, leaving the hull to chafe.

Corpach from south. The loading gantry for the Pulp Mill is on the left, and the canal entrance in the centre.

Camas nan Gall – various craft and equipment on moorings. McLean Rock buoy right of centre. Caledonian Canal upper left.

The canal operates Mondays to Saturdays from 0800 to 1200 and from 1300 to 1645. The sea lock is operated only from four hours before to four hours after HW. Charges (1987) for a single day are £2 per metre, and for a through passage over three days £4 per metre.

It is intended to install VHF R/T at Corpach in 1987. Corpach lock office, ☎ Corpach (039 77) 249; Canal office, ☎ Inverness (0463) 233140.

Supplies and services

Shops, hotels and garages in Fort William. Early closing Wednesday. In Corpach, a shop on the north side of the main road is open late some evenings, and open Sunday.

Corpach Chandlers has moorings, diesel, *Calor Gas*, chandlery, repairs, cranage (in canal basin). ☎ Corpach (039 77) 245 or 467.

Communications Post office, phone boxes, bus to Glasgow, Mallaig and Inverness, train to Glasgow and Mallaig.

Loch Eil

56°51′N 5°14′W

Entered through Annat Narrows, south of the pulp mill. In the narrows the tide runs at 5 knots at springs. The west-going stream begins −0435 Oban (+0220 Dover); the east-going stream begins +0130 Oban (−0400 Dover).

The shore generally dries up to ½ cable, and more in places, usually off the mouth of a burn. Shoals extend 2 cables off the north shore at the west end of the narrows. The head of the loch dries off 2 cables, and then quickly becomes deep.

IV. Sound of Mull

This is the usual route to the north and west, the alternative being along the exposed south side of Mull. The Sound of Mull is straightforward and the fairway is well marked and adequately lit. If you want to explore (or tack) close inshore you will need a large-scale chart, but if you keep generally at least 2 cables from the shore you could manage without it.

The southeast half of the sound has high hills on both sides, particularly on Mull, and the wind tends to funnel along the sound, with occasional squalls through valleys. About halfway along the sound, at Salen, there is a gap in the Mull hills and a southwest wind often divides, blowing northwest and southeast from there. I've seen the opposite happen as well – in what was basically a northeasterly wind two yachts approaching this point from opposite directions, both of them under spinnaker.

On the Morvern shore at the southeast end of the sound there are cliffs up to 250-metres high, and it is not uncommon for waterfalls on these cliffs (known locally as the 'Widow's Tresses') to be blown upwards in strong southwest winds.

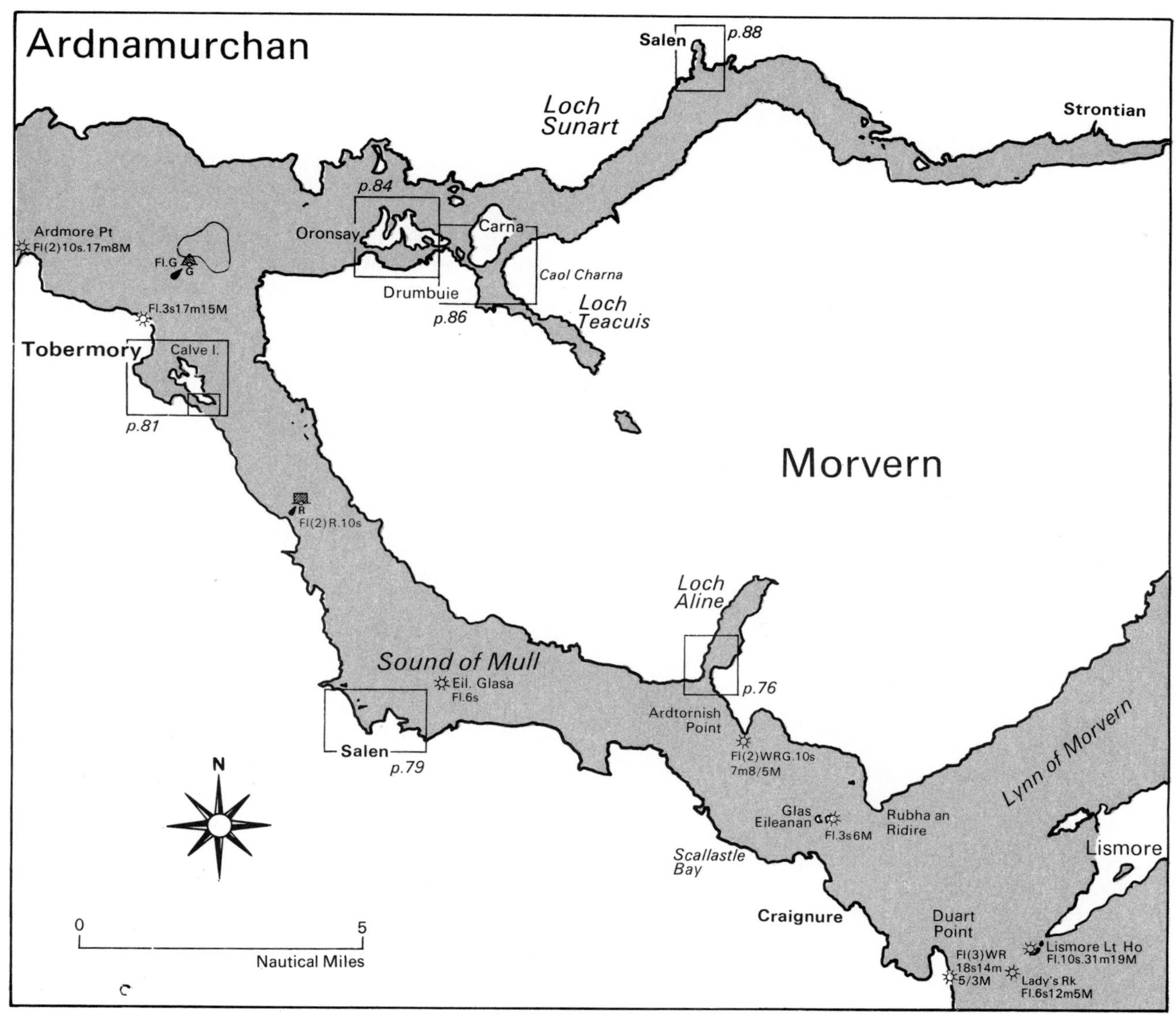

Charts

2390 (1:25,000); *2171 Sound of Mull and Approaches* (1:75,000).

Southeast entrance to the sound

56°30'N 5°42'W

The southeast entrance to the sound is between Rubha an Ridire on Morvern and Scallastle Point on Mull, but for convenience the passage between Lismore and Mull is included here.

Dangers and marks

Lismore lighthouse on Eilean Musdile, southwest of the south end of Lismore, is a very distinctive mark.

Half a mile southwest of the lighthouse is Lady's Rock, above water but with drying rocks up to half a cable round it, and a white light beacon on it, not always easily seen on a dull day.

Black's Memorial Tower, low on the Mull shore, is a miniature mock castle, nearly a mile west of Lady's Rock.

Duart Castle, also on Mull, is a classic picture-postcard castle on a low cliff 6 cables WNW of Black's Memorial tower; it is not visible from southeast.

Liath Sgeir, drying 3 metres, is just over a mile north of Lismore lighthouse halfway between the lighthouse and the southwest end of Bernera, and slightly to the west of a line joining these two points. This is a hazard if tacking, or making direct for the Lynn of Morvern from south of Lismore.

Tides

Constant +0015 Oban (−0515 Dover).

Height in metres at Craignure

MHWS	MHWN	MTL	MLWN	MLWS
4.0	3.0	2.3	1.7	0.6

The north-going stream begins −0545 Oban (+0110 Dover); the south-going stream begins +0025 Oban (−0505 Dover).

In the fairway between Lady's Rock and Mull tidal streams run at 3 knots springs, with overfalls at the windward end of the passage if the wind is against the tide. Between Lady's Rock and Lismore the ebb reaches 4 knots (the Admiralty pilot puts these figures at 4 and 6 knots respectively!).

On the flood there are eddies and severe turbulence northwest of Lismore lighthouse, which can be very uncomfortable in heavy weather.

On the ebb an eddy sets into Bernera Bay.

Directions

Except for Liath Sgeir there are no specific hazards and the main consideration is to carry a fair tide. With wind against tide there may be steep overfalls between Lismore and Mull.

Lights

At night the passage is well lit.

Lismore lighthouse Fl.10s31m19M
Lady's Rock Fl.6s12m5M
Black's Memorial Fl(3)WR.18s14m5/3M, showing red over Lady's Rock and 353° to shore, and white elsewhere.

Anchorages

Duart Bay, Mull, 56°27'N 5°40'W. Both parts of the head of the bay dry off nearly 4 cables and it rapidly becomes deep beyond the low-water line. Occasional anchorage off the slip at Torosay on the west side of the bay in 5 metres, clear of drying and submerged rocks 1 cable NNE of the slip, and leaving clear access to the slip for tourist launches.

Alternative temporary anchorage in very quiet weather off the jetty at Duart Castle on the east side of the bay, leaving clear access to the jetty. Both Torosay Castle, which is a Victorian mansion, and Duart Castle, which is ancient, are popular tourist attractions.

Craignure Bay, Mull, 56°28'N 5°42'W. The main car ferry terminal for Mull so the anchorage is likely to be disturbed. The west side of the bay dries and shoals for 1½ cables, but some shelter can be found anywhere in the bay in offshore winds, but leave space for ferries manoeuvring to the pier. Yachts may go alongside the pier clear of the link-span, but it is difficult to keep fenders in place on the concrete columns.

Light, F.R, at head of ferry pier. Leading lights are occasionally lit for ferries and commercial vessels.

Shop, post office, phone box, hotels, *Calor Gas*. Ferry to Oban; bus to Tobermory and southwest Mull.

Bernera Bay, 56°29'.5N 5°34'.5W, southeast of Bernera is suitable in northerly winds. There is a submerged rock 1 cable east of the rocks above water on the west side.

The Sound of Mull

56°32'N 5°54'W

Dangers and marks

The direction of buoyage is northwestward.

Throughout the sound there are unmarked rocks up to 2 cables off both shores.

In the middle of the southeast entrance, between Rubha an Ridire (Morvern) and Scallastle Point on Mull are the Grey Rocks (Glas Eileanan), two islets with a light beacon on the east one; the fairway is to the north.

Off Scallastle Point there is a group of rocks above water of which Sgeir nan Gobhar is the most northerly with a rock drying 0.5 metres 2 cables east of it.

7 cables WNW of the light beacon a red can buoy marks the north side of Yule Rocks, which are submerged.

Nearly 2 miles northwest of Grey Rocks Ardtornish Point, at the west end of the cliffs on the Morvern shore, has a ruined castle and a small white-painted light beacon low on the point itself.

The entrance to Loch Aline is about a mile northwest of Ardtornish.

A mile WSW of Ardtornish Point a red can buoy near the Mull shore marks Avon Rock over which the depth is 2.2 metres.

Green Island (Eileanan Glasa) is the largest of a group of islets 5½ miles west of Ardtornish, with a light beacon on the north islet. The main fairway is on the north side.

A mile ENE of the light beacon a green conical buoy 4 cables off the Morvern shore marks Fiunary Rocks, which can be awkward because of their position on the inside of the bend of the sound.

¾ mile SSW of the light beacon another green conical buoy is on the south side of a group of rocks, marking a channel between these rocks and Mull.

A red can light buoy 3½ miles northwest of Green Island, near the Mull shore, marks a wreck with 2.7 metres over it, and a green conical buoy over a mile further north marks drying rocks near the Morvern shore.

There are no other specific dangers outwith 2 cables from the shore until the sound opens out at the mouth of Loch Sunart. The west entrance to the Sound of Mull is described on page 82 below.

Tides

Tidal streams run at up to 2 knots at the southeast entrance to the sound, and up to 1 knot elsewhere.

At the southeast end of the sound the northwest-going stream begins about −0600 Oban (+0100 Dover); southeast-going stream begins about −0045 Oban (+0615 Dover).

3 miles southeast of Calve Island the northwest-going stream begins about +0500 Oban (−0030 Dover); southeast-going stream begins about −0045 Oban (+0615 Dover).

Note that the stream runs northwest for about 5¼ hours at the southeast end and 6¾ hours at the northwest end of the sound.

Constant throughout averages +0015 Oban (−0515 Dover).

Height in metres at Craignure

MHWS	MHWN	MTL	MLWN	MLWS
4.0	3.0	2.3	1.7	0.6

Height in metres at Tobermory

MHWS	MHWN	MTL	MLWN	MLWS
4.4	3.3	2.5	1.8	0.7

The times quoted are all interpolated from more comprehensive data, for which refer to almanacs or Admiralty tide tables.

Directions

The passage is straightforward but, unless you have the large-scale chart, keep north of Grey Rocks and Green Island and at least 2 cables offshore.

Lights

At night, the following lights give sufficient guidance.

Lismore lighthouse Fl.10s19M
Grey Rocks Fl.3s6M
Ardtornish Point Fl(2)WRG.10s8–5M; white over fairway in both directions with green sectors to the north and red sectors to the south, with a further white sector between the red.
Green Island Fl.6s8M
Red buoy Fl(2)R.10s
Rubha nan Gall lighthouse Fl.3s15M

Lismore lighthouse in line with Grey Rocks gives a useful line to pass Ardtornish. Rubha nan Gall lighthouse is obscured by Calve Island southwest of the centre of the sound.

Ardtornish light beacon is not very bright and in poor weather the coloured sectors will not be visible from the west from as far as Eileanan Glasa.

Anchorages – southeast part of the sound

Rubha an Ridire, 56°30′N 5°42′W. There is an occasional anchorage at the northeast point of the island west of Rubha an Ridire, the north point of the entrance to the sound. The island has drying rocks off its east and northwest sides: approaching from southeast keep closer to the mainland than to the island; approaching by the north of the island keep well over a cable off it. Anchor in 5 metres near the northeast tip of the island with Grey Rocks beacon over the northwest tangent of the island.

Scallastle Bay, Mull, 56°29′N 5°44′W. Good anchorage in offshore winds but the approach from eastward needs care. There are drying patches 2 cables off the west side of the bay and up to 1 cable elsewhere.

Approaching from southeast steer towards Grey Rocks to avoid the rock which dries 0.5 metres referred to earlier (page 74), and keep northeast of the middle of the channel between Grey Rocks and Sgeir nan Gobhar. Approaching by the north of Grey Rocks needs more careful chartwork. From northwest there is little problem.

Ardtornish Bay, east of Ardtornish Point on Morvern, provides good shelter from southwest to northeast, and is an inviting place to wait if the weather is particularly unpleasant further up the sound. Anchor off the boathouse in the northwest corner. The head of the bay is shoal.

Eilean Rubha an Ridire, looking southwest. A yacht is anchored close to the northwest tip of the island. Mull beyond is partly hidden by cloud.

Loch Aline

56°33′N 5°46′W

The best anchorage between Oban and Tobermory, and in many ways better than either, Loch Aline has a variety of sheltered places within and is fairly easy to enter, even at night, and can provide most essential supplies. The shores are steep and thickly wooded.

The entrance is a cable wide but the least depth in the fairway is only 2.1 metres, and the tide runs at about 2½ knots in the narrows. Just inside the loch there is a mine producing high quality silica sand which is taken away by coasters several times a week from a loading jetty on the west shore. Look out for the coasters, which have no room to manoeuvre once they are in the narrows, as well as for the car ferry which runs frequently to Mull from a slip on the west side of the narrows.

Ardtornish Estate appears to positively welcome visitors and there are several pleasant walks, particularly to Lochaline Castle at the head of the loch on the west side, and to Ardtornish Castle, southeastward along the Sound of Mull. The gardens of Ardtornish House are usually open to visitors; there is a box at the gate for donations. Respect the courteously worded notices which restrict access to parts of the estate at certain times, so that visitors will continue to be welcome.

The church, half a mile northwest of the village, has an excellent collection of medieval carved stones. Visits to the sand mine, which has 30 miles of tunnels, can be arranged for groups of people in mid-week.

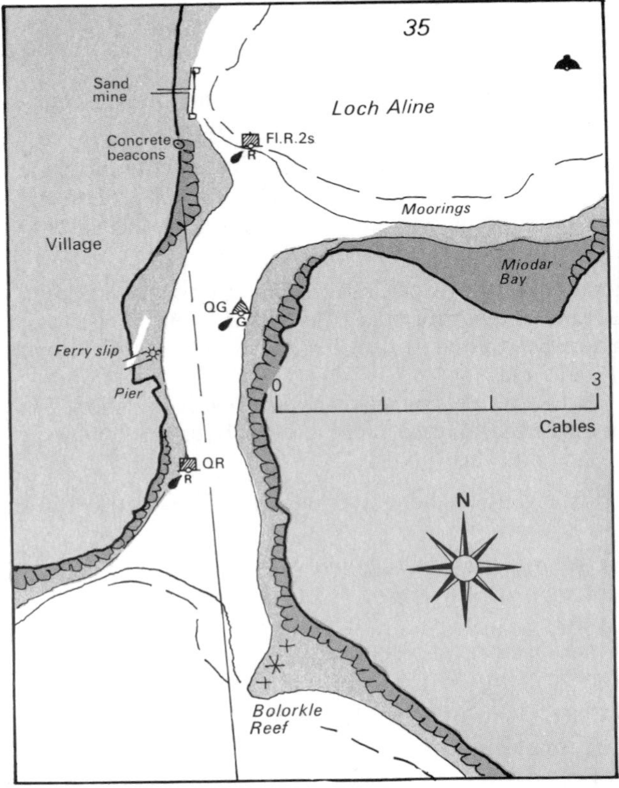

Loch Aline

Loch Aline entrance from southwest.

Tides

Constant +0012 Oban (−0518 Dover).

Height in metres

MHWS	MHWN
4.5	4.3

Dangers and marks

Outside the entrance Bolorkle Reef (Bogha Lurcain), which dries nearly a cable from the east shore, is unmarked but leading marks at the root of the loading jetty at the mine lead clear of it. The front mark is a concrete pillar, originally painted orange, but faded, and the back mark is an orange stripe on the structure of the jetty.

Three light buoys in the narrows are usually easier to pick out than the leading marks. The marks lead east of the first red can buoy, which is often the best guide to finding them. During the last few years these buoys have come and gone and been replaced again, and have only recently been re-lit; at one time there was a buoy off Bolorkle Reef, but there is not one at present. The buoys may have been changed yet again by the time you arrive.

Half a mile within the loch on the east side a yellow iron beacon with a spherical topmark marks a reef, and half a mile further a similar beacon off the west shore marks the east end of a more extensive reef. The head of the loch dries for about half a mile.

Approach

From southeast keep 2 cables offshore until the leading line is identified before turning into the entrance.

From west keep a cable offshore until the leading line is seen to the east of the first red buoy. Each buoy should be left on the appropriate side; they are intended for commercial vessels, and there is a little space for yachts to tack inshore of them.

By night the buoys are lit (Q.R, Q.G, Fl.R.2s) and there are fixed white lights on the leading marks, but there is sometimes a much brighter light on the head of the jetty, and it has been known, on a quiet night, for a helmsman to steer for this light, carefully keeping it in line above its own reflection.

There are lights, 2F.R(vert), at the end of the ferry slip.

Late in the summer of 1986 Nigel Gardner took some Yachtmaster students into Loch Aline as a night exercise and found that only one buoy and one leading light were lit, which added to the interest of the exercise. He says that the southeast face of the screen structure at the ferry jetty (which shows up well in the street lights) kept in line astern about 220° leads through the deeper water at the north end of the bar towards the fish cages on the east side which have low floodlighting.

Anchorages

Lochaline Pier is outwith the loch, 3 cables west of the entrance; yachts can berth temporarily alongside,

Coasters are often encountered in Loch Aline.

but should not be left unattended as fenders tend to shift in the wash from passing vessels. There are no ladders and it is in a ruinous state, and the car ferry is berthed here overnight. Coasters occasionally load timber at the pier. Water is laid on.

An alternative temporary berth is at the old stone pier on the west side of the entrance narrows, except within an hour of LW springs; however, the face of this pier is very rough.

The most convenient anchorage is on the west side, north of the loading jetty. The immediate surroundings are not attractive and there are several moorings, but the wooded shore provides good shelter in westerly winds and it is convenient for the village. There is reported to be less water than charted. Keep clear of the approach to the jetty.

Miodar Bay in the southeast corner of the loch. It is best to anchor beyond the moorings, but the bottom shelves abruptly just off the low-water line, so take care not to swing over it at low tide.

The fish cages further north, which have low floodlighting, are a useful guide at night. There is a good anchorage between the cages and the first yellow beacon.

East shore There is also a good anchorage beyond the first beacon, towards the slipway and moorings. Leave swinging room clear of shoal water inshore.

West shore A stony shelf extends a cable off the mouth of a burn to the SSW of the second yellow beacon, but there is a good anchorage between the burn and the beacon.

Beyond the beacon there is an anchorage between the beacon and a stone jetty on the west shore further north, but there are rocky patches on the bottom with poor holding. After heavy rain the outflowing stream from the river here will hold a yacht's stern to a strong southwest wind – even a ketch with the mizzen set, which can be discouraging if rain is still falling. The heavily wooded shore provides excellent shelter, but the steep hillside cuts out any sun quite early in the evening.

Supplies and services

Shop in the village, on the west side of the narrows. Hotel at Lochaline Pier, ¼ mile west of the entrance. Ardtornish Estate market garden at the northeast corner of the loch sells home-grown fruit and vegetables, as well as eggs, venison and fresh baking.

Petrol pumps up hill beyond the shop; ask at the shop first. *Calor Gas* at the shop.

John Hodgson, boatbuilder, has a workshop and slipway on the east side of the loch beyond the first beacon. Some moorings are provided and a pontoon is being installed at which fuel and water will be available. Most repairs can be carried out. ☎ Morvern (096 784) 242/204.

Loch Aline approach from southwest.

Communications Post office and phone box in the village. Ferry to Mull; the quickest way to Oban is to take this ferry, then a bus or a lift, and then a ferry at Craignure.

Anchorages – middle part of the sound

Fishnish Bay, Mull, 56°31′N 5°50′W, occasional anchorage in offshore winds. The head of the bay dries off ¼ mile and the sides of the bay are steep-to. Anchor towards the head of the bay around the 5-metre line.

Salen

56°31′.5N 5°57′W

Southwest of Green Island, this is a fairly good anchorage with HIDB visitors' moorings, but it needs to be approached carefully because of several groups of rocks in the way.

Approach

From east keep at least ¼ mile offshore to avoid the drying banks at the mouth of the Forsa river. The 10-metre contour is close to the low-water line here. Allowing for it to range around its mooring, the green conical buoy in line with houses at the root of the pier on the north side of Rubha Mor at the east side of the bay lead clear of this bank.

Pass south of the buoy, which is on the south side of a group of submerged and drying rocks, or at least ¼ mile north of the buoy, keeping north of the 5-metre contour. Enter the bay between the point and a red can buoy less than 2 cables WNW of it. Anchor on the southeast side of the bay, with the most easterly rocks at Green Island open of Rubha Mor.

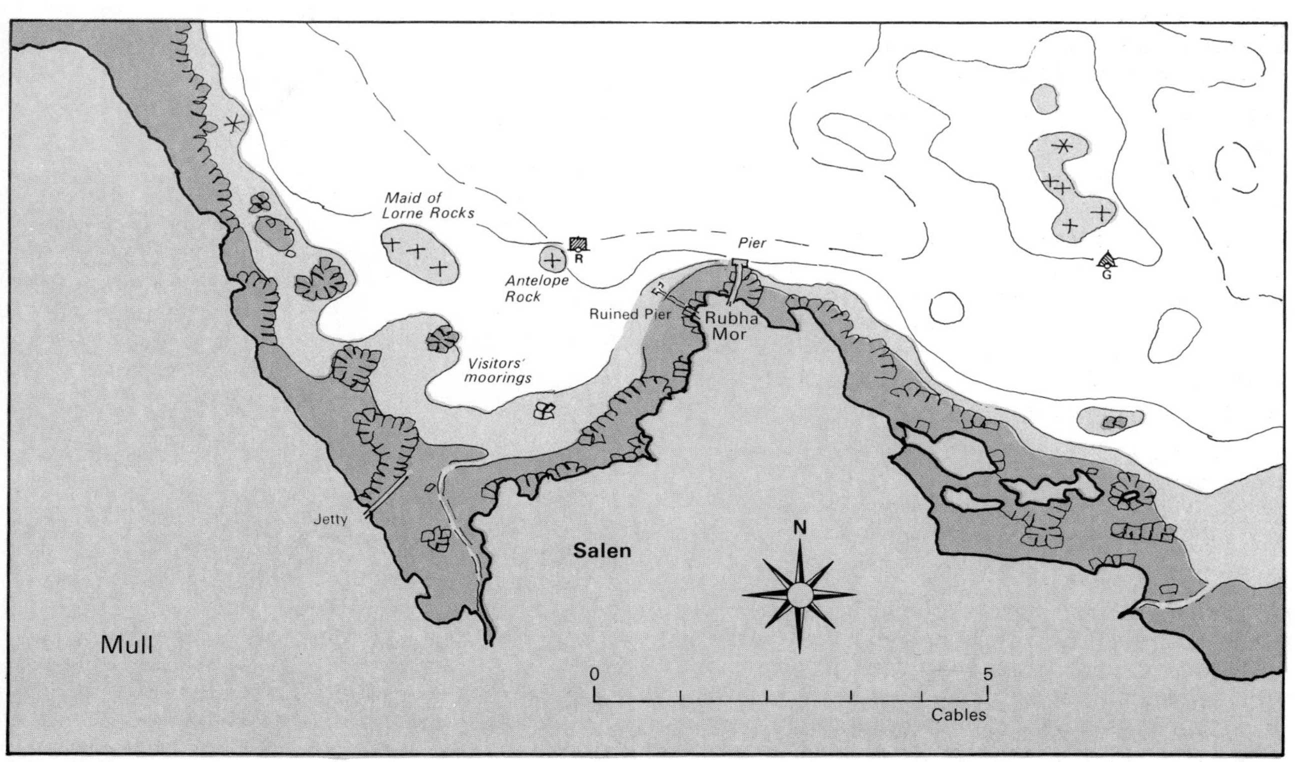

Salen, Mull

Salen, Mull; the passage inside the Bo Rocks; the buoy in line with houses at the root of the pier.

From north either pass east of the red buoy, or about a cable west of it to pass between Antelope Rock and the Maid of Lorne Rocks; are these named after boats which first found them the hard way?.

Land at the stone jetty west of the river mouth on the south side of the bay.

Supplies

Shops, post office, hotel, restaurant, phone box. Bus to Tobermory and Craignure.

Tobermory

56°37′N 6°03′W

Few yachts pass by Tobermory without stopping there. It is well known for its sheltered natural harbour and as one of the few attractive towns on the west coast of Scotland. There is a selection of pubs whose reputation is one of its main attractions, and probably the best range of shops between Oban and Stornoway. The HIDB moorings (sometimes occupied by fishing boats) have been laid in what used to be the best position for anchoring; you may have to anchor in back-breakingly deep water on very soft mud through which the anchor has a tendency to drag. If you can bear to miss an evening in the pub, the best plan is possibly to anchor temporarily inshore on a rising tide and leave again before you are stranded.

Tides

Constant +0020 Oban (−0510 Dover).

Height in metres

MHWS	MHWN	MTL	MLWN	MLWS
4.4	3.3	2.5	1.8	0.7

Approach

In the main entrance, north of Calve Island, there are no dangers other than fishing boat and ferry traffic.

The Doirlinn, the passage southwest of Calve Island, dries at its southeast end. Two beacons mark rocks, a tripod in the middle of the southeast entrance and a cylindrical beacon on the northeast side. The passage between the beacons is charted as drying 1.0 metre, so that there should be 1.5 metres at half-tide. The solid bases of the beacons cover at about 3 metres rise. The traditional leading line is the church spire at Tobermory with the high-water line on the southwest side of the channel.

Tobermory, looking northeast about half-tide; Macbraynes Pier at the top, Mishnish Pier in the middle.

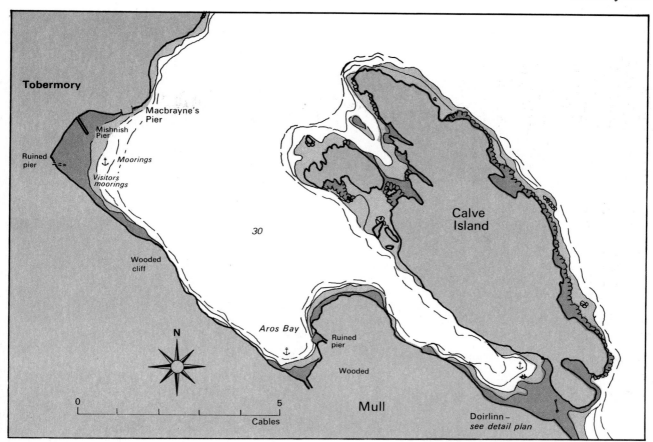

Tobermory Bay

A sunken fishing boat at the southeast end of the Doirlinn is usually marked by a small red float; it is just north of the drying bar, and very close northeast of the leading line described above. The masts uncover at LW, and it is best to keep southwest of the leading line as soon as the channel opens up northwest of the bar.

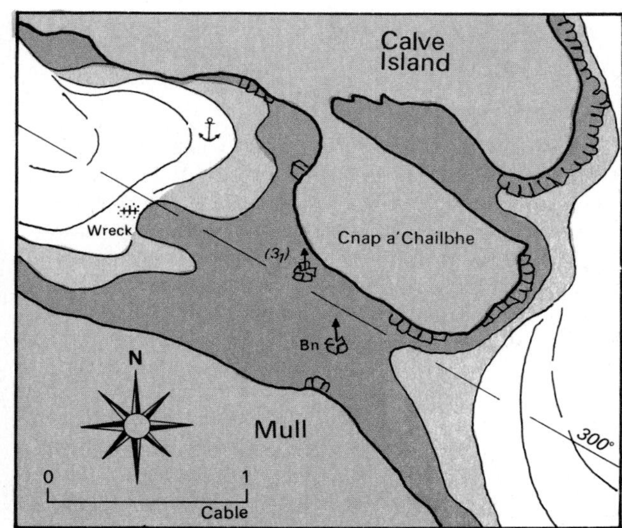

Doirlinn

Anchorages

West side of the bay, as close to it as depth and moorings and other anchored boats allow. In normal weather there is usually space to anchor inshore of the HIDB moorings.

For a short visit, if the tide is rising or with a shoal-draught boat it may be possible to anchor inshore of other boats, close to the town.

Old Pier is the property of the Mull Fishermen's Association and permission should be sought (ask any fisherman there) before leaving a yacht alongside. The pier dries completely.

Tobermory (Macbraynes) Pier is heavily used by ferries and fishing and diving boats. Yachts can usually go alongside to take on water and provisions, but must not be left unattended. The pier is cleared when a ferry is due. An area within which vessels may not anchor is marked with buoys to leave space for ferries to manoeuvre when approaching the pier.

Aros Bay is mostly very deep but reasonable depths can be found off the ruined pier on the east side. Part of the bay may be occupied by fish farming.

The Doirlinn The anchorage is near the southeast end, but you have to be sure of clearing the fishing boat wreck which is usually marked by a small red float. Show an anchor light – fishing boats sometimes come through at HW by night.

Doirlinn passage from southeast at LW.

Services and supplies

Shops, bank, hotels, laundrette, *Calor Gas* (halfway up the hill). Chandlery and chart agent (Seafare). Water, diesel, paraffin and petrol at Macbraynes Pier. Divers available (ask at Seafare).

Communications Post office, phone box, bus to Craignure, ferry to Kilchoan (Ardnamurchan).
☎ Piermaster (0688) 2131
Seafare (0688) 2277 (also Ch M VHF)

Northwest entrance to the Sound of Mull

56°39′N 6°04′W

Charts

2392 1:25,000. *2394* (see below, *Loch Sunart*) shows the main group of rocks.

Tides

Off Rubha nan Gall, the northwest-going stream begins +0400 Oban (−0130 Dover); the southeast-going stream begins −0045 Oban (−0615 Dover). The spring rate is about 1 knot.

Approach

The entrance itself is completely clear, but north of Tobermory there is a large area of rocks, with a clear passage nearly a mile wide between Mull and a green conical light buoy which marks their south side. The buoy is about five miles from the entrance and the passage should present no difficulty in moderate weather. If tacking, look out for the most southeasterly rock, Little Stirk, which dries 3.7 metres. Even when uncovered it is not easily seen if there is a slight sea.

Lights

Rubha nan Gall lighthouse Fl.3s17m15M
Ardmore Point Fl(2)10s17m8M (2¼M WNW of Rubha nan Gall)
New Rocks buoy Fl.G.6s (NNE of Rubha nan Gall)

Anchorages – Kilchoan

56°41′.5N 6°07′W

Kilchoan Bay is on the east side of Sron Bheag, the east end of the cliffs which stand on the south side of Ardnamurchan Point. A drying rock in the middle of the bay is marked by an isolated danger beacon with shoal water half a cable west of it. There is a red and white beacon, in position between May and September, on the southeast end of a drying reef a cable off the north shore. There are drying rocks up to a cable off the west shore, and up to 1½ cables off the east shore. It should only be entered in quiet settled weather, passing a cable west and northwest of the isolated danger beacon.

1½ miles east of Sron Bheag a pier on the northeast side of a small promontory is used by the ferry from Tobermory.

Mingary Castle is half a mile east of the ferry pier. There is temporary anchorage in settled weather on the northeast side of a promontory, Rubh' a' Mhile, close east of the castle.

Loch Sunart

56°41′N 5°48′W

One of the most picturesque of West Coast lochs, with successive ranks of mountains and islands arranged as in a Victorian engraving of Highland scenery. There are several attractive anchorages and some spectacular bits of rock-dodging for those who have a taste for that sort of thing. Even in the main fairway of the loch a lot of anxiety will be spared by having chart *2394*. However, the popular anchorage at Drumbuie on the south side of the loch can be reached without any difficulty.

Chart

2394 (1:25,000)

Tides

Streams run generally at less than 1 knot.

The in-going stream begins about −0500 Oban (+0200 Dover); out-going stream begins about +0130 Oban (−0400 Dover).

At Salen (Loch Sunart) the constant is as Oban.

Height in metres

MHWS	MHWN	MTL	MLWN	MLWS
4.6	3.4	2.6	1.7	0.6

Dangers

From the south, and from Tobermory, the Stirks, 6 cables off the west end of Morvern, must be identified. Big Stirk, the more northerly of the two, is above all except extra high spring tides, Little Stirk, which dries 3.7 metres, 2 cables south of Big Stirk, is east of a line from Tobermory to the Big Stirk.

From the west the main dangers are Red Rocks and Sligneach Mor and Sligneach Beag. Red Rocks are the most northerly of the group of rocks at the junction of Loch Sunart with the Sound of Mull, nearly a mile ENE of the green conical buoy, these dry 2.8 metres, showing about half-tide.

Sligneach Mor is ¼ mile southwest of Rubha Aird Shlignich, the north point of the entrance to Loch Sunart, and is only 0.6 metre high, drying up to a cable on all sides. Sligneach Beag, half a mile west of Sligneach Mor, dries 3.3 metres, with other drying rocks up to a cable off its north side.

Approach

The traditional clearing mark is the summit of Risga in line with the north point of Oronsay, 083°, but Risga may be difficult to identify. If you can't make out this line, steer towards Maclean's Nose at the base of Ben Hiant, the highest hill on the north side of the entrance; then towards a waterfall east of Auliston Point, the south point of the entrance, and when you have identified Sligneach Mor, head for the entrance.

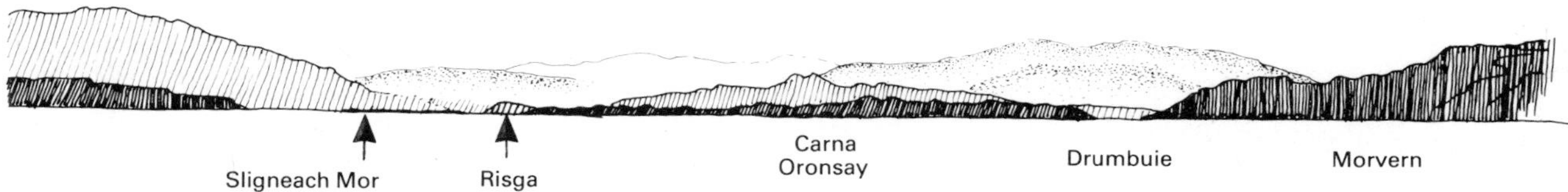

Loch Sunart approach from the west.

Drumbuie

56°39′N 5°56′W

This is the popular rendering of Loch na Droma Buidhe, the name of the basin south of the island of Oronsay, 2 miles east of Auliston Point on the south side of the entrance to Loch Sunart.

The entrance is ¾ cable wide but clean almost to the steep rocky sides of the channel. North of the entrance drying rocks extend up to a cable off the west point of Oronsay. About a cable inside the entrance is a submerged rock, with less than 0.5 metre over it, just south of the line of the south side of the entrance. The north side of the rock is cleared by keeping the west end of the south side of the entrance open.

During or after strong westerly winds some sea runs in through the entrance. While this does not affect the anchorage, going out may be a matter of some anxiety.

Anchorages

There is shelter somewhere in the loch from any wind, but allow for possible changes in wind direction. Strong southeasterlies tend to be deflected to blow from east. The most popular anchorage is in the southwest corner, but there is a drying bank off the mouth of the burn, and the bottom quickly drops away.

The next bay to the east, halfway between a burn and a promontory, is also suitable. Beyond this promontory the loch is mostly shoal and drying.

The view from the highest point of a track on the

Drumbuie from south; Sailean Mor is on the far side of Oronsay, with Eilean Mor beyond.

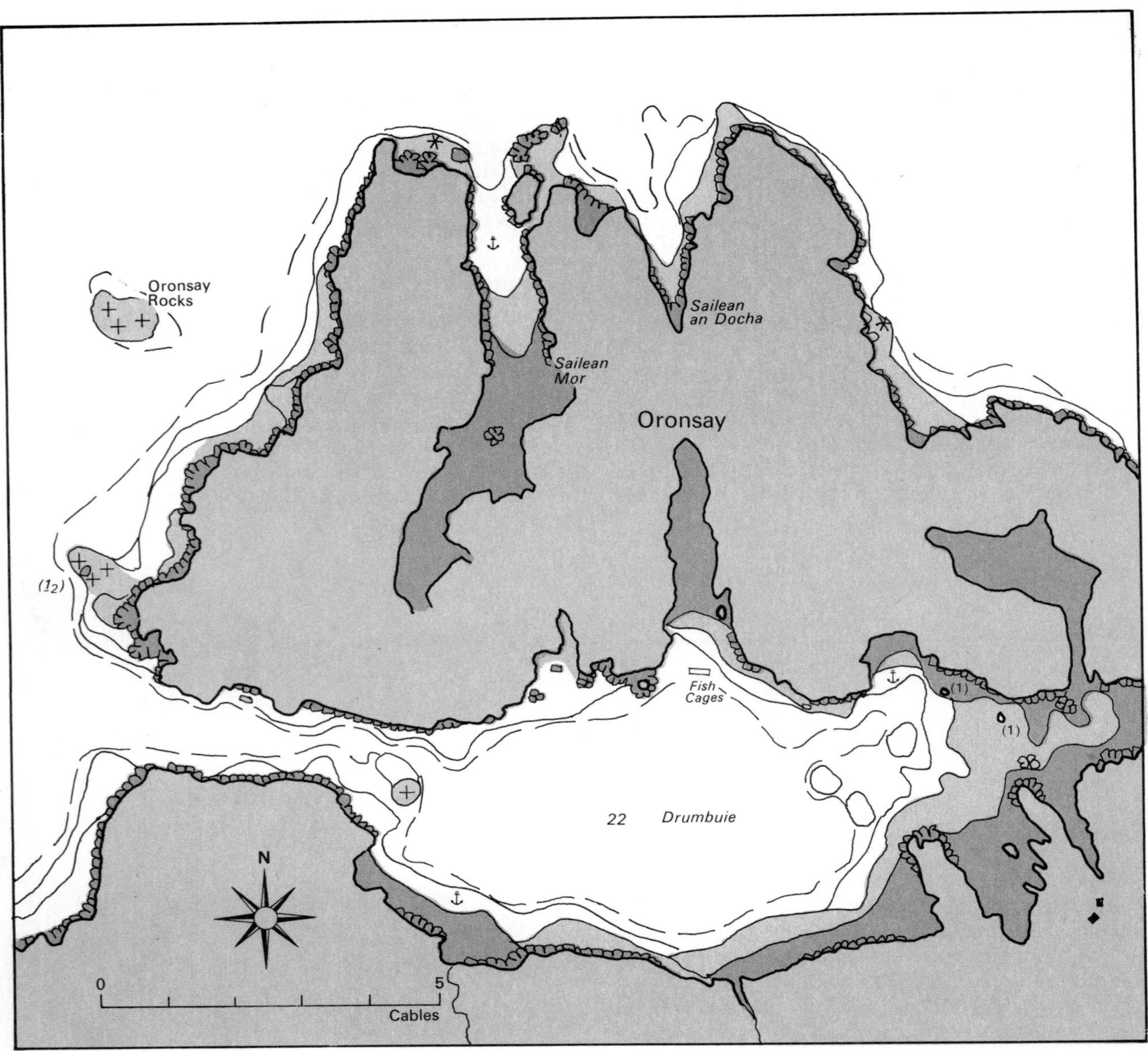

Oronsay and Drumbuie

south side of the loch is well worth the effort of scrambling up the hillside.

On the north side the mouth of the second inlet, east of the highest point of Oronsay, is now obstructed by fish cages, and most of the inlet itself dries out.

The next bay to the east, north of the promontory towards the head of the loch on the south side, and west of a 1-metre high rock, is clean.

Anchorages north of Oronsay

These can be reached without any difficult pilotage, but Oronsay Rocks on which there is a least depth of 1.5 metres, 2 cables off the middle of the west side of Oronsay, must be avoided.

Sailean Mor (56°40′N 5°56′W), a narrow inlet on the north side of Oronsay, dries over 3 cables at the head but there is depth for anchoring 1 cable within the entrance. Note the drying rocks over ½ cable north of the east point of the entrance.

Sailean an Docha, the next inlet to the east, is less sheltered but adequate in offshore winds. Keep clear of the drying rocks just referred to above.

The bay on the northeast side of Oronsay provides reasonable shelter in offshore winds, but there is fish-farming equipment at both ends of the bay.

Glenmore Bay on the north side of Loch Sunart provides shelter on the east side of Eilean Mor, which is effectively a peninsula except at HW springs. Rocks up to ¾ cable off the east side of Eilean Mor are normally above water, and there is a submerged rock over a cable northeast of them. There are fish cages and yachts and workboats on permanent moorings. Pass ½ cable east and northeast of the visible rocks and anchor north of them.

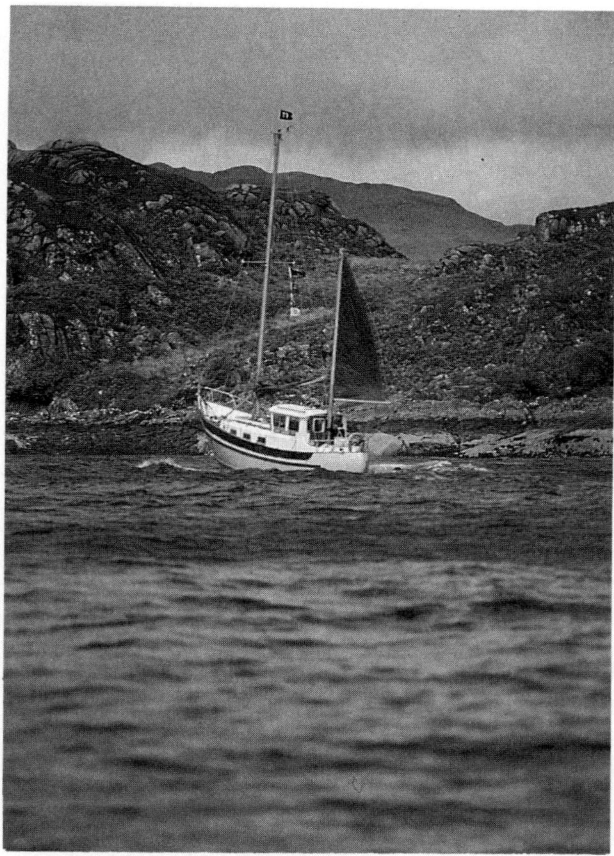
Leaving Drumbuie after a westerly gale.

Loch Sunart – central section

56°41′N 5°48′W

A mile east of Oronsay on the south side of Loch Sunart, Carna sits in the mouth of Loch Teacuis, while on the north side between Oronsay and Carna is the small island of Risga; the main channel twists and turns between them.

The passage north of Risga is clear but there are submerged rocks on its north side, as well as rocks both submerged and drying outwith each end on the south side.

A further mile from the east side of Carna the islet of Dun Ghallain off the north shore marks the beginning of a straightforward reach leading northeast to Salen.

Tides

Streams run generally at less than 1 knot, but north of Carna, and in the entrances to Loch Teacuis, they run at 2½ knots. At Laudale Narrows, 4 miles from the head of the loch, the streams run at 3 to 3½ knots.

The in-going stream begins about −0500 Oban (+0200 Dover); out-going stream begins about +0130 Oban (−0400 Dover).

At Salen (Loch Sunart) the constant is as Oban.

Height in metres

MHWS	MHWN	MTL	MLWN	MLWS
4.6	3.4	2.6	1.7	0.6

Dangers

Oronsay Rocks with a least depth of 1.5 metres, 2 cables west of Oronsay.

A rock with a least depth of 2.1 metres, 1 cable WNW of Risga.

Ross Rock with a least depth of 0.3 metre, 1 cable south of Risga.

There are drying and submerged rocks ¾ cable east of Risga.

Broad Rock, with a least depth of 0.3 metres, almost exactly halfway between Risga and Carna.

Bo Crithean and other drying rocks within ½ cable of the west side of Carna.

South of Dun Ghallain is a rock drying 2.4 metres, and Dun Ghallain Rock, awash, is ¾ cable south of the east end of Dun Ghallain.

Directions

Only Ross Rock and Broad Rock are at all close to the fairway, and for most of us will only be a hazard within 2½ hours of LW. The first can be avoided by keeping well over a cable south of Risga, and the second by keeping well away from mid-channel, preferably towards Carna to avoid the rocks east of Risga.

Carna

The main anchorages are in Loch Teacuis and the passages on either side of Carna, and at Salen, but other occasional anchorages can be found on the chart.

Loch Sunart – clearing mark for Ross Rock.

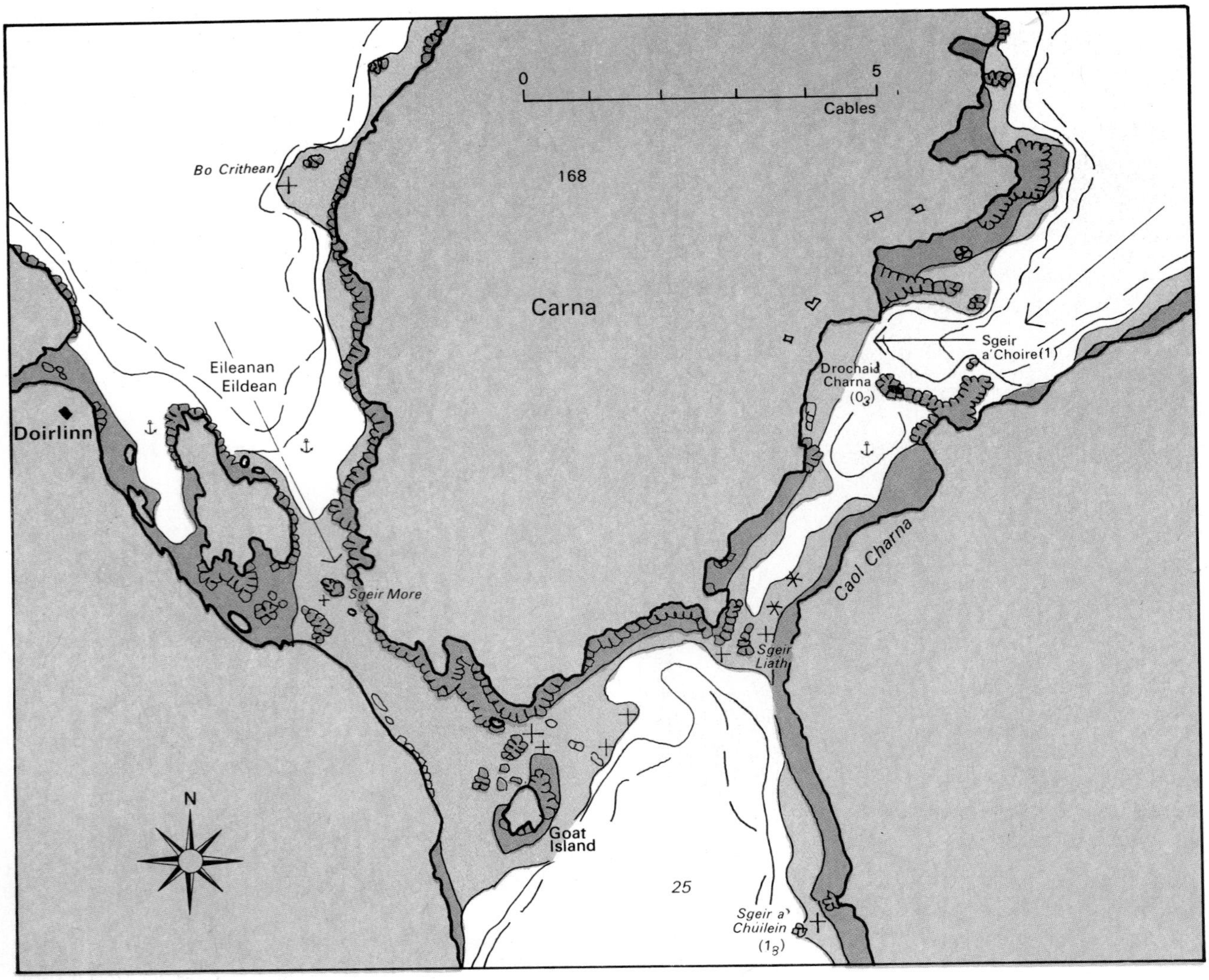

Carna

The passages either side of Carna are among the trickiest bits of rock-dodging anywhere on the West Coast, and there is still some doubt about the position of some of the rocks. In both passages the tidal streams run at 2½ knots springs. The channel east of Carna is the easier to follow as there are more rocks above water by which to establish your position.

West Kyle of Carna

56°39′.5N 5°54′W

Named on charts as Caol Achadh Lic, which translates as something like 'the channel of the field of stones'. The cleanest passage seems to be between Carna and the mid-channel rock, Sgeir More, which dries about 1.7 metres.

The pilotage is easiest before Sgeir More covers; the ideal time would be just before LW neaps. Keep at least a cable off the west side of Carna to avoid Bo Crithean,

West Kyle of Carna – Sgeir More and rocks beyond just showing.

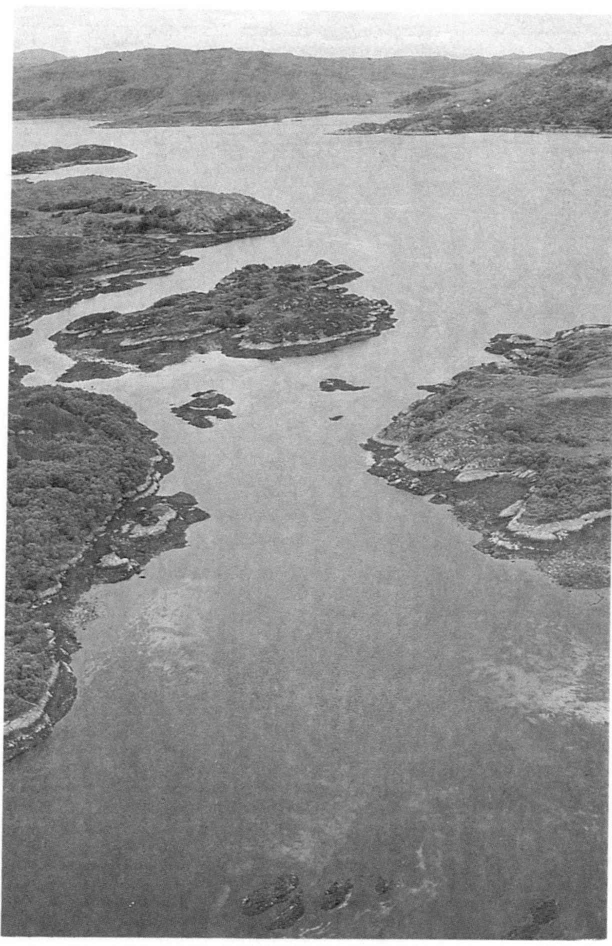

West Kyle of Carna looking NNW at LWS, showing Sgeir More.

and make for the east side of Eilean nan Eildean. Near the south end of that island cross to the Carna shore and keep about 20 metres off it as there are also submerged rocks about 10 metres off Carna. After this keep closer to the mainland to avoid rocks which cover northwest of Goat Island (Eilean nan Gabhar).

Anchorages

Doirlinn, west of Eilean nan Eildean; sandy bottom, limited swinging room. There is a mooring ring on the second tidal islet southeast of a white cottage on the mainland.

The north entrance to the kyle is a good anchorage; within the kyle the tide runs more strongly but the shelter is better.

Caol Charna

56°39'.5N 5°52'W

The passage east of Carna is more straightforward than that to the west. A ridge of rock, Drochaid Charna ('bridge of Carna') extends over halfway across the passage from the southeast side, and its middle point is just above MHWS. Sgeir a' Choire, on the northeast side of Drochaid Charna, is about a metre high, and there are various drying and submerged rocks north of it, near the shore of Carna. In the channel between Carna and the northwest end of Drochaid Charna the greatest depth is just over 2 metres.

At the next narrows, 3½ cables southwest of Drochaid Charna, there is a long rock close to the southeast point of Carna and, towards mid-channel,

Caol Charna from east.

Sgeir Liath, which covers but is marked by a small concrete pillar. Northeast of Sgeir Liath is a submerged rock (1.5 metres) nearer to the mainland shore, and there are two drying rocks further northeast.

Directions

Identify and steer for Sgeir a' Choire and when about ¼ cable from it, turn to pass between Drochaid Charna and the promontory on Carna close north of it, steering for the most southerly house on Carna. Pass midway between Drochaid Charna and Carna. At the next narrows identify Sgeir Liath and pass southeast of it, closer to the rock than to the mainland.

Anchorage

The pool southwest of Drochaid Charna is said to provide good shelter even in strong northeast winds.

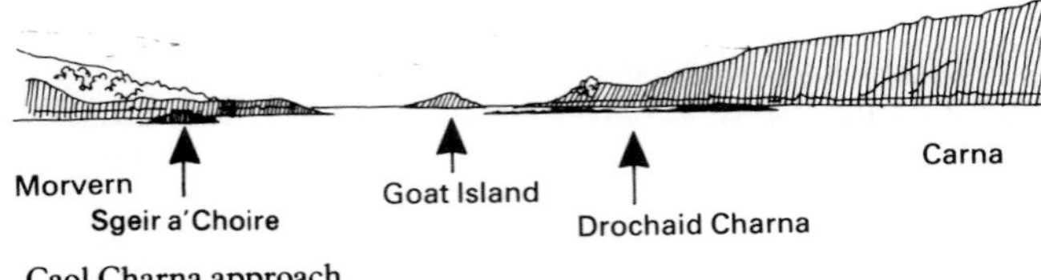

Caol Charna approach.

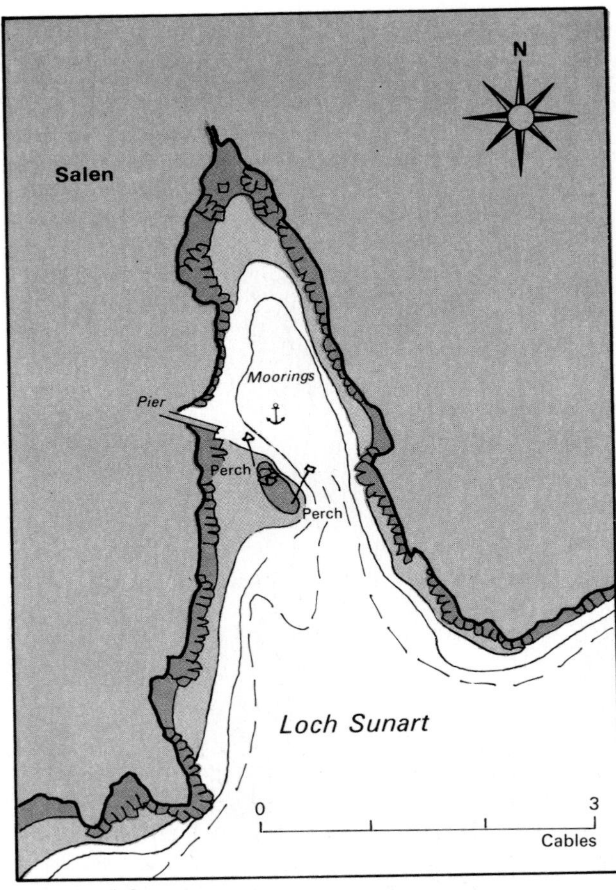

Salen, Loch Sunart

Loch Teacuis

56°38′N 5°50′W

The basin south of Carna is entered by either of the passages described above. Sgeir a' Chuilein, ½ cable off the east side of the basin, dries 1.8 metres with an uncharted submerged rock ¼ cable southwest of it, and the south side of the basin dries off ¼ mile.

A mile southeast of Goat Island the rock-infested narrows of Rahoy (Caolas Rahuaidh) lead to the head of Loch Teacuis. Generally this passage should be taken just northeast of mid-channel. At the narrowest part there is a rock, drying 1.2 metres, south of mid-channel.

The inner basin is over a mile long with a narrower part about the middle of its length. Between this narrow part and the head of the loch, about a cable off the southwest side, an uncharted rock awash was found by Hilary King in 1985. Its approximate position is close south of the 4-metre sounding on chart *2394*. The head of this basin dries off 2 cables, and the sides about ½ cable. Depths are otherwise moderate throughout the southeast part of the basin, and the bottom is mud.

Salen

56°43′N 5°46′W

A convenient anchorage on the north side of Loch Sunart 4½ miles beyond Carna, with some provisions and a hotel. A drying reef west of the middle of the bay is marked by a pole with a triangular topmark on its west side and one with a rectangular topmark on the east side; the main passage is east of the reef. There are several moorings so that you should buoy your anchor. The jetty on the west side of the bay dries and its side is uneven in places.

Tides

The constant is as Oban.

Height in metres

MHWS	MHWN	MTL	MLWN	MLWS
4.6	3.4	2.6	1.7	0.6

Supplies

Shop, post office, phone box, hotel; water at pier. Limited chandlery. Visitors' moorings (10 tons maximum). The Jetty Shop can arrange delivery of provisions by 1800 hours on the same day, given reasonable notice, and delivery of *Calor Gas* the following morning. The Jetty Shop, ☎ Salen (096 785) 648; VHF Ch M.

Loch Sunart – upper part

56°41′N 5°36′W

The loch continues for a further 8 miles beyond Salen and it is in this part that the large-scale chart *2394* will be most needed. For the first two miles beyond Salen, as the loch bends round to the southeast, there are submerged and drying rocks up to 2 cables off the south shore. In the next mile, off two islands on the northeast side, there are several submerged rocks disposed at random (one of them having been reported in 1979 at a point where the chart shows a depth of 25 metres). To most yachts these are probably only a hazard within 2 hours of LW springs or 1 hour of LW neaps.

A cable west of Garbh Eilean, the larger and more southerly of the two islands, a rock dries 3.3 metres.

Rubha an Daimh, 4 cables southeast of Eilean Garbh, has drying rocks extending up to 2 cables southwest of it. Opposite this point at the mouth of the Laudale river, a bank of stones dries off 2 cables, and on both sides of the loch between Rubha an Daimh and Laudale Narrows, a mile further southeast, the foreshore dries up to ¼ mile in the bays on either side of the loch.

Immediately before Laudale Narrows Glas Eilean has a shoal bank with a least depth of 1.2 metres extending 2 cables WNW of it. From Laudale Narrows to the head of the loch the south shore is generally clean, but on the north side there are drying banks at the mouths of rivers, particularly at Strontian. Eilean a' Mhuirich, ¾ mile west of Strontian, has a rock drying 1.8 metres ¼ cable off its south side. The head of the loch dries for half a mile.

Anchorages

Camas na h'Airbhe, on the southwest shore 1½ miles west of Laudale Narrows, has suitable depths close to the west side, but quickly becomes very deep away from the shore.

Garbh Eilean has reasonable depths off its southeast side.

Liddesdale, on the south shore 1½ miles east of Laudale Narrows, has reasonable depths east of the mouth of the valley, but there is probably no space clear of fish cages.

Strontian The bay at the mouth of the river dries out a long way. Anchor beyond a concrete slip with a green shed east of a granite obelisk which stands on a low cliff east of the village. In easterly winds there are violent squalls from the head of the loch.

Supplies

At Strontian, a shop, hotel, post office, phone box, and *Calor Gas*.

V. The west coast of Mull

The areas described in the previous chapters have been for the most part enclosed by hills or at least sheltered behind islands. The west of Mull is predominantly open to the Atlantic and the landscape is more rugged. On the Ross of Mull and Iona the shore is mostly granite, often pink in colour, with brilliant white sand. There are several good anchorages, a few of them excellent, and many attractive occasional ones.

The easiest approach is from the Sound of Mull, but in clear and moderate weather with careful pilotage you can sail there from the Sound of Islay or the Firth of Lorne by the south side of Mull, but you have to negotiate the passage between Mull and the Torran Rocks. This will be described with the approach to the Sound of Iona on page 107.

Charts

2171 (1:75,000) covers most of the west of Mull except the south of the Ross of Mull. You should have *2652* (1:25,000) for Loch na Keal and the offlying islands, and *2617* (1:25,000) is absolutely essential for the Sound of Iona and the Ross of Mull. With these two, if you have the Imray *C65*, you could do without *2171*. *2392* (1:25,000) covers the northwest coast of Mull, and *2771* (1:25,000) covers Loch Scridain.

Tides

Off Caliach Point and Rubh' a' Chaoil, the next point to the south, tidal streams run at up to 2½ knots.

The north-going stream begins −0510 Oban (+0145 Dover); the south-going stream begins +0115 Oban (−0415 Dover).

There are strong tidal streams around the Treshnish Isles, but not generally elsewhere. Those in the Sound of Iona will be described separately.

Tidal constants are, on average: at Bunessan on the north side of the Ross of Mull, −0015 Oban (−0545 Dover); at Arinagour, Coll, +0020 Oban (−0510 Dover).

Height in metres at Bunessan

MHWS	MHWN	MTL	MLWN	MLWS
4.3	3.0	2.4	1.8	0.6

Passage notes and dangers

In the passage from the Sound of Mull to Iona there are, with the exceptions described below, no dangers outwith a quarter of a mile from the shore, and no artificial marks; you need to be able to identify various islands, and features on Mull. The dangers beyond ¼ mile from the shore are as follows.

Sgeir Mhor, 3 miles ENE of Caliach Point, is ¾ mile from the shore in the mouth of Loch a' Chumhainn.

East of the Treshnish Isles, there are many drying rocks up to ½ mile outwith the line of the ESE side of the islands.

WSW of Staffa, drying rocks up to ½ mile.

The 20-metre contour will generally keep you out of trouble, although sometimes by only a small margin, and a few shallower banks further out may give you a fright, but the echo sounder will be some help in this area in combination with the chart.

The most prominent point of this side of Mull is Caliach Point (56°36′N 6°20′W) and very heavy seas can be met with off it, particularly with wind against tide. It is worth taking care to be there at the most favourable time, particularly at springs or in fresh or strong winds; otherwise stand a couple of miles offshore. A drying reef extends nearly 2 cables from Rubh' a' Chaoil, the point 2½ miles south of Caliach point.

Anchorages – northwest Mull

Loch Mingary (56°38′N 6°13′W) can only be considered as even a temporary anchorage on the rare occasions when there is no onshore swell, but given the right conditions a visit there will be memorable. The entrance is little over ½ cable wide between the islets south of Cuan Mor and drying reefs on the southwest side of the entrance. Be prepared to clear out sharpish if the wind or swell start to come onshore.

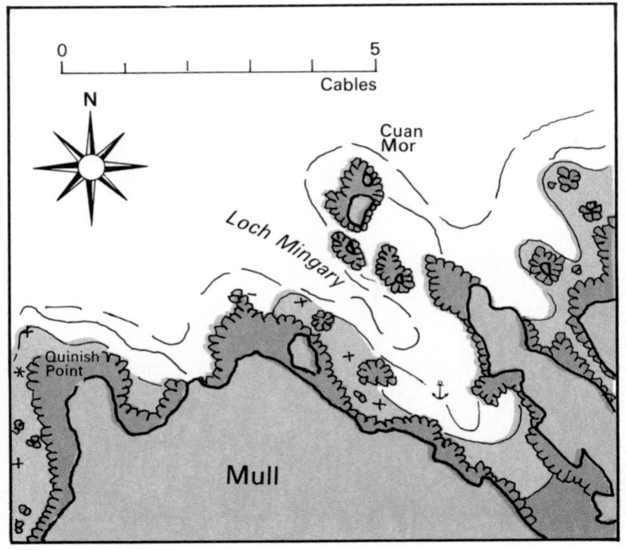

Loch Mingary

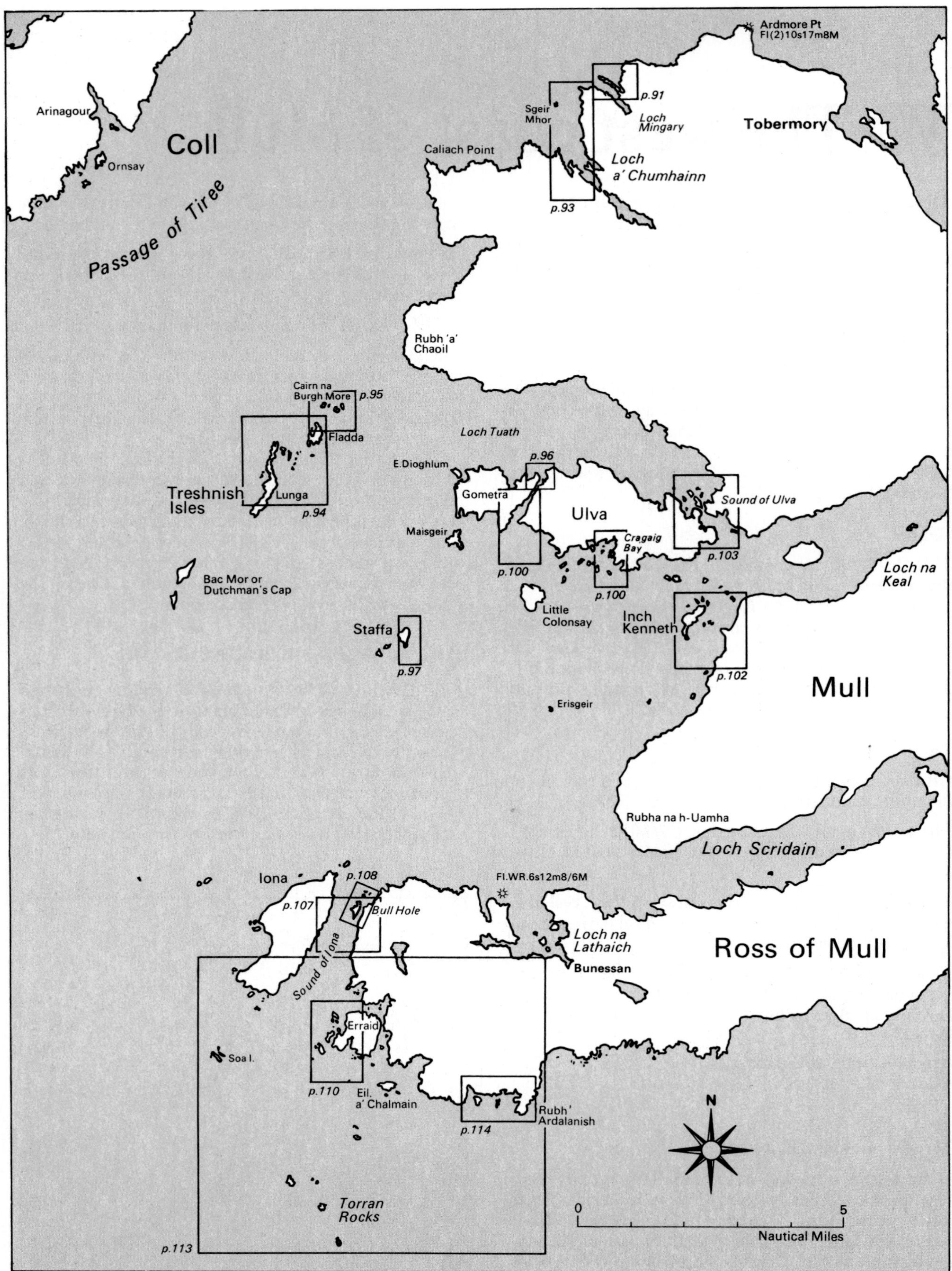
Ardmore Pt
Fl(2)10s17m8M
p.91
Sgeir
Mhor
Loch
Mingary
Tobermory
Arinagour
Coll
Ornsay
Caliach Point
Loch
a' Chumhainn
p.93
Passage of Tiree
Rubh 'a'
Chaoil
Cairn na
Burgh More
p.95
Fladda
Loch Tuath
p.96
E.Dioghlum
Treshnish
Isles
Lunga
p.94
Gometra
Ulva
Sound of Ulva
Maisgeir
Cragaig
Bay
p.103
p.100
p.100
Loch na
Keal
Bac Mor or
Dutchman's Cap
Little
Colonsay
Inch
Kenneth
Staffa
p.97
p.102
Mull
Erisgeir
Rubha na h-Uamha
Loch Scridain
Iona
p.108
Fl.WR.6s12m8/6M
p.107
Bull Hole
Sound of Iona
Loch na
Lathaich
Ross of Mull
Bunessan
Erraid
Soa I.
p.110
Eil.
a' Chalmain
p.114
Rubh'
Ardalanish
N
Torran
Rocks
0
5
Nautical Miles
p.113

Loch Cuan

56°37′N 6°14′W

Loch a' Chumhainn on current charts, this is only better than Loch Mingary in that there is more space, but it could be almost as much of a trap in an onshore wind; however, a shoal-draught boat would find more shelter further in than at either of the anchorages suggested below.

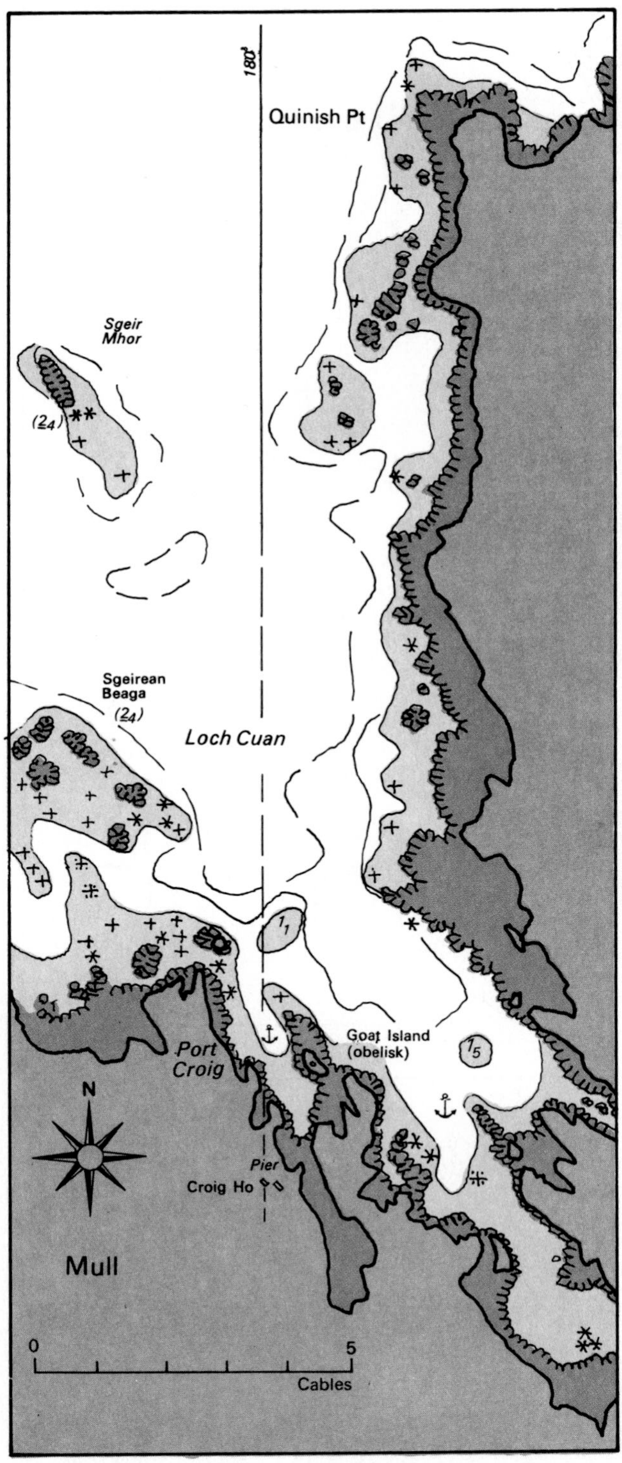

Loch Cuan

It is best to approach before half-flood at which time Sgeir Mhor covers, although the swell will usually reveal it after that. Sgeirean Beaga cover at the same time, so an approach can be made from northwest, or from north, passing 2 cables east of Sgeir Mhor. If Croig House can be identified among the trees it should be kept in line with the summit of Carn Mor, the highest hill to the south, bearing 180°. Otherwise the only mark is a stone obelisk on Eilean nan Gobhar (Goat Island), on the south side of the loch.

Anchorages If near LW springs, avoid the 1-metre patch nearly ¼ mile north of the obelisk and anchor either east of the promontory southeast of the obelisk, or in Port Croig, the creek northwest of Goat Island, but this has very little swinging room.

Provisions Shop, hotel and post office at Dervaig, 2 miles by dinghy or 3 miles by road.

Calgary Bay, 2 miles south of Caliach Point, is another temporary anchorage if there is no swell, but perhaps less attractive than the two above in that it is accessible by road and fairly popular. Drying reefs extend ¼ mile southwest from the north point of the entrance, and there are submerged and drying rocks up to 1½ cables from the southeast side of the bay.

Treshnish Isles

56°30′N 6°25′W

These interesting and attractive islands are a breeding ground for grey seals and for many sea birds. The rocks and islets provide some shelter but they are rarely free from swell. The approach, particularly from the north, needs careful pilotage, and the tide runs strongly between the islands.

The main islands are, from south to north, Bac Mor, whose summit is a pronounced knob; Lunga, the largest and highest; Fladda, which is flat; and Cairn na Burgh More, which has ruins of a chapel and a castle on it.

In very quiet weather the Cairn na Burgh Islands are interesting to visit, but the tides run very strongly here and there is no shelter.

Approach and clearing marks

North Rock (Bogha Tuath) and the drying rocks west of Cairn na Burgh More are cleared by keeping the summit of Bac Mor bearing 214° open west of Tighchoie, the northwesternmost rock with a prominent rectangular block 8 metres high.

From north identify Tighchoie and the leading beacons on Lunga which are stone cairns, one close to the shore and one on the summit, bearing about 195°; they may be difficult to identify against the sky. Pass between Tighchoie and the Irishman's Rock (Sgeir Eirionnaich), the flat-topped island east of it, keeping the beacons in line. About midway along the Irishman's Rock alter course to the east of the line as it leads over rocks east of Sgeir a' Chaisteil and steer for the east point of Lunga.

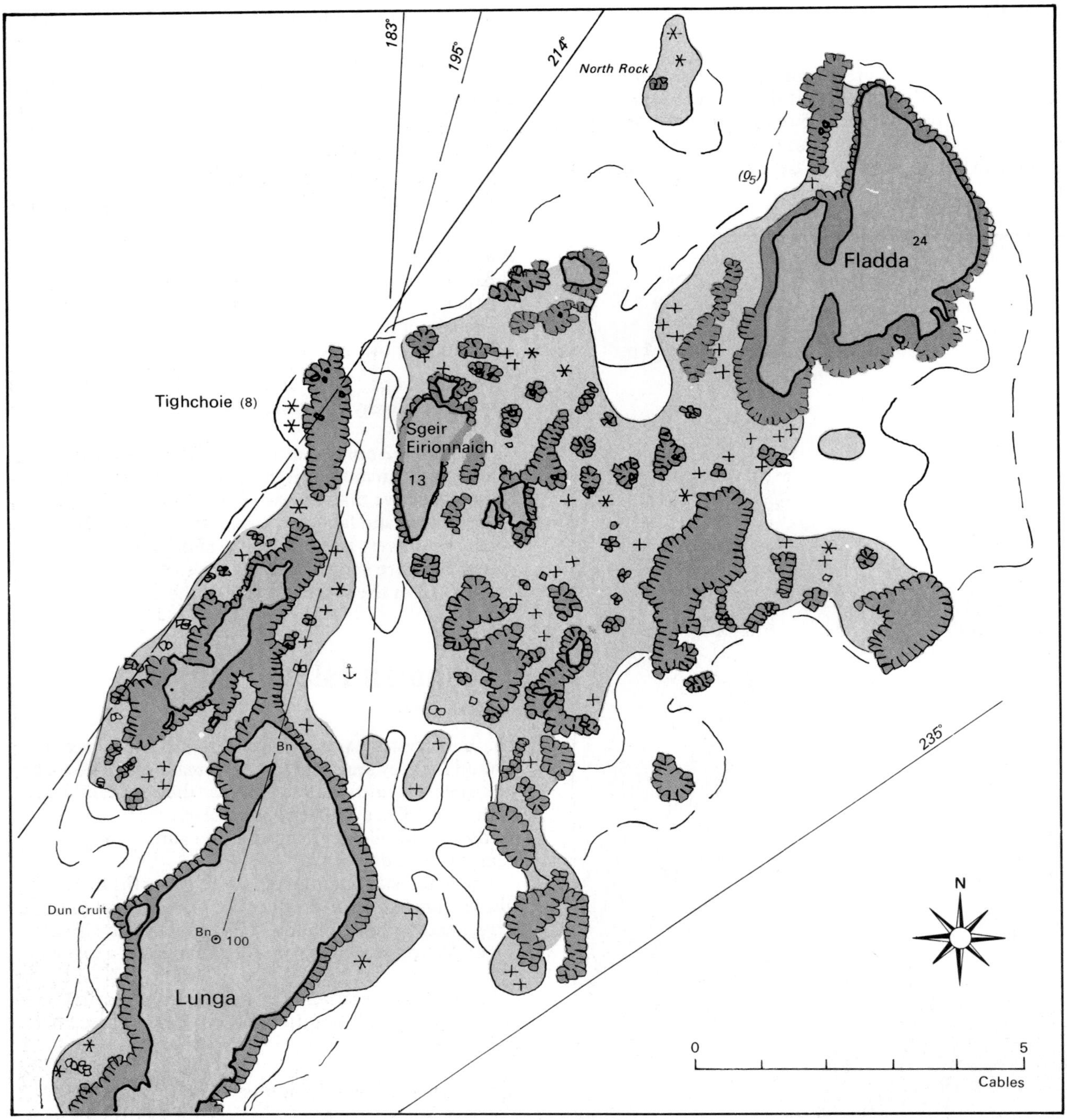

Treshnish Isles

Treshnish Isles north entrance. Sgeir Eirionnaich is on the left and Tighchoie on the right, with the summit of Bac Mor showing beyond.

Treshnish Isles; Lunga from the north with the position of the leading beacons shown.

Rocks on the east side of the group are cleared by keeping the south point of Lunga open of the north point of Bac Mor, bearing 235°.

From east approach with Staffa astern: The mouth of a prominent cave on the shore below the summit of Lunga kept open bearing 300° leads south of drying rocks east of Lunga. A submerged rock 1 cable east of Lunga is a danger near LW. North of the position of this rock keep within a cable of Lunga to clear a very shoal patch (0.4 metre), 1½ cables northeast of Lunga; there is also a 1.8-metre patch ½ cable WNW of the 0.4-metre patch.

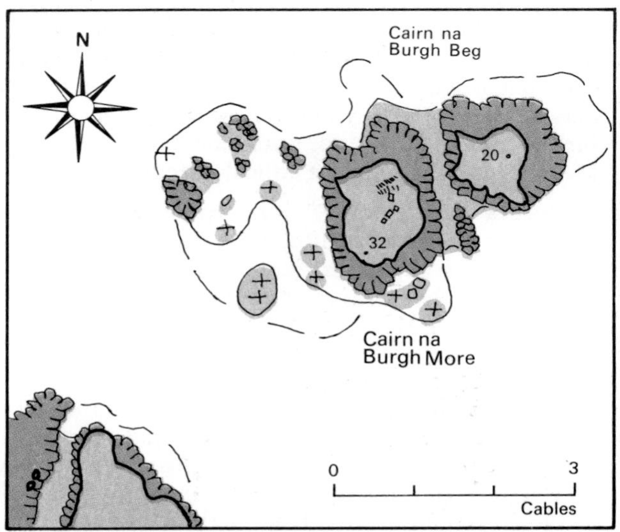

Cairn na Burgh Islands

Anchorage

Anchor east of the boulder spit between Lunga and Sgeir a' Chaisteil. Small boats also anchor in a pool between Sgeir a' Chaisteil and the reef southeast of it.

Treshnish Isles; Lunga from the southeast.

Loch Tuath

56°31′N 6°13′W

Although not a particularly interesting loch it is pleasant enough. Loch na Keal can be reached from the head of Loch Tuath through the Sound of Ulva but the passage should only be attempted above half-tide and even then at a very cautious pace. The approach to the Sound of Ulva from the south is easier, and both entrances are described on pages 101-5.

Tides

For the Sound of Ulva the constant is −0010 Oban (−0540 Dover).

Height in metres

MHWS	MHWN	MTL	MLWN	MLWS
4.4	3.2	2.5	1.8	0.6

Dangers

Sgeir Dubhail, which dries 2.6 metres is in the middle of the loch, a mile and a quarter from its head. There are many rocks around the approach to the Sound of Ulva, and the head of the loch should be avoided entirely unless you have the large-scale chart, *2652*.

Anchorages

Acairseid Mhor, Gometra (56°30′N 6°18′W) A popular anchorage on the northwest corner of Gometra at the south point of the entrance to Loch Tuath. Most of the inlet is too shallow for yachts of moderate draught, and shoal-draught boats have a great advantage here.

Keep towards the east side on entering to avoid drying rocks on the west side outside the entrance, some of which are showing in the photo, but don't overdo it as there is a drying shelf of rocks and boulders at the east side. Anchor near the east side, no further in than abreast the north end of the islet (unless it is neaps or you have a shoal-draught boat).

Port Rainich (56°31′N 6°12′W) is not named even on the large-scale chart and is difficult to find. It is behind Eilean Rainich on the north side of Loch Tuath about 4 miles from the entrance and is best found by identifying Torloisk House, a large house among trees on the hillside, from which Port Rainich is ESE. Swinging room is very limited.

An Carraigean, the rock at the outer end of the reef on the south side of the entrance does not normally cover. Enter from southwest rather closer to An Carraigean than to Eilean Rainich to avoid drying rocks at the south end of the island, and then turn north towards the head of the inlet, keeping closer to Eilean Rainich. Anchor when the south high-water line of Eilean Rainich is in line with the north point of Eilean Dioghlum at the south side of the entrance to the loch.

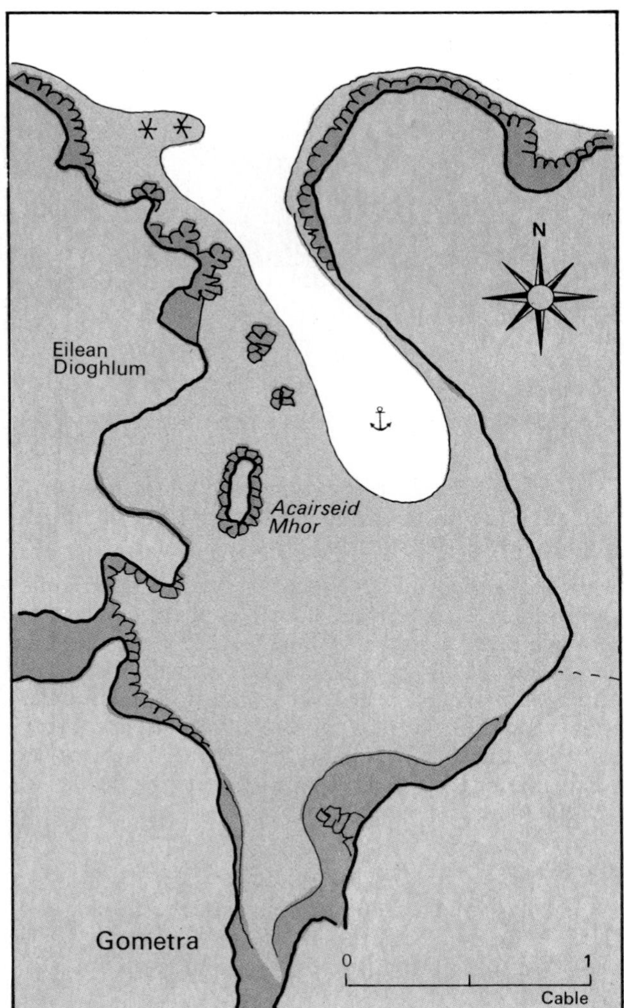

Acairseid Mhor, Gometra

Acairseid Mhor, Gometra, from north. The drying rocks outside the west side of the entrance are showing. Those on the west side within the entrance cover at HW.

Port Rainich from the west.

Soriby Bay (56°29′N 6°11′W) at the southeast of Loch Tuath has a good reputation for shelter but seems open to northwest (in fact, recently, the owner of a 25-footer found its reputation to be distinctly overrated). There are drying and submerged rocks over a cable WNW of Eilean Liath which is in about the middle of the south shore of the bay. Anchor at the south end of the west side of the bay, or in the mouth of the inlet in the southeast corner of the bay, but not far in as there are submerged and drying rocks.

Staffa

56°26′N 6°20′W

With its basalt columns and several sea caves, of which Fingal's Cave is the best known, Staffa is one of the most spectacular natural features anywhere. The island has no adequate anchorage and yachts have to take their chances outside some drying rocks off the landing place on the east shore. The island itself provides little shelter and the slightest sea will make a visit a matter of anxiety for the skipper.

I have been lucky in being able to visit the island several times, but one was distinctly marginal. The wind was easterly, and the skipper of a tourist launch chose to land his passengers inside Fingal's Cave itself, rather than at the landing place. On another occasion it was so quiet that a large MFV-type charter yacht was taken right alongside the landing place itself. The wind and sea can get up quickly and an eye should be kept on the boat at all times.

Dangers and anchorages

The plan shows the rocks on the east side of the island, and the photos show the ones which uncover near the landing place.

The usual anchorage is off the landing place at the north end of the Buachaille, but there are no marks for avoiding any of the rocks; the bottom is rocky and falls away sharply.

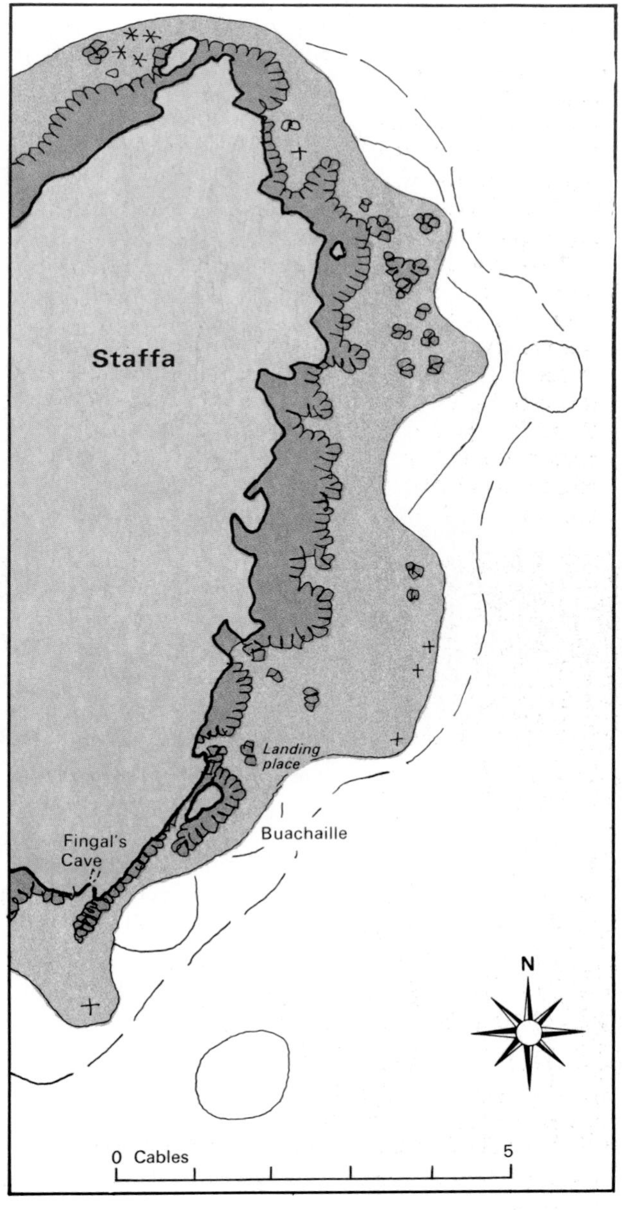

Staffa

South end of Staffa from east.

Staffa – the landing place looking north. All the detached rocks cover.

A gap in the rocks 2 cables NNE of the landing place, with moderate depths, might be less affected by seas from the west but the bottom is covered with weed.

At the northeast end of the island is a small beach sheltered from south and southwest suitable for landing a dinghy, but a yacht would have to stand off.

In easterly winds the bay on the southwest side of the island may provide shelter, but no easy landing place. Its name. Port an Fhasgaidh, is translated as a shelter or refuge (or alternatively, such are the ambiguities of Gaelic at least for anyone who does not speak it, as a search for vermin).

Loch na Keal

56°23′N 6°04′W

In terms of anchorages this is the main inlet on the west coast of Mull but there are so many rocks that it would be unwise to enter without chart *2652* or, at the least, *2171*. There are no villages around this loch and the main interest is in the pilotage and the anchorages themselves. Climbers will want to have a go at Ben More, which is the only island mountain over 915 metres (3000 feet) apart from the Cuillins of Skye.

Tides

Ulva Ferry constant −0010 Oban (−0540 Dover).

Height in metres

MHWS	MHWN	MTL	MLWN	MLWS
4.4	3.2	2.5	1.8	0.6

Tidal streams are not significant.

Dangers

Off the south side of Ulva and Gometra there is a mass of rocks which will be described in greater detail in relation to each anchorage. Maisgeir, most of which is above water, extends 6 cables south of the west end of Gometra; however it is black and low-lying and difficult to see at dusk or in hazy weather.

The passage 4 cables wide northeast of Little Colonsay is clear except for drying rocks over a cable north of its west end, a 2.1-metre patch 2 cables off its north side, and a 1-metre high rock 1½ cables north of its east end.

Erisgeir, 2¼ miles south of Little Colonsay, is a conspicuous islet 22-metres high with drying rocks over ½ cable off its north and west sides, and a detached rock drying 4.4 metres over a cable south of it.

On the southeast side of the loch, up to 2 miles SSW of Inch Kenneth, there are several submerged and drying rocks, all of which are avoided by keeping the east point of Ulva open of the northwest side of Inch Kenneth 027°.

Rocks above water and drying extend 4 cables north of Inch Kenneth. The light beacon at the entrance to Loch na Lathaich on the Ross of Mull bearing 208°, open of the northwest side of Inch Kenneth leads close west of these.

Geasgill Islands between Ulva and Inch Kenneth have rocks drying up to ½ cable all round, except south of Geasgill Mor, the larger island, and a drying reef extends 1 cable east of the southeast point of Geasgill Mor.

MacQuarrie's Rock which dries 0.8 metres, ½ mile south of the east point of Ulva, is the most dangerous rock in the loch. Various transits using the Geasgill Islands and other islands lead clear of it. The 'official' clearing mark is the south extremity of Garbh Eilean, northeast of Little Colonsay, touching the north extremity of Geasgill Beag 266°; an easier line to identify is the south side of Geasgill Mor with the south side of Little Colonsay 259°.

I have passed north of MacQuarrie's Rock, keeping the south side of Little Colonsay open north of Geasgill Beag 255°. MacQuarrie's Rock is passed when the west side of the Sound of Ulva begins to show north of the east extremity of Ulva, bearing 348°.

In the inner part of Loch na Keal Eorsa has drying rocks up to a cable off its east end, and Scarisdale Rocks extend east from a point 1¼ miles east of Eorsa.

Directions

The straightforward approach is south of Little Colonsay and north of Erisgeir; pass a cable south of Geasgill Mor and choose a suitable clearing mark to avoid MacQuarrie's Rock. If continuing to the head of the loch pass either side of Eorsa but then keep to the north side of the loch which is clean outside a cable from the shore. Alternative passages should be tried only with chart *2652*.

Anchorages

Gometra Harbour

56°29′N 6°16′W

The inlet between Ulva and Gometra continues NNE as a drying channel separating the two islands. There are drying rocks up to a cable off the east side of Rubha Bhrisdeadh-ramh (Broken Oar Point), the promontory on the west side of the entrance. Sgeir na Skeineadh, a detached rock 3 cables east of the promontory, dries 3.2

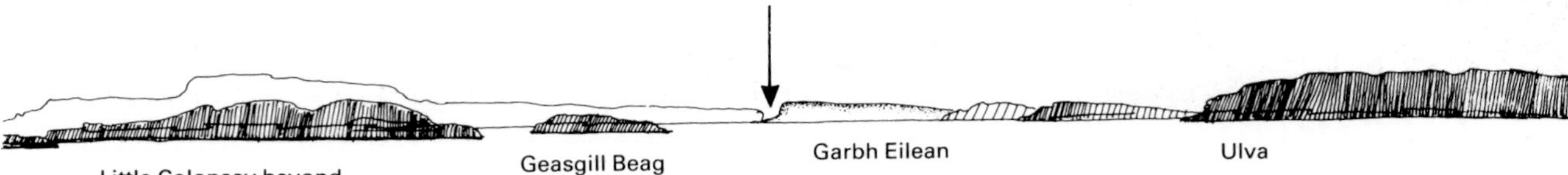

Garbh Eilean and Geasgill Beag 266°.

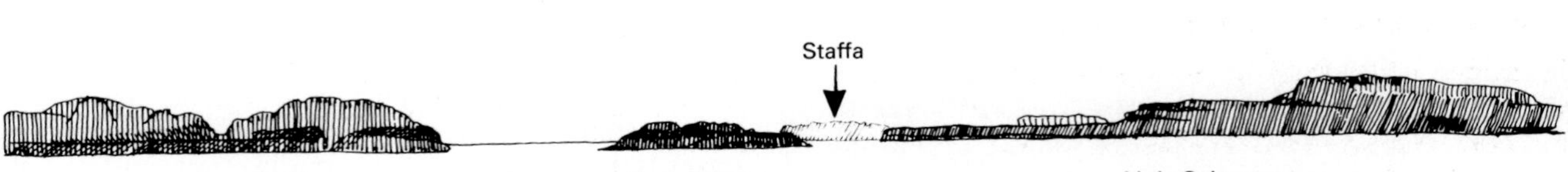

Little Colonsay and Geasgill Mor 259°.

N
Gometra
Ulva
Rubha Bhrisdeadh-ramh
Sgeir na Skeineadh
Bogha Ludden
0
5
Cables

Gometra Harbour

Gometra Harbour from south. Sgeir na Skeineadh is in the right foreground.

metres, and there are submerged rocks 2 cables further southeast. Don't mistake the next bay to the west for Gometra Harbour.

Approach with the Sound of Iona astern between Staffa and Little Colonsay and pass 1 to 2 cables east of Broken Oar Point. A dark bluff on the northwest side of the basin in line with the middle of the entrance leads clear.

Anchor in the basin beyond the narrow entrance, near the east shore, which is the cleanest; there are rocks drying up to a cable from the west side and ¼ mile from the head of the inlet. Substantial seas come in with strong southerly winds.

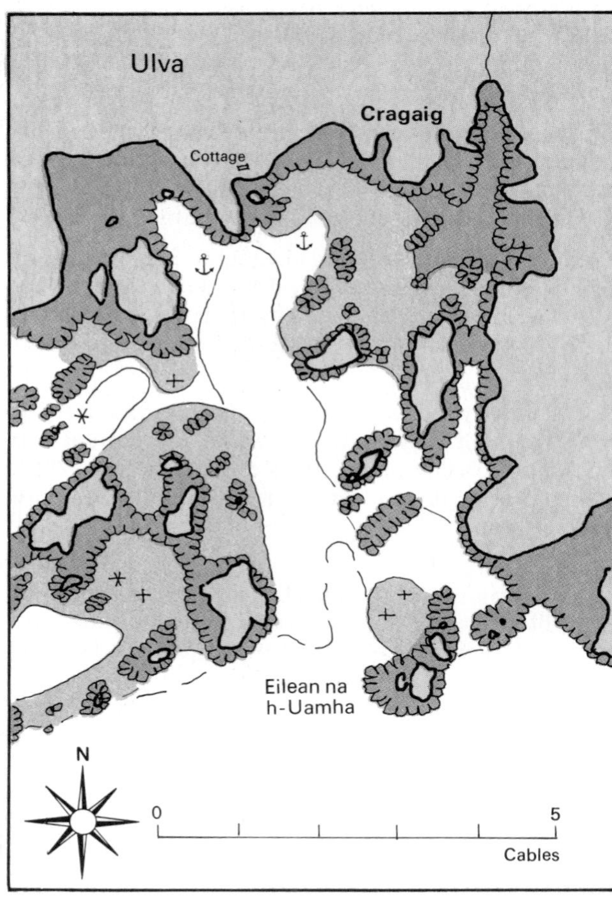

Cragaig Bay

Cragaig Bay

56°28′N 6°13′W

Northeast of Little Colonsay, Cragaig Bay is filled with islets, one or two of which have sandy beaches attached to them. The entrance is east of Eilean na h-Uamha which is grass-topped, 1¼ miles ENE of Little Colonsay. As you sail past the islets the entrance opens up, leading to an inconspicuous stone cottage under the more easterly of the twin peaks of Ulva. Anchor towards the head of this inlet, southwest or southeast of the promontory south of the cottage. Some sea comes in with strong southerly winds.

Cragaig Bay.

Many other pools can be found, particularly with a dinghy or shoal-draught yacht. There is a large basin in the northwest of the bay, but no simple way of reaching it.

An abandoned village on the northeast side of the bay with the ruins of a water mill in the northeast corner, is best seen early in the summer before the bracken takes over.

Inch Kenneth

56°27′N 6°09′W

The usual anchorage is east of the island, approached from the north. Rocks extend 4 cables north of Inch Kenneth; Sunday Rock (Maol an Domhnaich), the broad rock 3 cables from the island, rarely covers (dries 4.4 metres) but there are other drying and submerged rocks a cable further northwest. Rocks drying and awash 2 cables northwest of Samalan Island on the east side of the entrance are cleared by keeping a white shed open west of rocks on the west side of the island 130°.

Approach from NNW keeping one of two white cottages on the southeast shore bearing 150° midway between visible rocks. When the big house on Inch Kenneth is open south of the cliffs on the south side of the northeast part of the island, bearing 240°, turn towards the island and anchor in about 5 metres; the bottom shoals abruptly further in. Holding is said to be poor.

The anchorage east of the south point of the island has been used and may be suitable in quiet weather. The outermost of rocks southeast of the point rarely cover.

Either of these anchorages is subject to violent squalls from the cliffs of Mull in southeast winds.

Sound of Ulva

56°28′.5N 6°08′W

An attractive anchorage between Ulva and Mull, but parts of it are shallow, and even though the cliffs on the south side of Loch na Keal are two miles away it is subject to fierce squalls in southerly winds. The intricate passage through from Loch Tuath should only be taken above half-tide and even then at a cautious pace. It is far from certain that all the rocks in this passage have been charted.

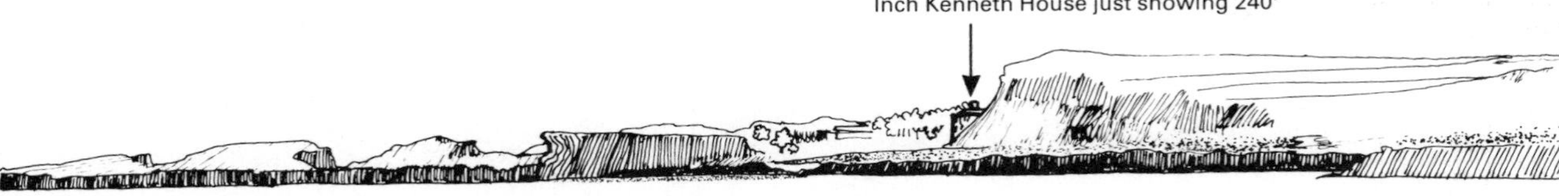

Inch Kenneth House just showing beyond cliffs 240°.

Inch Kenneth – approach from NNW at HW springs. From left to right, a white shed, 'white cottage', *Clachandhu*, more white houses. Maol an Domhnaich spreads across the foreground.

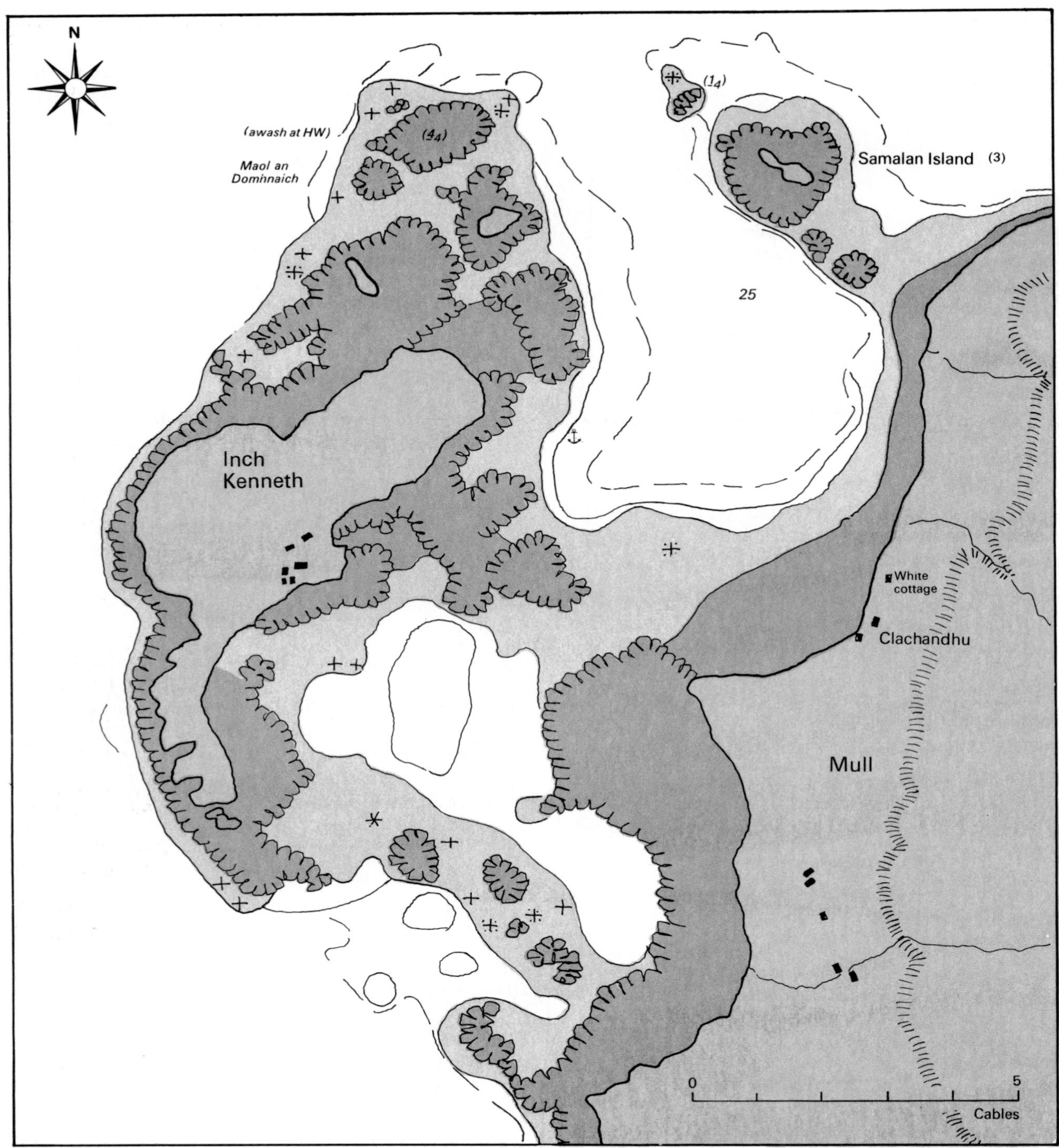

Inch Kenneth

Tides

Sound of Ulva constant −0010 Oban (−0540 Dover).

Height in metres

MHWS	MHWN	MTL	MLWN	MLWS
4.4	3.2	2.5	1.8	0.6

Flood runs northwestwards but tidal streams are not significant.

Dangers and marks

For MacQuarrie's Rock see under *Loch na Keal* page 99. In the mouth of the sound, where it narrows to 2 cables north of the east point of Ulva, Sgeir Beul a' Chaolais (which means 'the rock at the mouth of the sound') dries 4.4 metres with a low concrete beacon on it. Northeast of it drying rocks extend a cable south of the north point of the entrance to the sound.

Sgeir Dubhail, ½ mile NNW of the northwest entrance, dries 2.6 metres. The northwest entrance is between a rock 1 metre high off Torr Ardalum on Ulva,

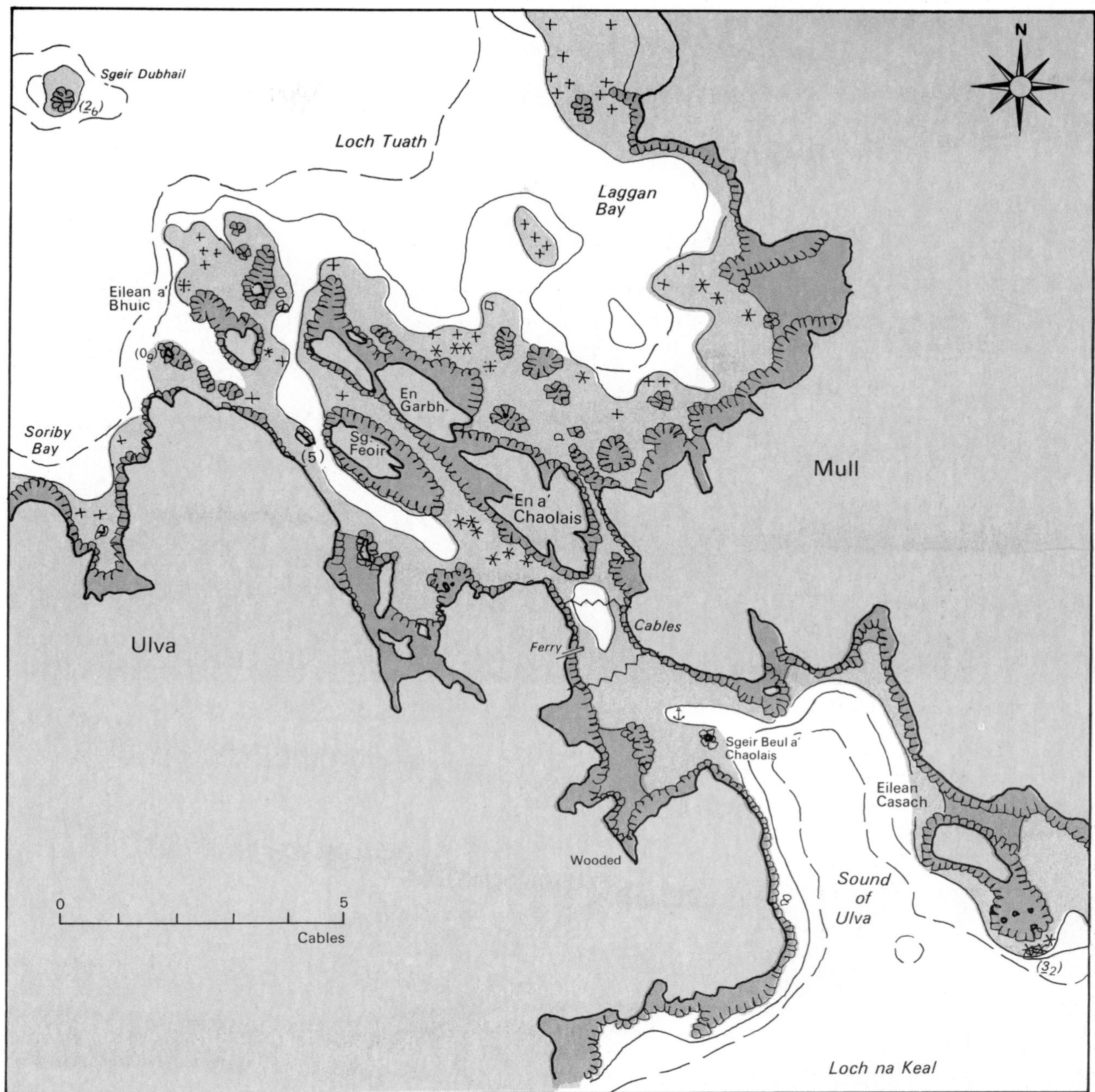

Ulva Ferry

and Eilean a' Bhuic. South of this island there are drying rocks on the south side of the channel. Two cables southeast of Eilean a' Bhuic is a 5-metre islet with a larger, but lower, islet (Sgeir Feoir) close to its east side. Half a mile southeast of the 5-metre islet is a passage about a third of a cable wide leading to the Ulva Ferry passage. In the basin between the 5-metre islet and the narrows there are many submerged and drying rocks.

Directions – through passage

From south, pass close northeast of Sgeir Beul a' Chaolais and head for the ferry house on Ulva. Pass southwest of moorings and keep south of the middle of the narrow passage north of the cable beacon on Ulva. Head initially south of the south point of the northwest entrance and come round gradually towards the point. Pass east of the 5-metre islet off Ulva and then within 20 metres of Eilean a' Bhuic to avoid rocks on the south side of the channel, and pass north of the 1-metre rock. Continue on the same course for a mile to be sure of avoiding Sgeir Dubhail.

From northwest, identify Eilean a' Bhuic and keep the summit of Ben More south of it bearing 126°. Pass north of the 1-metre high rock and 20 metres south of Eilean a' Bhuic, then east of the 5-metre islet and come round gradually to head for the narrows ½ mile southeast; do not steer directly for the narrows. Keep

Sound of Ulva from north at LW. Some of the drying rocks in the passage may not be charted.

Sound of Ulva from southeast.

Sound of Ulva, northwest entrance.

south of the middle of the narrows, pass southwest of the moorings and come round gradually to pass north of Sgeir Beul a' Chaolais.

Anchorages

WNW of Sgeir Beul a' Chaolais, clear of Sgeir Lach and rocks on the north side, and cables crossing the sound.

In settled weather only, east of the drying rocks off the point of Mull northeast of Sgeir Beul a' Chaolais.

The pool northeast of the ferry house is taken up with moorings for local boats, and underwater cables cross the sound north and south of the ferry.

Water is available, and there is a pay phone in an outbuilding at the ferry house on Ulva.

Anchorages – upper Loch na Keal

Eorsa ENE of the island on the 5-metre line. Keep at least a cable off the southeast and east sides of the island to avoid drying rocks.

Dhiseig Temporary anchorage southeast of Eorsa to land a party to climb Ben More. There is a stony bank at the mouth of the two burns, outside which the bottom falls away steeply; it slopes more moderately ½ mile ENE.

Scarisdale provides better anchorage if you can find your way in south of the main group of rocks. A' Chrannag on Ulva over the north edge of Eorsa leads between submerged rocks to a pool ¼ mile across south of Scarisdale Rocks.

Loch Scridain

56°22′N 6°05′W

Loch Scridain, running 5 miles ENE on the north side of the Ross of Mull, has no really good anchorages. The north side is fairly clean but on the south side there are several groups of drying rocks extending for half a mile from the shore; of these the most important are detailed below.

Chart

2771 (1:25,000) is hardly necessary except for exploring close inshore.

Dangers and clearing marks

Bogha Mor dries 0.6 metres, 3 cables off the entrance to a bay on the south side of the entrance to the loch, with a submerged rock 2 cables ENE of it. Meall nan Carn, a conspicuous conical hill, 64 metres in height on the north side of the Ross of Mull, over the extremity of Ardtun, the nearest point to the west, 271°, leads close north of Bogha Mor.

An Carraigean, 3 miles further east, dries 0.6 metres, 3 cables offshore, ¾ mile ENE of the promontory Ard Fada.

Bogh' an Rubha dries 2.1 metres, ¾ mile ENE of An Carraigean, 2 cables offshore. Ardchrishnish House open of Ard Fada 249°, leads close north of both An Carraigean and Bogh' an Rubha.

Sgeir Alltach, a reef drying 3 metres, extends 4 cables from the shore, with other drying rocks east of it, 4 miles from the entrance, opposite Kilfinichen Bay. Dun I, the highest hill on Iona, over the high-water line of the north point of the entrance of the loch, 263°, leads close north of Sgeir Alltach.

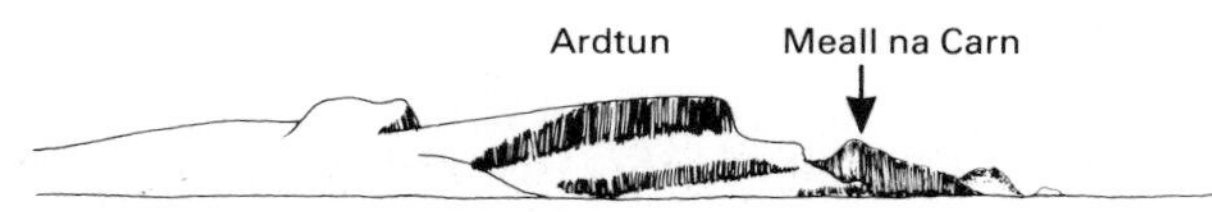

Loch Scridain – clearing mark for Bogha Mor 271°.

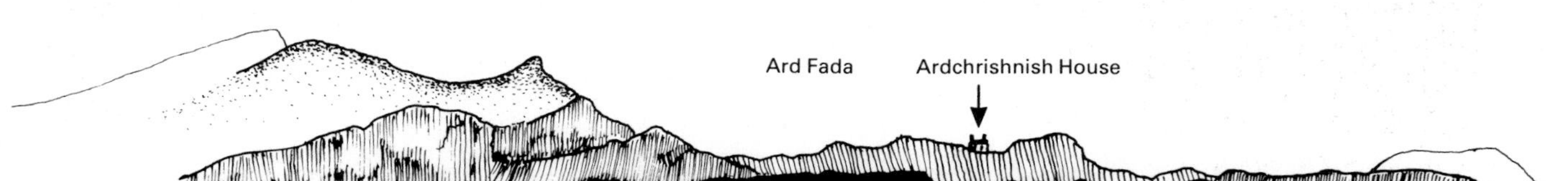

Loch Scridain – clearing mark for Bogh' an Rubha 249°.

Loch Scridain – clearing mark for Sgeir Alltach 263°.

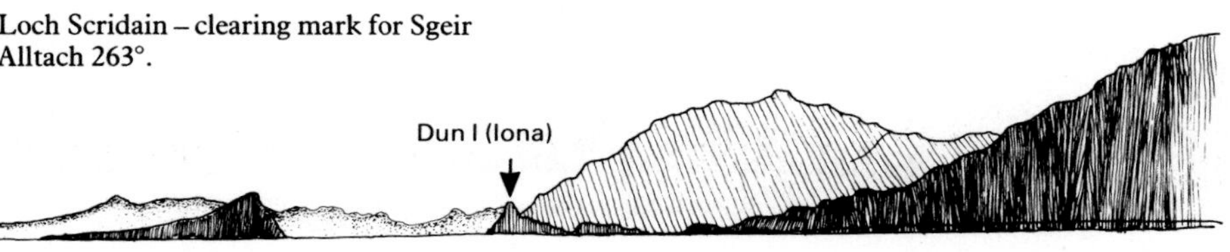

Anchorages

Bun an Leoib (which appears on chart *2617*), on the south side of the entrance to Loch Scridain, provides shelter from the west behind the above-water rocks Sgeir Leathen and Sgeir Mor, but little shelter from northwest and north. Enter ½ to 1 cable north of Sgeir Mor to pass inside Bogha Mor, and anchor either on the south side of the bay or NNE of a tidal islet ¾ cable off the southwest side of the bay. A drying reef extends a cable east of the islet, with other drying rocks between the reef and the south shore.

Sgeir Alltach, 5 miles from the mouth of Loch Scridain, provides some shelter on its east side. The outermost rock dries 3 metres; nearly 2 cables northwest of the above-water part of the reef Sgeir Chailleach dries 0.9 metres. Sgeir na Rad, 3½ cables east of the islet, dries 2.1 metres, with lesser drying rocks within ½ cable WSW of it. This anchorage should only be approached within 2½ hours of LW, when Sgeir na Rad shows, to give some guide to the position of the other rocks.

Kilfinichen Bay, on the north side of the loch, is a suitable anchorage for quiet settled weather. Keep a cable off the west point of the entrance to the bay to avoid drying rocks there.

Loch Beg, at the north side of the head of the loch, is the most satisfactory anchorage in Loch Scridain. A post with a red reflective topmark of a triangle in a circle stands on the shore 3 cables south of the entrance.

Most of the basin dries out and there is only depth to anchor within a couple of cables of the entrance. It is subject to any sea running up Loch Scridain, and violent squalls in easterly winds.

Loch na Lathaich (Bunessan)

56°20′N 6°16′W

A well sheltered inlet on the north side of the Ross of Mull, halfway between Loch Scridain and the Sound of Iona. It has a straightforward entrance, with the only light beacon on the west coast of Mull; a boatyard, shop and hotel, and a bus service to the Oban ferry at Craignure.

Tides

Constant −0015 Oban (−0545 Dover).

Height in metres

MHWS	MHWN	MTL	MLWN	MLWS
4.3	3.0	2.4	1.8	0.6

Dangers and marks

Eileanan na Liathanaich is a group of islands and rocks off the west side of the entrance of the loch. The largest and most easterly has a light beacon on its south side. Rocks above water and drying extend a cable WNW of the west island, and there is a detached drying rock ½ cable northeast of the east island.

Ionain Rock, drying 3.4 metres, extends 1½ cables from the east side of the loch. Towards the southeast corner of the loch are two islets, Eilean nam Meann and Eilean Ban, which is the larger and further southeast. Eilean nam Meann in line with a prominent hill on the south side of the loch, Cnoc an t-Suidhe 173°, leads west of Ionain Rock.

Approach either side of Eileanan na Liathanaich, but look out for lobster pot floats around the islands.

Light

At night Eileanan na Liathanaich, Fl.WR.6s12m8/6M, shows red to the west between 088° and 108° and white elsewhere.

Anchorages

Southwest corner in 3 to 4 metres clear of moorings. Nigel Burgess, the owner of Bendoran Boatyard, has carried out a survey and has found that, apart from an individual wreck with a least depth of over 3 metres, the obstructions as charted no longer exist. This part of the loch is now well used for mooring and anchoring.

Southeast corner south of Eilean Ban, clear of approach to the pier, and no further east than a line between the pier and the east side of Eilean Ban as it is shoal and drying beyond this. The bottom is mud with increasing weed. Show an anchor light at night. The pier has a lot of fishing traffic in the evening and at night, but its ramp is a good place to land a dinghy, ¼ mile from the village.

Loch na Lathaich – Eilean nam Meann below Cnoc an t-Suidhe 173°.

Services and supplies

Bendoran Boatyard in the southwest corner of the loch has a pontoon with a depth of over 2 metres alongside for 4 hours either side of HW springs, and supplies diesel, water and *Calor Gas*, and provides showers. Moorings, laying up, repairs. Petrol at Bunessan. Shops and hotel at Bunessan in the southeast corner of the loch.

Communications Post office and phone box at Bunessan. Bus service to Oban ferry and Iona ferry. Bendoran Boatyard, ☎ Fionnphort (068 17) 435.

Camas Tuath is an occasional anchorage ¾ mile west of Loch na Lathaich. The granite quarry there supplied the stone for building Skerryvore and Ardnamurchan lighthouses.

Sound of Iona

56°20′N 6°23′W

The west end of the Ross of Mull consists mainly of pink granite with brilliant white sands and the sea shading from jade green at the edges to indigo further out; add a blue sky overhead, the white sails of yachts and the occasional paddle steamer, and you have all that the Tourist Board could ask for – quite apart from a fine, although heavily restored, cathedral. Iona has a heavy traffic in day visitors, and it is well worth arranging to go ashore there early in the day, or after most of the visitors have left.

Most of the width of the sound is blocked by a shoal which, the chart indicates, consists of sand, black shingle and coral, and below half-tide this needs careful pilotage. Tidal streams in the sound according to the chart are 'probably' 2½ knots and apart from any swell from the open sea, the tide over the shallows generates its own sea. The anchorage off the village at Iona is usually unsettled except very close inshore.

The passage between the Firth of Lorne and the Sound of Iona is described on page 112.

Iona – it's worth waiting until after the day-visitors have gone.

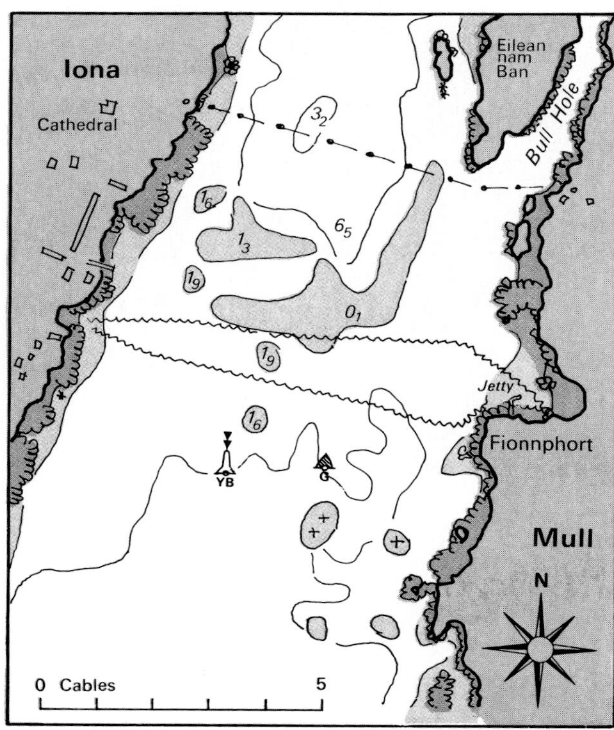

Sound of Iona

Chart

2617 (1:25,000) is essential.

Tides

At Iona the constant is −0005 Oban (−0535 Dover).

Height in metres

MHWS	MHWN	MTL	MLWN	MLWS
4.0	3.0	2.2	1.5	0.5

Tidal streams in the sound run at up to 2½ knots.

There is some uncertainty about the times at which the tides turn, but the following is a guide: north-going stream begins +0515 Oban (−0015 Dover); south-going stream begins −0015 Oban (−0545 Dover).

Dangers and marks

The most conspicuous reference marks are the cathedral on Iona north of the village, and the hill Dun I, 99 metres, ½ mile NNW of the cathedral.

The main hazard is the shoal bank which stretches across the middle of the sound from Iona village to Eilean nam Ban, ½ mile north of Fionnphort, with only 0.1 metres on it in places.

North of the bank rocks dry up to a cable off either shore, and Breug, an isolated rock 1½ cables west of the north end of Eilean nam Ban, covers at HW.

South of the bank are an unlit south cardinal buoy, and a green conical buoy on the north side of a submerged rock ¼ mile off the Mull shore.

Further south there are many rocks up to 3 cables off the Mull shore, and two cables off Iona. A green conical buoy, a mile south of the buoys just referred to above, marks a 3-metre rock and is 2 cables west of the nearest drying rocks.

Directions

From north keep 2 cables off either shore unless you are carefully following the large-scale chart. The course you take at the mid-sound bank will depend on your draught and the state of the tide. Yachts over 2-metres draught, if it is near LW springs, should pass no more than ½ cable southwest of the south end of Eilean nam Ban, then parallel to the Mull shore for half a mile keeping Bull Hole just open astern, before altering course to pass between the green conical buoy and the south cardinal. The shallowest part of the bank is close west of this line.

Yachts of moderate draught, and deep-draught yachts within 4 hours of HW springs, can pass about a cable off the Iona shore between a point abreast of the cathedral and the south end of the village. There is a short steep sea here when the tide turns against the wind.

Towards the south end of the sound keep west of a line joining the two green conical buoys.

From south pass west of both green conical buoys and if over 2-metres draught and near LW springs turn to head obliquely towards the Mull shore to keep Bull Hole just open, until Eilean Annraidh at the north end of Iona is touching Eilean Liath, west of Eilean nam Ban. Then pass ½ cable southwest of Eilean nam Ban and continue towards the middle of the sound. Otherwise pass west of the south cardinal buoy and a cable from Iona until past the cathedral.

For the passage along the south coast of Mull see p.112.

Iona village.

Anchorages

Two underwater telephone cables cross the sound from Fionnphort to Martyrs' Bay, south of the ferry jetty on Iona, and a water pipeline crosses from the south end of Eilean nam Ban to a point south of the cathedral. Yachts usually anchor south of the jetty – often, probably, over the telephone cables – but you should take care to avoid both the cables and the ferry's line of approach to the jetty.

A more peaceful anchorage with less tide may be found clear north of the pipeline beacon, ENE of the cathedral. Further north again there is a an underwater electricity cable.

Fionnphort Temporary anchorage WNW of the ferry jetty, avoiding both the cables and the approach to the jetty.

Supplies

Shops and phone box at both Iona and Fionnphort. Hotels (unlicensed) and post office on Iona. Water tap on the end wall of public toilet at the jetty on Iona. Other supplies at Bunessan.

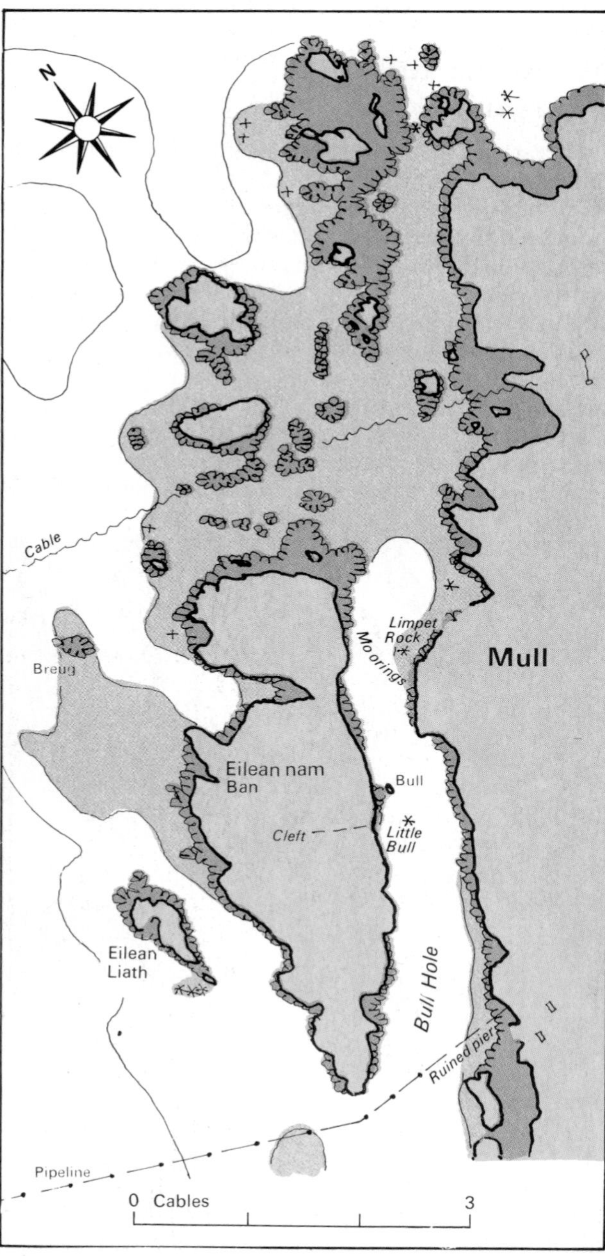

Bull Hole

Bull Hole from northeast.

Bull Hole

56°20′N 6°22′W

Between Eilean nam Ban and Mull, near the north end of the sound. Much of the basin at the north end is too shallow except for shoal-draught yachts other than at neaps, and most of the deeper water is taken up with moorings. An underwater pipeline to Iona crosses the entrance. If space can be found the best anchorage is close to the Mull shore east of the north end of Eilean nam Ban, taking care to avoid the Limpet rock. In approaching the upper part of Bull Hole take care to avoid the Little Bull rock which dries 0.5 metres, south of the Bull rock, which is above water, and in line with a cleft in the rocks on Eilean nam Ban.

An alternative anchorage, more subject to swell, is north of the ruined pier near the south entrance, but take care to avoid the underwater pipeline, and leave a clear passage for the ferry, whose mooring is north of the Bull. Fionnphort is ½ mile by footpath from the pier.

Dedicated rock-dodgers will find it possible to leave Bull Hole on a rising tide by one of several passages, which are shown on the air photo, but no other guidance is available.

Tinker's Hole

56°17′.5N 6°23′W

One of the most popular anchorages on the West Coast, although one visitor likened it to a half-flooded quarry. Tinker's Hole is between Eilean Dubh and the west side of Erraid at the south end of the Sound of Iona. It is in places less than ½ cable wide and on the east side the shore consists of walls of pink granite. R. L. Stevenson visited Erraid when his uncle was building Dubh Artach lighthouse, and knew this as Fiddler's Hole.

The cottages here were built for the shore station for Dubh Artach lighthouse and are now occupied by the Findhorn Community.

Tides

At Iona the constant is −0005 Oban (−0535 Dover).

Height in metres

MHWS	MHWN	MTL	MLWN	MLWS
4.0	3.0	2.2	1.5	0.5

In Tinker's Hole the north-going stream begins about +0445 Oban (−0045 Dover); and the south-going stream begins about −0130 Oban (+0530 Dover).

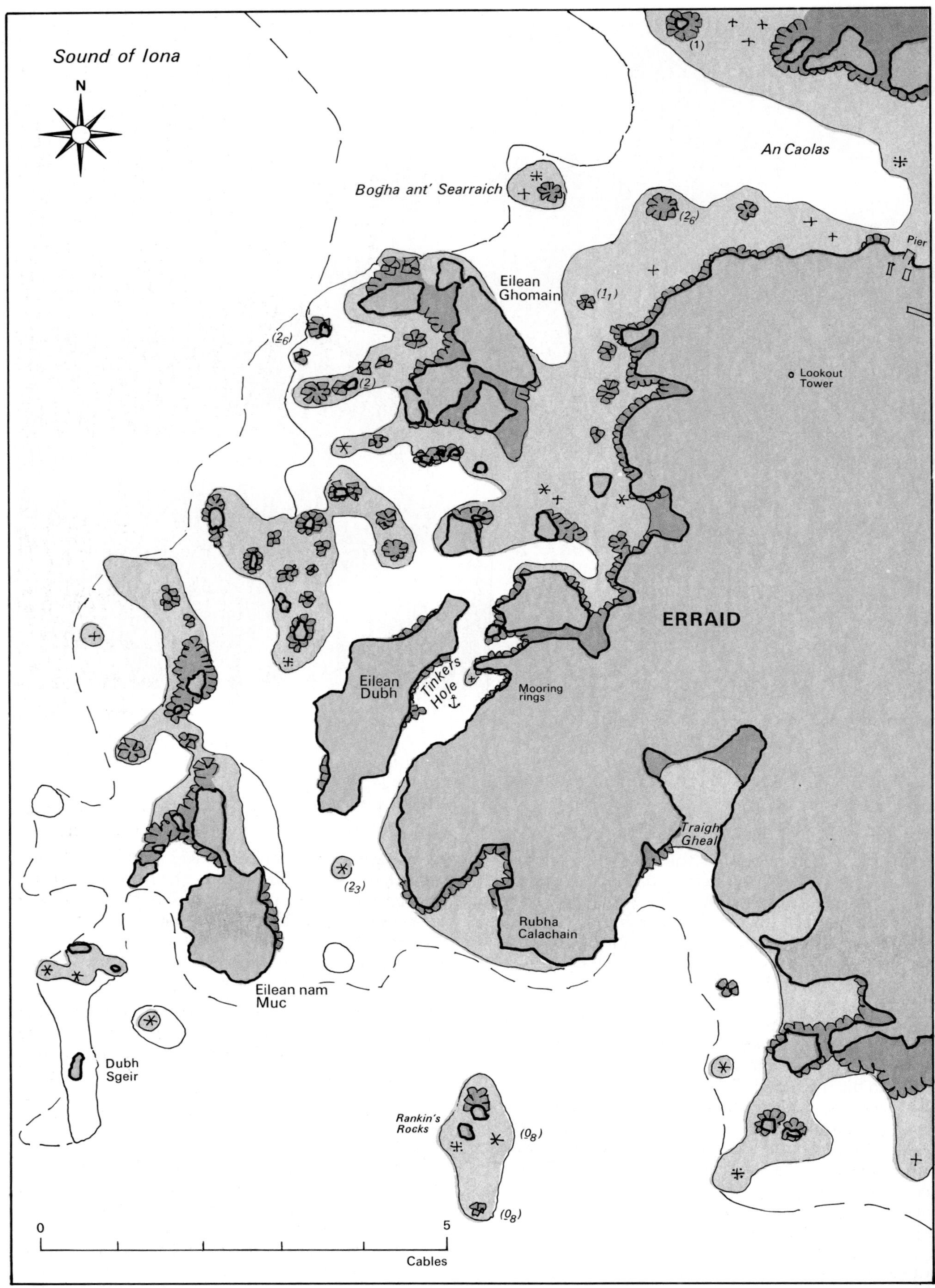

Tinker's Hole and Erraid

Tinker's Hole from the south. Eilean Dubh is in the centre with the Hole to the right, and Eilean nam Muc bottom left.

Tinker's Hole from southwest. The drying rock shows clearly right of centre – it's more alarming when you can't see it.

Dangers

The south entrance, which is the usual approach, is from a passage between Eilean Dubh and Eilean nam Muc, a cable further southwest. In the middle of this entrance is a rock drying 2.3 metres.

Rankin's Rocks, in the approach to this passage from southeast, are 1 and 2 metres high, with drying rocks around them. Take care not to confuse Sgeir na Caillich with Rankin's Rocks. At the northwest end of the passage there are so many rocks and islets that the main difficulty is finding it in the first place. The key is to identify Eilean nam Muc and look for the clear passage inside it as you approach; note the rock drying 4.2 metres on the south side of the northwest entrance, which is not normally covered.

The approach to Tinker's Hole from the north is not difficult above half-tide. Keep within ½ cable northeast of Eilean Ghomain to avoid drying rocks further off. If your charts have not been corrected, note there is no longer a beacon on Bogha ant'searraich, 1½ cables NNE of Eilean Ghomain. The main hazard is a drying rock a cable SSE of Eilean Ghomain; steer to bring the east side of Eilean Dubh in line with the west side of Erraid 198° – if you can see the east end of Eilean nam Muc you will probably go over the rock.

There is slightly deeper water inshore close to Erraid but there is no alternative to feeling your way here, but the bottom is clear white sand – see the air photo.

Some yachts have used the passage from the west but there is at least one uncharted rock, on the north side of the entrance, and no clear leading line.

Anchorages

Between Eilean Dubh and Erraid, wherever convenient. At times the tidal stream runs strongly here. Mooring rings at the head of the bight on the Erraid side are maintained by CCC members. A submerged reef extends 20 metres south from the northwest point of this bight. This point defines the edge of the tidal stream. Lobster keep-boxes are sometimes moored in the fairway.

The large pool immediately north of Tinker's Hole is an alternative anchorage; others may be found among the skerries north and northwest of Eilean Dubh, particularly by shoal-draught boats, or others at neaps; also close northeast of Eilean Ghomain or towards the pier on the north side of Erraid.

The passage inside Eilean nam Muc looking northwest; the drying rock off the entrance to Tinker's Hole is showing; the northwest entrance of the passage is beyond it.

Eilean nam Muc and the passage inside it from the north.

Leading line for entrance to Tinker's Hole from the north.

Traigh Gheal on the south side of Erraid, known as David Balfour's Bay after the hero of *Kidnapped*, is a delightful daytime anchorage, but a trap if the wind strengthens from between south and southwest.

South coast of the Ross of Mull and the Torran Rocks

56°15′N 6°22′W

Admiralty chart *2617* is essential for this passage, and the plan here should be treated as diagrammatic only, to illustrate the transits described.

A direct passage can be made from the Firth of Lorne to the Sound of Iona by the south side of Mull, but it is a lee shore to the prevailing southwest wind and there is no good sheltered anchorage on the way. Another approach is from the Sound of Islay passing east and north of Colonsay.

The usual passage is between Mull and the Torran Rocks which extend over an area 4 miles by 4 miles, southwest of Mull. The nearest of them to Mull, the unpronounceable Bogha nan Ramfhear, dries 1.4 metres and is 7 cables south of the east end of Eilean a' Chalmain. The only way to establish your position is by reference to various natural features together with a stone beacon on one of the Torran Rocks; good visibility is needed to identify these features at a range of several miles.

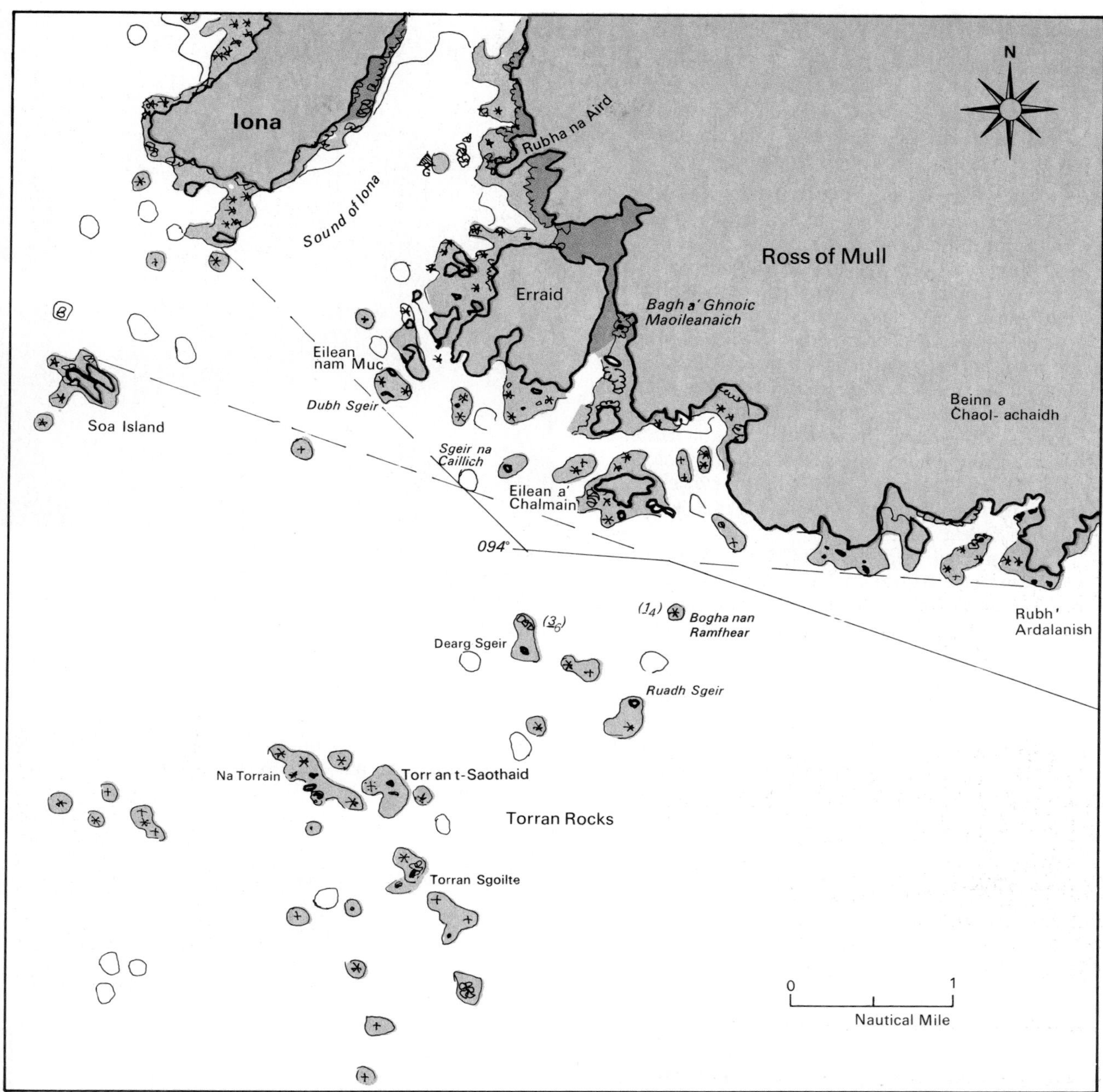

Torran Rocks

Landmarks – from east to west

Rubh' Ardalanish, the most southerly point of the Ross of Mull with, to the north, Beinn a' Chaol-achaidh, the highest hill in the west part of the Ross. To the east of Ardalanish the rocks are grey; to the west they are mostly pink.

Eilean a' Chalmain 3 miles west of Ardalanish, has a drying rock nearly a cable southwest of its south point. An islet 2 cables southwest of Eilean a' Chalmain, although unnamed, is a useful reference point.

Sgeir na Caillich is an islet 6 cables west of Eilean a' Chalmain.

Dubh Sgeir 2 cables southwest of Eilean nam Muc, is the most southwesterly island off Erraid.

Soa Island, 34 metres, is 1½ miles SSW of Iona.

Ruadh Sgeir, on which there is the stump of a stone beacon, the most easterly of the Torran Rocks and must be clearly identified in approaching from the east.

Na Torrain is a group of three above-water rocks in the middle of the Torran Rocks and provide the key to pilotage within the area. From the south these are 23, 15 and 19 metres high, and Torr an t-Saothaid, ½ mile east of Na Torrain, is about 18 metres high. These are sometimes mistaken at a distance from the east for Soa Island.

Dubh Artach lighthouse, 10 miles southwest of the Torran Rocks, has a broad red band round it.

Directions

From the Sound of Islay pass east of Colonsay and steer 330° for Beinn a' Chaol-achaidh, the highest hill of the west part of the Ross of Mull, and continue as below. Yachtsmen familiar with the area take other passages through the Torran Rocks.

From the east steer to pass outside Ardalanish. Identify Ruadh Sgeir and Na Torrain. These two in line will provide a preliminary position line. Head along the Mull shore and bring Soa Island not more than its own width open of the islet southwest of Eilean a' Chalmain, the islet bearing 295°.

A further useful position line is Na Maoil Mhora in line with the rocks south of Rubh' Ardalanish 094°.

If you are tacking, it is essential to know your position relative to the Torran Rocks in general and Bogha nan Ramfhear in particular. Bogha nan Ramfhear is safely passed when Dearg Sgeir, which is ¾ mile WNW of Ruadh Sgeir, is in line with Na Torrain. There is a large rock drying 3.6 metres 2 cables north of Dearg Sgeir.

Pass south of Sgeir na Caillich and Dubh Sgeir, southwest of Eilean nam Muc, and alter course for the Sound of Iona; keep over ¼ mile west of the islands on the east side of the sound to avoid rocks at a depth of 1.9 metres. The east end of the former Free Church (now a house but identified by the belfry at its east end) in line with the cathedral tower about 012° leads west of these rocks.

Bogha hun a Chuhoil about 6 cables southwest of Dubh Sgeir has a depth of 1.6 metres. The line described above leads close east of it.

Bagh a' Ghnoic Mhaoileanaich, between Erraid and Mull, from the south.

For the alternative passage north of Eilean nam Muc see under *Tinker's Hole*, on page 109.

The passage eastward is generally easier than going westward as you are closer to each of the features which need to be identified.

Bagh a' Ghnoic Mhaoileanaich, between Erraid and Mull, provides an occasional anchorage in settled weather.

Ruadh Sgeir
Na Torrain
Dearg Sgeir
Bogha nan Ramfhear

Torran Rocks – general view from northeast.

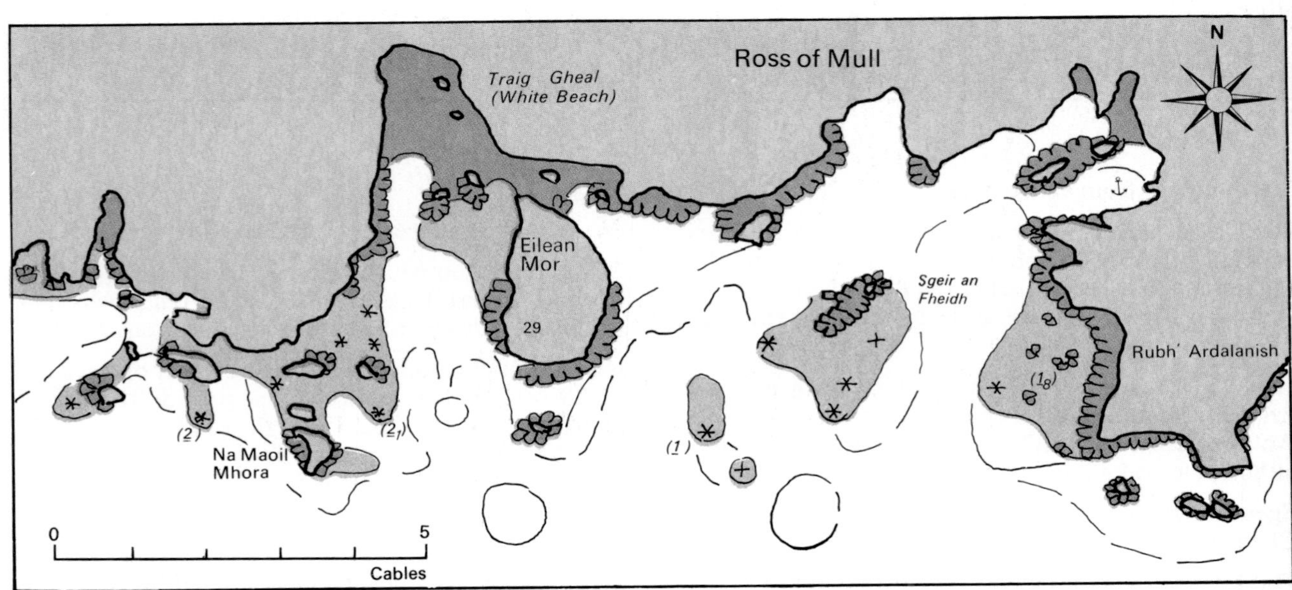

Ardalanish

Rubh' Ardalanish

56°16'N 6°17'W

The inlet on the west side of Rubh' Ardalanish is particularly attractive in settled conditions. It has been spoken of as safe in a gale, but I haven't put this to the test, and it would not be safe to enter or leave if there were much sea running.

Do not cross the 20-metre contour until you have identified Sgeir an Fheidh which at most states of the tide appears to be two separate rocks; approach with the rock in line with a deep valley 350°, and then pass midway between the rock and the west side of Rubh' Ardalanish. It may be easier to find your way in ESE of Eilean Mor and north of Sgeir an Fheidh.

There are two inlets at the north end of the west side of the promontory, and the more southerly of them is the more sheltered.

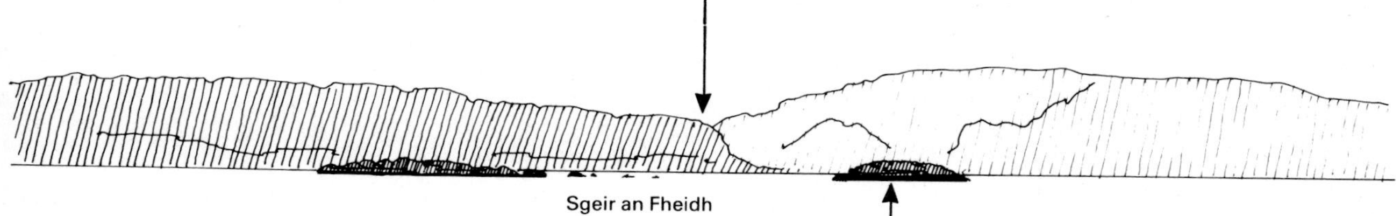

Ardalanish approach – the northeast part of Sgeir an Fheidh is to the right of the mouth of the small valley beyond.

Ardalanish anchorage.

VI. Coll and Tiree

These two islands are mostly low-lying and exposed, and neither of them has an anchorage which is secure, let alone comfortable in winds from all directions. There is more of an edge-of-the-world feeling about these islands than about any other area covered by this book. Loch Eatharna (Arinagour) on Coll is only 7 miles from Caliach Point on the west side of Mull and has a clean sandy bottom and a welcoming hotel, but if the wind is from anywhere between ENE and SSW, you will pitch and roll more or less uncomfortably, depending on its strength. Likewise, Gott Bay which is the main anchorage on Tiree will be uncomfortable in any wind between ENE and south. Either can be dangerous in strong winds from these directions.

Both islands may be visited from the Sound of Mull or from Iona, or from anchorages in between, the distance from Tobermory to Arinagour, or from Iona to Gott Bay being about 20 miles.

Chart

Apart from large-scale plans referred to at individual anchorages and passages, *2171* (1:75,000) is the largest-scale Admiralty chart to show any part of Coll and Tiree; this covers none of the southwest part of Tiree. Ordnance Survey map *46* may be found helpful.

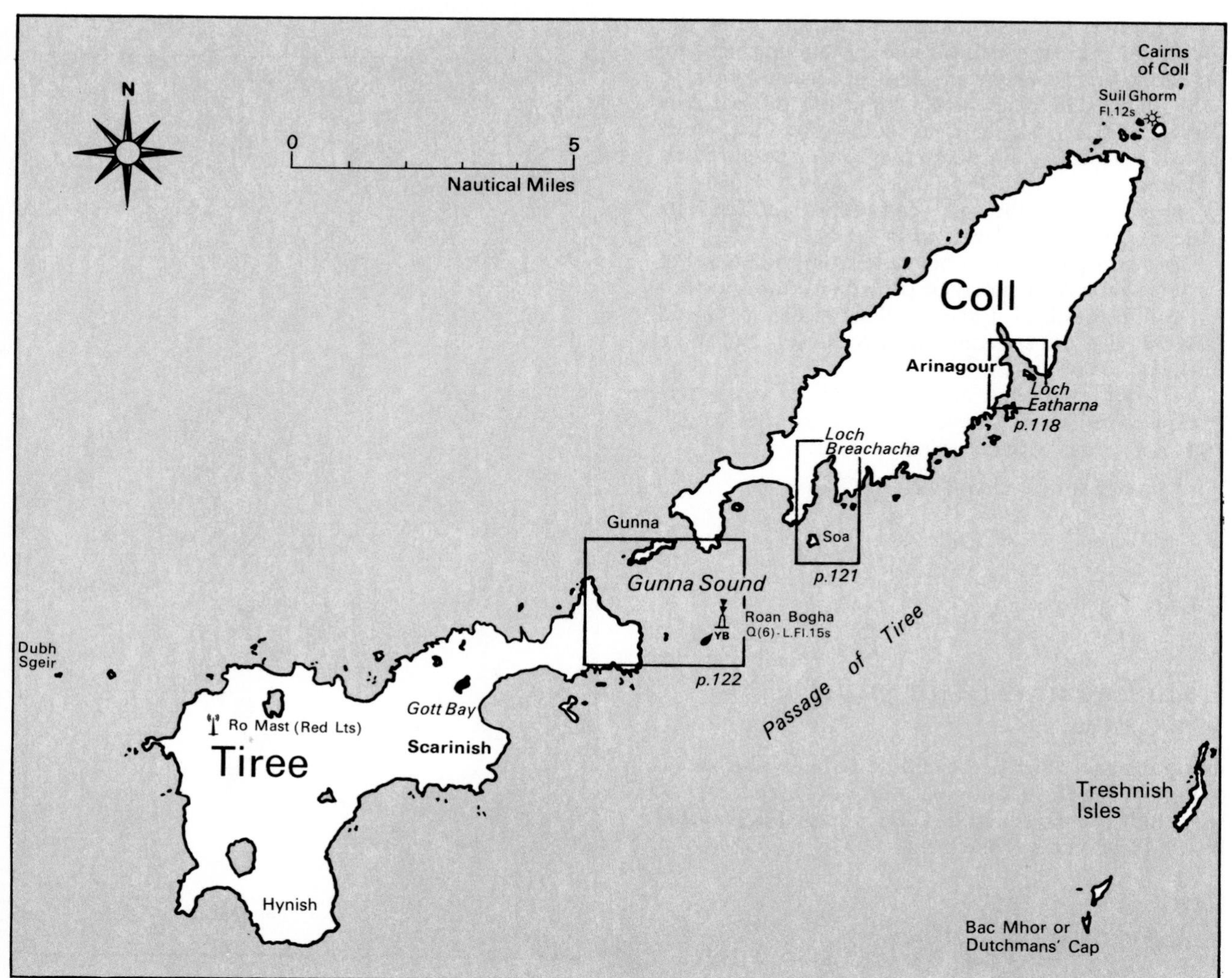

Tides

In the Passage of Tiree, the channel between Coll and Tiree and Mull, tidal streams run at up to 1½ knots at springs – enough to cause a very unpleasant sea with wind against tide. Off Caliach Point and around the Treshnish Isles tidal streams increase to 2½ knots.

Off the middle of the southeast side of Coll, the northeast-going stream begins −0430 Oban (+0230 Dover); the southwest-going stream begins +0200 Oban (−0330 Dover).

Towards the south end of Tiree, the northeast-going stream begins +0600 Oban (+0030 Dover); the southwest-going stream begins at HW Oban (−0530 Dover).

Passage notes

Between the Sound of Mull and Arinagour there are no particular hazards apart from drying rocks within the line of headlands on the northwest coast of Mull. There is no way of identifying Arinagour until you are fairly close to it, when houses will begin to appear. Bearing in mind that you will be approaching the coast of Coll obliquely, make for a point about a quarter of its apparent length from the south end of the island.

Approaching Tiree from southeast The most conspicuous features on the island are Beinn Hough on the west side (119m) with a radar installation near its summit, and Ben Hynish (138m) at the south point of the island. There is a small latticed communications tower at Scarinish, ½ mile southwest of the south point of Gott Bay and about 5 miles northeast of Ben Hynish.

Crossing from the north end of the Sound of Iona there are no particular hazards.

A direct passage can be made from the Sound of Islay. Dubh Artach may be passed on either side but if you go north of it keep well south of the Torran Rocks, as there are submerged rocks south of those which are visible.

For ten miles west of Iona there is an area where the bottom is very uneven, causing overfalls which are dangerous with any wind or swell.

For Gunna Sound see page 121.

Coll

Loch Eatharna (Arinagour)

56°37′N 6°31′W

A popular anchorage in the middle of the southeast side of Coll with a clean sandy bottom, but exposed to any sea running, even along the coast, which is aggravated by the shallowness of the loch.

Chart

Plan (1:10,000) on chart *2474*.

Tides

Constant is +0017 Oban (−0513 Dover).

Height in metres

MHWS	MHWN
4.4	3.2

Approach and anchorages

The main anchorage is west of Eilean Eatharna and there are HIDB visitors' moorings north of the concrete pier on the west side of the loch. If approaching from southwest keep over a cable off Ornsay at the southwest point of the entrance, to avoid a submerged rock there.

From any direction identify Bogha Mor green conical buoy and leave it to starboard. Steer to pass close east of the head of the concrete pier to avoid unmarked drying rocks opposite, keeping the right side of the hotel in line above the root of the stone pier at Arinagour village.

The most northwesterly of drying rocks off Eilean Eatharna has a stone beacon on it. Anchor between the beacon and the stone pier. The deepest water is towards the beacon; at neaps a medium-draught yacht can lie fairly close to the pier. There is limited space to the northeast of the beacon.

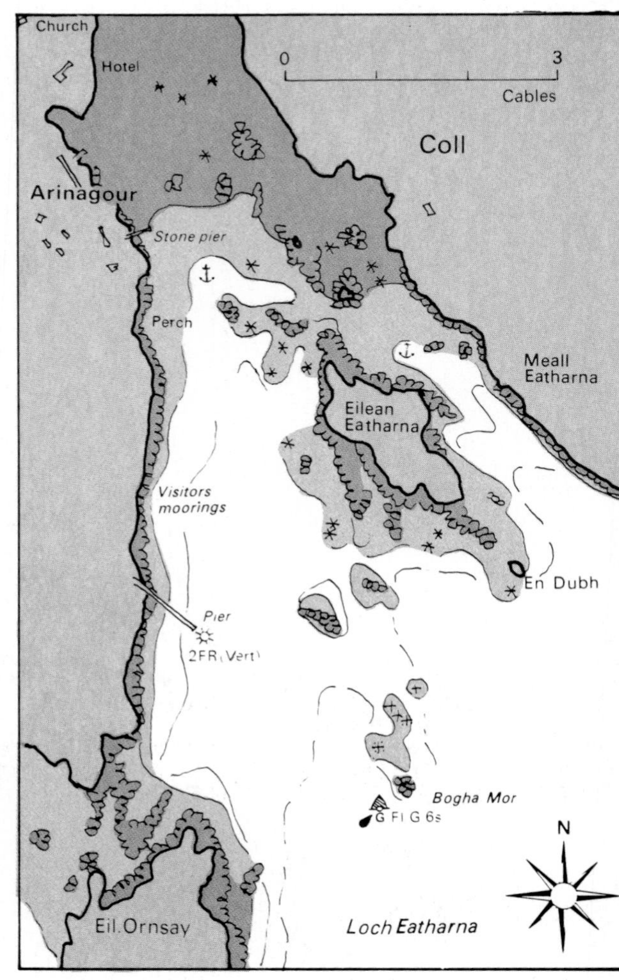

Loch Eatharna

Arinagour from the east shore of Loch Eatharna.

East of Eilean Eatharna keep closer to the northeast shore until near the most northeasterly point of Eilean Eatharna, then keep the left side of the hotel in line above the left-hand edge of the low islet ahead 309° to clear a rock drying 1.2 metres, ½ cable off the northeast shore. At neaps the best shelter is north of Eilean Eatharna; otherwise anchor further southeast, clear of the rocks shown.

A half-tide passage north of Eilean Eatharna can be used – with great caution – in quiet weather.

Lights

At night Bogha Mor buoy is lit Fl.G.6s and the head of the concrete pier has lights 2F.R(vert), so that the approach as far as the visitors' moorings is fairly simple.

Supplies

Shop, hotel, laundrette, showers, *Calor Gas*. Diesel and petrol (not always available). Post office; phone box at stone pier. Water tap in a field behind the stone pier. Bicycle hire from Coll Hotel, ☎ Coll (087 93) 334.

The hotel, the church, and the stone pier.

Loch Eatharna from southeast. The drying rock east of the concrete pier is on the left, so Bogha Mor is well below the bottom of the photo.

Entering the western arm of Loch Eatharna. The church is on the skyline, with the hotel below it.

Eastern arm of Loch Eatharna; left-hand side of islet in line with the hotel.

Loch Breachacha

56°35′N 6°37′W

An occasional anchorage towards the southwest end of Coll, identifiable initially by Soa Island, 15m high, and nearer at hand by the old and new castles, of which the 'new' one is a grey castellated 19th-century building with symmetrical wings and small corner turrets. The inlet is sandy and open to any southerly swell. There are many rocks on both sides of the entrance and inside the loch.

Approach and anchorage

The 20-metre contour clears all dangers. Steer with the highest point of the sand dunes to the west of the loch bearing 330°. When the 'new' castle appears clear west of above-water rocks at the east point of the entrance, all rocks to the south of that point are cleared.

The line to clear rocks within the loch is to keep the middle window of a cottage behind the 'old' castle just open of the left-hand side of that castle 360°; this line leads rather close to drying rocks in the middle of the loch.

The loch shoals very gradually; anchor as far in as depth allows.

Gunna Sound

56°33′N 6°43′W

The passage between Coll and Tiree is used by boats on passage to the Outer Hebrides from south of Mull. There are several dangerous rocks but the two worst are marked by light buoys.

Chart

2475 has a plan of Gunna Sound at 1:25,000.

Tides

Tidal streams run at up to 3 knots causing heavy overfalls at the windward end with an opposing tide.

The northwest-going stream begins +0535 Oban (+0005 Dover); the northeast-going stream begins −0120 Oban (+0540 Dover).

Directions

From south and east identify Roan Bogha south cardinal buoy and pass either south or ¼ mile north of it. Identify Placaid Bogha green conical buoy and pass south of it.

From southward, an alternative course is to pass a cable west of Creachasdal Mor heading 360°. Do not alter course northwest until Placaid Bogha appears about the middle of the northwest entrance so as to clear Bogha Hoshmish, a rock drying 2.3 metres 2 cables off the northeast point of Tiree.

From north and west make for the centre of the channel to avoid rocks on either hand, but especially drying rocks up to 2 cables all round the north point of Tiree. Identify and pass south of Placaid Bogha buoy and follow the reverse of the directions above.

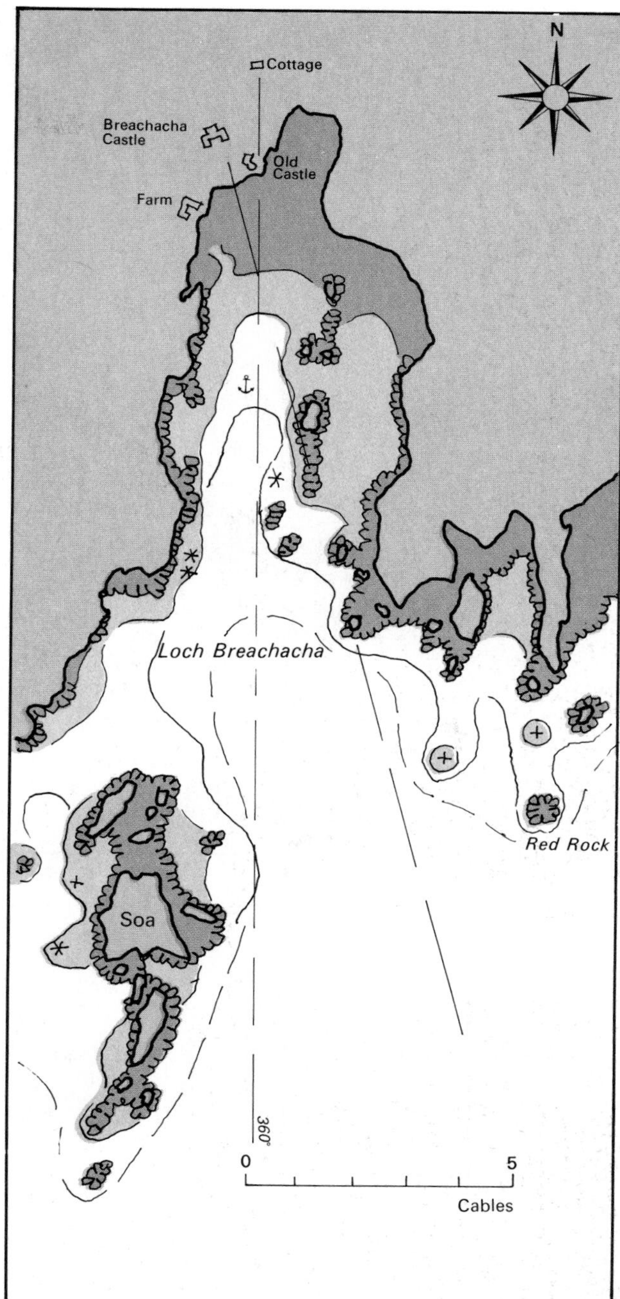

Loch Breachacha

Anchorage

Clach Chuirr on the southwest side of the sound gives some shelter from south and west. An underwater power cable marked by a beacon on the southwest side of the bay runs ENE towards Coll, but there is space to anchor on either side of it in 3 metres, sand. Another cable beacon inshore from the south side of the bay marks a cable which crosses the sound from the southeast point of the bay.

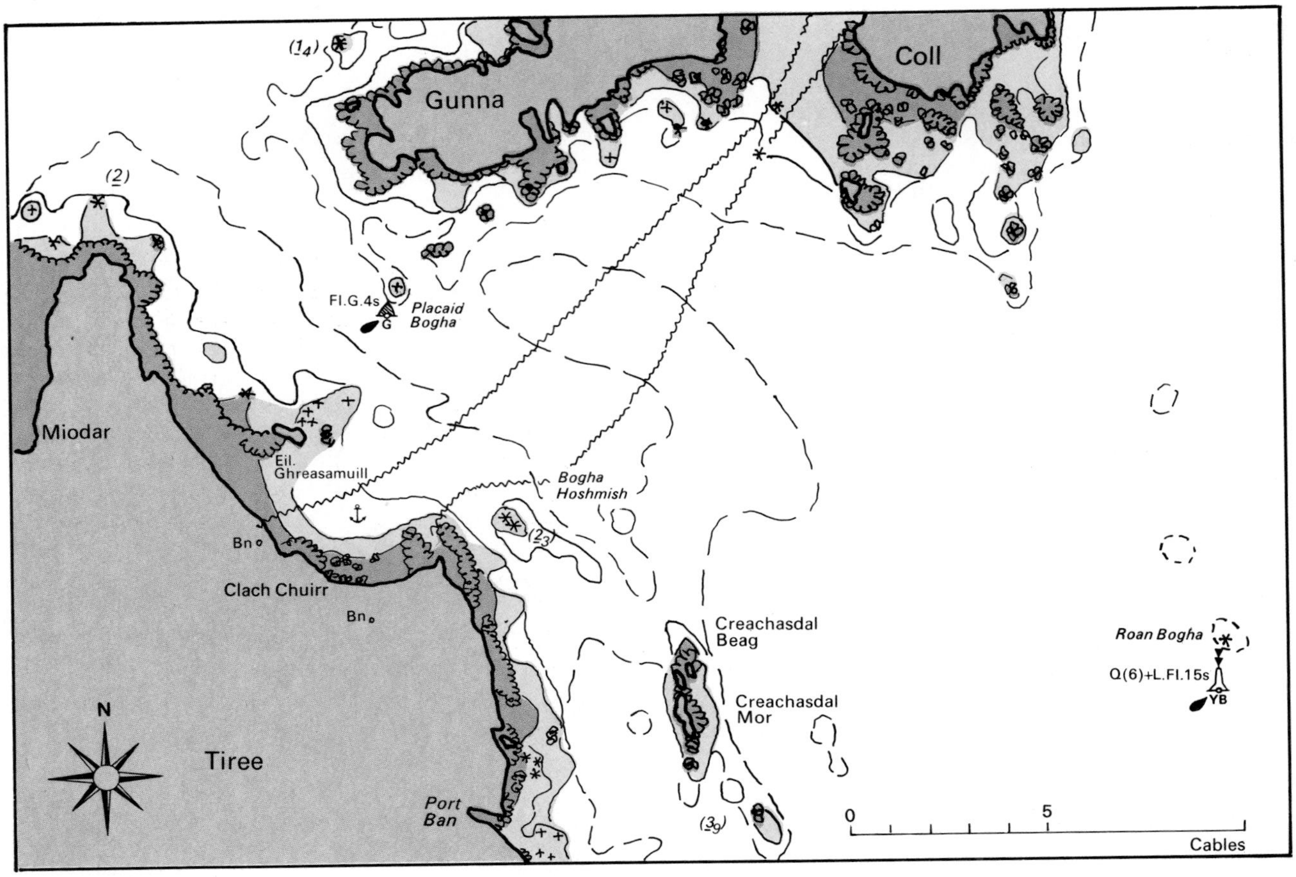

Gunna Sound

Clach Chuirr from the north.

Tiree

Gott Bay

56°31′N 6°47′W

A broad sandy bay towards the northeast end of the southeast side of Tiree exposed over a wide area and only suitable for anchoring overnight in settled westerly or calm weather. It is initially identified by the latticed communications tower ¼ mile south of Scarinish. There are submerged and drying rocks ¼ mile southwest of Soa at the northeast side of the entrance. Anchor northwest of the pier on the southwest side of the bay, as close inshore as depth permits.

Chart

Plan (1:15,000) on chart *2474*.

Tides

The constant is +0007 Oban (−0523 Dover).

Height in metres

MHWS	MHWN	MTL	MLWN	MLWS
4.1	3.0	2.3	1.7	0.6

Scarinish

This is the main village on Tiree but the creek and its drying harbour can only occasionally be used by yachts if there is no sea coming in. Towards HW or at neaps there might be a temporary berth at the old pier, or anchored in the middle of the creek, but avoid obstructing access to the drying harbour.

Cul Bo dries 1.8 metres nearly a cable south of the east point of the entrance. The east end of a white house with a red roof at the head of the creek bearing 330°, over the west end of the jetty at the harbour, leads clear WSW of this rock.

Supplies

Shops, post office, phone box, hotel.

Gott Bay pier from the north.

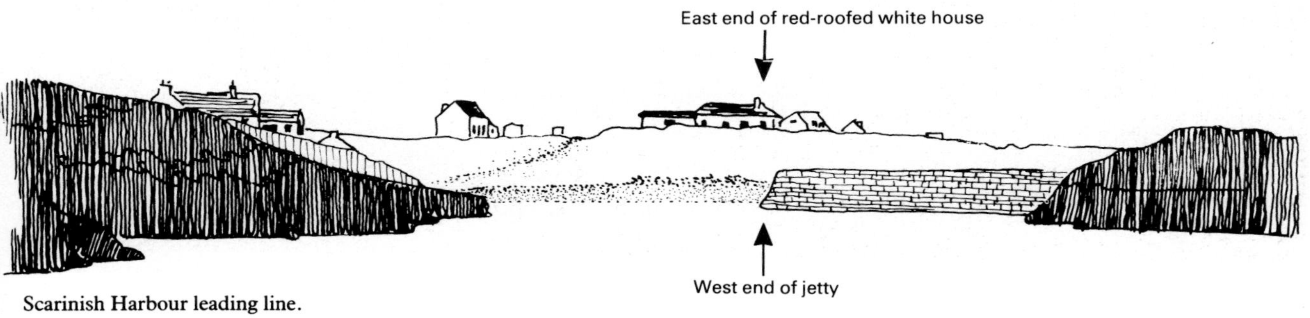

Scarinish Harbour leading line.

Scarinish Harbour from the west. The lighthouse is the small white rectangle to the right of the entrance.

Hynish pier.

Hynish

56°27′N 6°53′W

On the northeast side of the south point of Tiree, east of Ben Hynish, is a masonry pier and dock built as a shore station for Skerryvore lighthouse, and the buildings are now used as a lighthouse museum.

Hynish has been visited by yachts on rare occasions in very settled weather; some shelter from southward is given by the point Am Barradhu and there are rocks drying up to ¼ mile south of this point. The pier dries alongside and the dock fills with sand, but a reservoir built to retain water to flush out the sand has been restored to working order.

Skerryvore lighthouse

56°19′N 7°06′W

On a group of drying rocks ten miles SSW of Tiree, Skerryvore lighthouse is only likely to be of interest to yachts on a direct passage from Islay to the Outer Hebrides. There are drying rocks 3 miles southwest and 1 mile northeast of the lighthouse, and the bottom between the lighthouse and Tiree is very uneven with rocks both submerged and awash.

Strong tides run round Skerryvore with overfalls, and yachts should pass at least 5 miles southwest of the lighthouse in a depth of not less than 15 metres.

VII. Ardnamurchan to Mallaig

It used to be customary for any cruising yacht which had been beyond Ardnamurchan to display a bunch of heather at the end of her bowsprit as a token of having been round this exposed headland. Ardnamurchan is a key point in any cruise on the West Coast, partly because of the exposure, but mainly by contrast with the sheltered waters of the Sound of Mull. The point itself has none of the hazards associated with headlands elsewhere, like Portland Bill or Land's End; there are no offlying rocks or shoals, nor strong tides, but the bottom is uneven and beating against such tide as there is can be very unpleasant. As the prevailing wind is from the southwest these conditions are most likely to arise on your way home, and the possibility should be allowed for in planning a cruise.

Beyond Ardnamurchan the scale of the landscape is, for the most part, more dramatic, and there are fewer of the intimate anchorages associated with the southern part of the West Coast. There are several extremely sheltered places, but some of them will give you anxious moments before you are safely inside; these are mostly on the mainland.

After a yacht has rounded Ardnamurchan the passage NNE towards the Sound of Sleat gradually takes her into more sheltered water, but there are rocks both marked and unmarked up to a couple of miles offshore. Tidal streams run at up to 4 knots in places with relatively shoal banks which can cause an unpleasant sea. Most of the lochs between Ardnamurchan and Mallaig are difficult to find the way into, but some of them are outstandingly attractive and well worth the effort.

The north side of the Ardnamurchan peninsula has no shelter, except in moderate offshore winds in Loch Ceann Traigh (Kentra) at its east end, and there are several dangerous rocks along this shore.

Loch Moidart, between the Ardnamurchan peninsula and the major inlet of the Sound of Arisaig, is very difficult to enter. The Sound of Arisaig itself divides into Loch Ailort and Loch nan Uamh, both of which involve intricate pilotage, but in the mouth of Loch Ailort there is an island behind which it is feasible to run for shelter given reasonable visibility.

North of Rubh' Arisaig on the north side of the Sound of Arisaig is Loch nan Ceall (Arisaig Harbour), entrance to which would be almost impossible without the beacons erected by the owner of the yacht centre there. Note that Arisaig Harbour and the Sound of Arisaig are entirely separate places.

Mallaig, towards the entrance of the Sound of Sleat, is a busy fishing and ferry harbour, fairly easily entered by day or night, good for supplies but otherwise unattractive.

Charts

The only relevant Admiralty chart is *2207* at a scale of 1:50,000, but its northern margin is a mile short of Mallaig. *2208* will probably be needed for the continuation northward in any case. *C65* extends to Mallaig.

Tides

Off Ardnamurchan the flood stream runs northeastwards, and the spring rate is 1½ knots. On the ebb an eddy sets inshore south of the point. Heavy seas build up with onshore winds, especially with wind against tide, and it is best to keep 2 miles off the point.

Between Eigg and the mainland tidal streams run as follows: NNE-going stream begins −0530 Oban (+0130 Dover); SSW-going stream begins +0100 Oban (−0430 Dover).

The maximum rate is generally 1 knot, but near the east shore of Eigg the rate is up to 4 knots; in the bight between the north side of Ardnamurchan and Rubh' Arisaig the rate is negligible.

Dangers and marks

The lighthouse at Ardnamurchan is very conspicuous, but if approaching from the Sound of Mull it is not visible until it bears 001°.

Bo Kora Ben, a submerged rock with a least depth of 1.8 metres, is 6 cables NNE of Ardnamurchan lighthouse and 2 cables offshore.

Bo Faskadale, a group of drying and submerged rocks 6 miles northeast of Ardnamurchan lighthouse, and over 2 miles offshore, is marked on its northwest side by a green conical light buoy which is often difficult to identify if there is any sea running.

The only other artificial mark is the white light beacon on Eilean Chathastail at the southeast point of Eigg.

Off the Arisaig promontory, on the mainland east of Eigg; rocks above water and drying extend over half a mile from the shore, and further north many drying rocks are over a mile from the shore.

Several banks, although over 14 metres below chart datum, cause very heavy seas, particularly with wind against tide. The two most significant are Maxwell Bank, about a mile across, 1 mile southeast of Eigg, and Oberon Bank which is small in extent, 3 miles east of the southeast point of Eigg.

A local magnetic anomaly is charted east of Muck and south of Eigg.

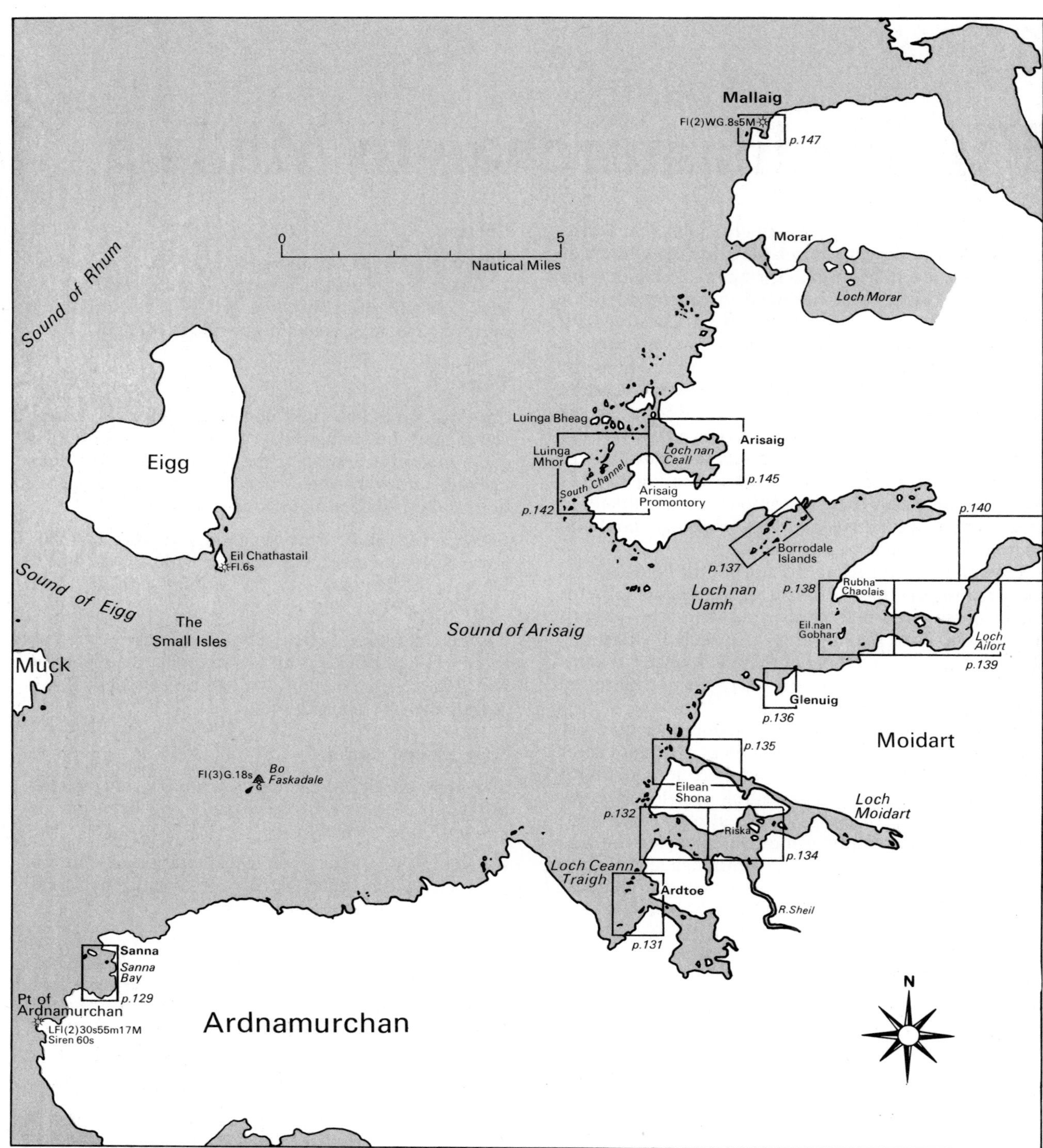

Passage notes

The passage from Ardnamurchan NNE towards the Sound of Sleat is straightforward enough in clear, moderate weather.

From a point 2 miles off Ardnamurchan steer 037° to clear the east side of Eigg. To avoid Maxwell Bank alter course more to the east, over 070°, when Bo Faskadale buoy has been identified, or when the southwest side of Rhum comes open north of Muck 322°.

Going south or southwest, particularly from Arisaig, tend towards Muck and Eigg until Bo Faskadale buoy is identified.

The passage along the north side of Ardnamurchan has two dangers which are fairly easily avoided although there are no specific clearing marks. The first danger is Elizabeth Rock with a least depth of 0.7 metre, 1 mile south of Bo Faskadale buoy and 1¼ miles

Approaching Moidart from the west. Sgeir Charrach is on the left and Rubha Aird Druimnich on the right.

offshore. The second is Sgeir Charrach which dries 2.6 metres (at approximately half-tide), ¼ mile off Rubha Aird Druimnich which is the most northerly point on the peninsula.

Soundings are very irregular here and give no guide to position. Steer to keep Rubha Aird Druimnich bearing 083° until Bo Faskadale buoy is abaft the beam, then steer to keep Rubh' a' Phuill Bhig, the south point of the Sound of Arisaig, bearing not less than 060°.

Lights

At night the following lights (in clear weather, as they are a long way apart) make a direct passage between Ardnamurchan and the Sound of Sleat reasonably straightforward.

Ardnamurchan lighthouse LFl(2)30s55m17M
Eilean Chathastail, southeast of Eigg, Fl.6s24m8M
Bo Faskadale buoy Fl(3)G.18s
Sleat Point light beacon Fl.3s20m9M

The harbour at Mallaig is well lit, but there are no lights at any other anchorage.

Anchorages

Sanna Bay

56°44′.5N 6°11′.5W

A delightful sandy bay 1½ miles northeast of Ardnamurchan lighthouse, sheltered to some extent by a reef projecting from its southwest side, Sanna Bay should probably be treated as only an occasional anchorage. From the south the bay immediately north of the lighthouse might be mistaken for Sanna Bay and from the north, White Sand Bay, which is east of Sanna Point, might be taken for it. Meall Sanna behind Sanna Bay is the highest land on this part of the coast; apart from this the bay can only be identified by reference to the lighthouse and Sanna Point, north of which the coast falls away to the east.

Tides

Constant at Loch Moidart +0022 Oban (−0508 Dover).

Height in metres at Loch Moidart

MHWS	MHWN	MTL	MLWN	MLWS
4.8	3.5	2.6	1.6	0.5

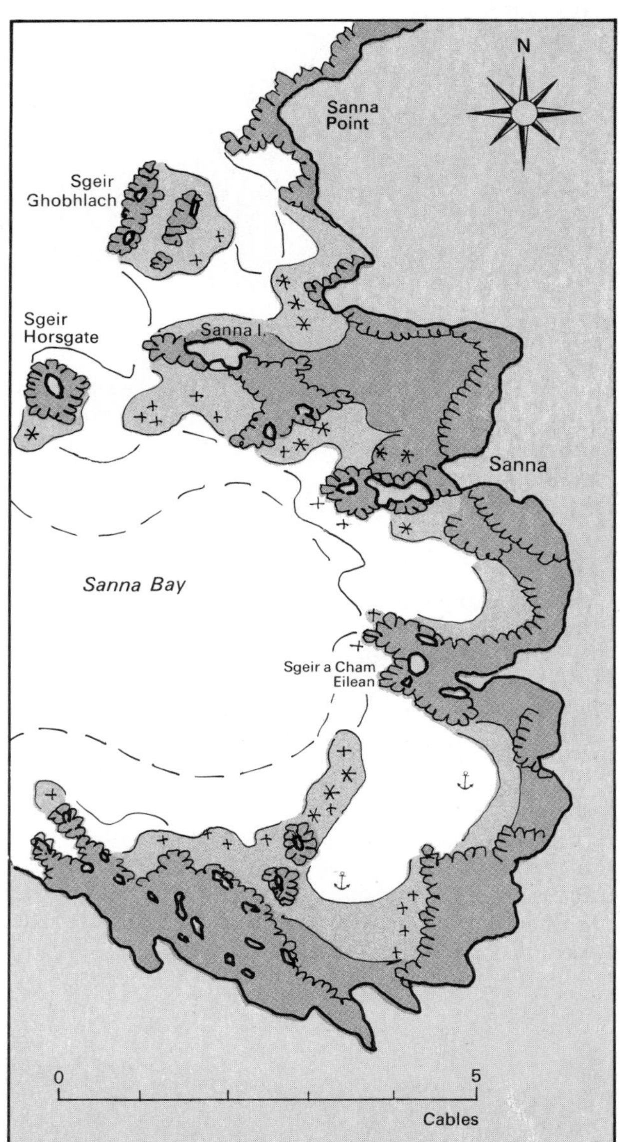

Sanna Bay

Dangers

Bo Kora Ben is a submerged rock, 1.8 metres, halfway between the lighthouse and the south point of Sanna Bay, 2 cables off the north point of the bay to the south of Sanna Bay. To the north of Sanna Bay drying rocks extend ¼ mile WSW of Sanna Point. A reef, parts of

Sanna Bay from the south. Part of the reef is uncovered.

which dry, extends at least two thirds of the way across the mouth of the southeast part of the bay from its southwest side. Even on the quietest day there is often a swell running into the bay, and the marks by which to avoid the reef are not easy to identify.

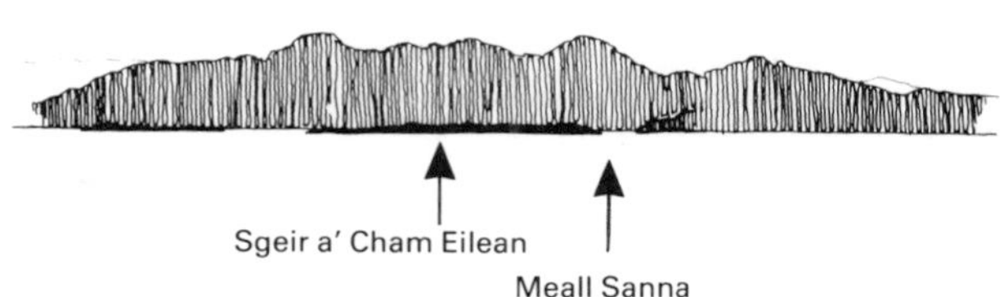

Sanna Bay approach from WNW.

Approach and anchorages

From south keep well over ¼ mile offshore until Sanna Bay is well open, to avoid Bo Kora Ben. Head towards Sgeir Horsgate on the north side of the bay and approach as from the north (see below) to be sure of avoiding the reef.

From north pass well over ¼ mile off Sanna Point, and southwest of Sgeir Horsgate. Head for the more southerly of two white sandy beaches ahead, below the south peak of Meall Sanna, bearing 110° to 120° (depending on how close you are to Sgeir Horsgate). Pass about ½ cable south of the rocky peninsula Sgeir a Cham Eilean and, for a short visit if there is little swell, anchor off the beach ahead.

To reach the inner anchorage, when about two thirds of the way along the detached part of Sgeir a Cham Eilean, turn to head about 204° towards a detached white cottage on the southeast shore with a stone barn to the left of it.

On a clear day the view over the Small Isles from Meall Sanna will make the climb well worthwhile.

No supplies. Phone box at south side of the bay.

The detached cottage on the south shore of Sanna Bay (left of centre).

Loch Ceann Traigh (Kentra)

56°46′N 5°53′W

A bay 1½ miles wide and 1½ miles deep at the east end of the Ardnamurchan peninsula, open to the north but providing occasional anchorage in offshore winds off sandy beaches at the south end.

Approach

From west follow the directions above for the north side of Ardnamurchan and, after clearing Sgeir Charrach, keep at least ½ mile off the east side of Rubha Aird Druimnich to avoid Bo Ruadh.

From north pass west of Sgeir an Eididh (11 metres high) off the east side of the bay and keep it in line with Rubh' Arisaig astern 353° to avoid a submerged rock, 1.3 metres, ¼ mile south of it.

Anchorage

Anchor in about 5 metres, south of Dubh Sgeir (1 metre high) towards the south end of the loch.

Caolas Ardtoe

A narrow inlet on the east side of Loch Ceann Traigh, ½ mile southeast of Sgeir an Eididh, leading to Kentra Bay which completely dries. There appears to be reasonable anchorage in the narrows in 3 metres, sand, but the tide runs quite strongly through, to and from Kentra Bay.

Approach

Approach heading ESE towards Rubha Lingan at the north side of the entrance and keep ¼ cable from that side until the entrance narrows to avoid drying rocks extending from the south side of the entrance.

Anchorage

Anchor a cable WNW of the islet ½ mile ESE of Rubha Lingan, or ½ cable south of it. Shoal-draught boats can take the ground on sand off the stone slip ¼ mile further southeast on the north side of the inlet (any yacht could dry out alongside for repairs if necessary).

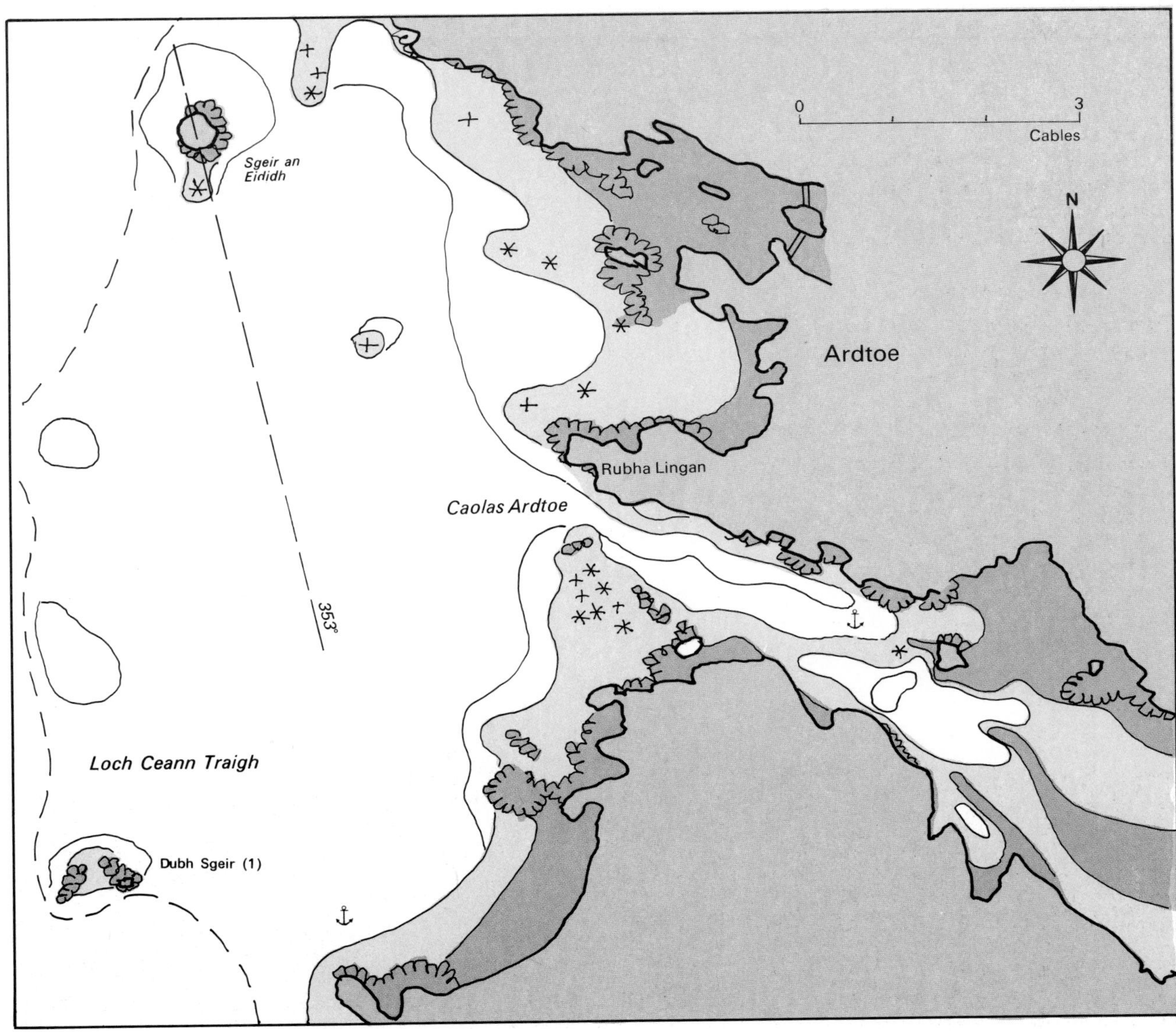

Caolas Ardtoe

Loch Moidart

56°47′N 5°52′W

One of the most picturesque of all West Coast lochs with sandy beaches between rocky headlands and, further in, a ruined castle on a tidal islet with thickly wooded shores on either side. It is however one of the most difficult of all lochs to enter with a labyrinth of islets and rocks, many of them submerged or drying, and the courses to be taken on transits of islets have to be quickly identified in turn.

A steep sea builds up in the entrance with the ebb running against a westerly wind, which is particularly likely to trouble a small yacht when leaving the loch.

The entrance is 3 miles SSW of the south point of the Sound of Arisaig and 2½ miles east of Rubha Aird Druimnich. Eilean Shona on the north side of the entrance is 263 metres high and merges with the hills behind it; it is easy to mistake either the north Channel or Caolas Ardtoe for the main entrance to Loch Moidart.

Charts

There is no current detailed chart of Loch Moidart although one has been planned for some years. Photocopies of a very old chart, *531*, will provide more detail than anything currently published.

Tides

Constant +0022 Oban (−0508 Dover).

Height in metres

MHWS	MHWN	MTL	MLWN	MLWS
4.8	3.5	2.6	1.6	0.5

Approach

From the west as for north side of Ardnamurchan (page 128 above); Rubha Aird Druimnich bearing 263° astern will lead direct to the entrance.

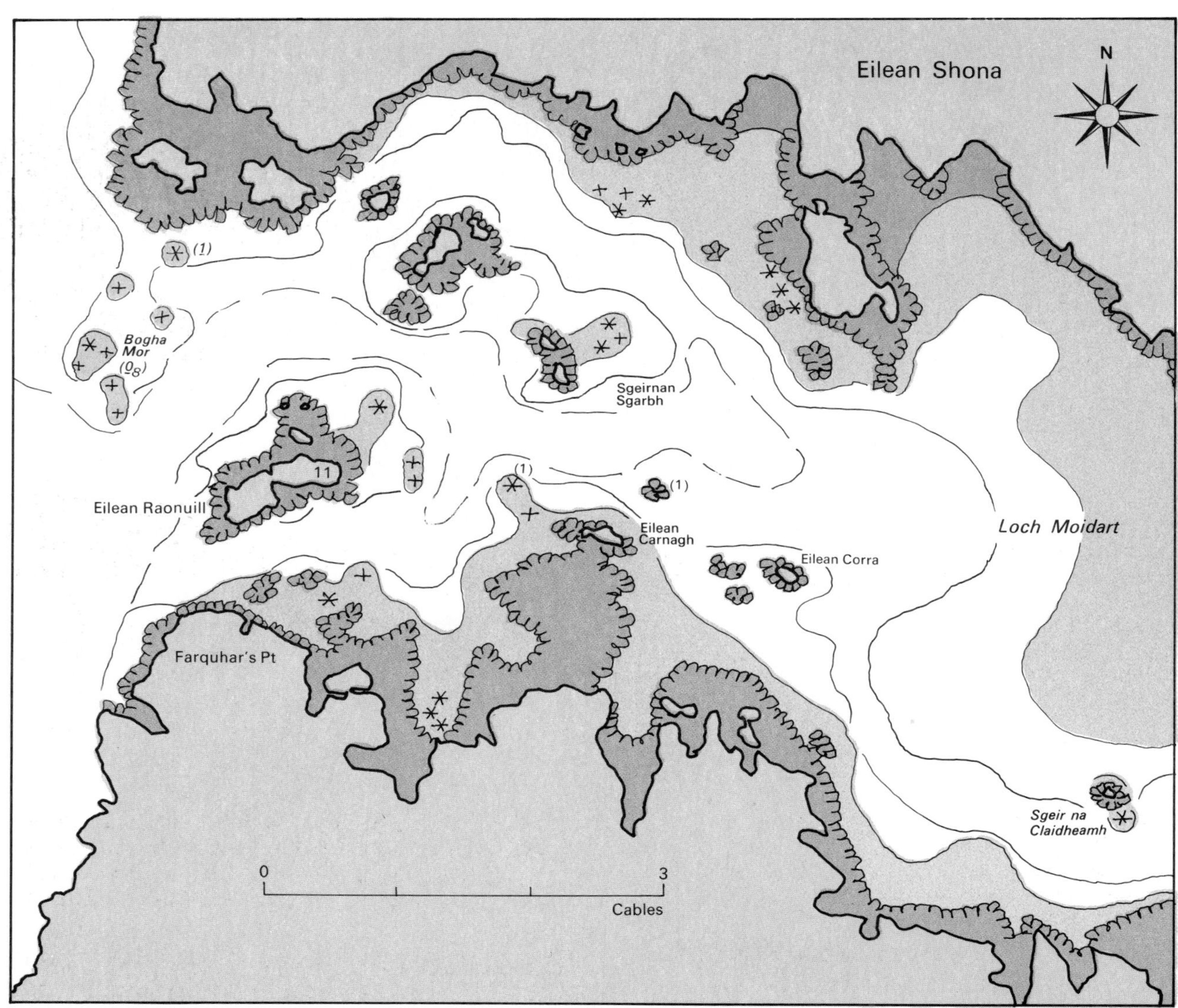

Loch Moidart entrance

From the north keep clear west of Howorth Rock which has a least depth of 1.9 metres, ¾ mile off the middle of Shona, unless you are satisfied that there is no swell and there is sufficient height of tide for your draught. The 20-metre contour is a safe guide here.

Eilean Raonuill in the middle of the entrance, 11 metres high with a thin perch on its summit, must be positively identified. Castle Tioram, 2 miles further east, shut in behind the island 094° leads south of rocks on the north side of the passage northwest of Raonuill. Eilean Raonuill can be passed on either side but the north side is the more straightforward.

To pass north of Eilean Raonuill steer northeast to pass ¼ cable north of rocks above water on a drying reef on the north side of Eilean Raonuill. When the east end of Eilean Raonuill is abeam head for Sgeir nan Sgarbh, a prominent rock above water 1¾ cables ENE of Eilean Raonuill, in line with the south point of Shona 097°, then pass ¼ cable south of Sgeir nan Sgarbh.

Identify Eilean Corra and Sgeir na Claidheamh ('clay') to the southeast and when Sgeir na Claidheamh is open east of Eilean Corra, turn to pass east of Eilean Corra and ½ cable south of Sgeir na Claidheamh to avoid a detached drying rock.

The passage south of Eilean Raonuill is narrower than that to the north with more dangers. Approach the centre of the passage heading 073° to avoid a drying reef off the southwest point of the island and drying rocks east of Farquhar's Point. Identify Eilean Carnagh and Eilean Corra ESE and when they are in line steer for the south point of Sgeir nan Sgarbh and then proceed as in the last paragraph above.

Several temporary anchorages can be found here but more satisfactory ones are further in.

To continue further up the loch approach to within about a cable of Shona. Close west of Riska a shallow bar of sand crosses the loch, and underwater cables cross the loch both east and west of Riska; their landing places are unmarked.

Loch Moidart entrance – looking ESE from the passage north of Eilean Raonuill. Castle Tioram shows over the point of Shona on the left; the drying rock northeast of Eilean Raonuill is right of centre, with Eilean Corra beyond and to the right of it.

Loch Moidart entrance, from close southeast of Sgeir nan Sgarbh. Eilean Corra is left of centre, with Sgeir na Claidheamh beyond and to the left of it.

Anchorages

The most straightforward is ½ cable east of the jetty on Shona but this is quite exposed in southerly winds, particularly at HW.

East of Riska, a cable northeast of a rock above water off the south point of the loch there.

South of Riska, off the east end of the castle island. If approaching from the west note that the sand bar is shallower southwest of Riska than northwest, and there are drying rocks off the southwest side of Riska.

In all cases take great care to avoid the lines of cables. Each of these anchorages is subject to fairly strong tides.

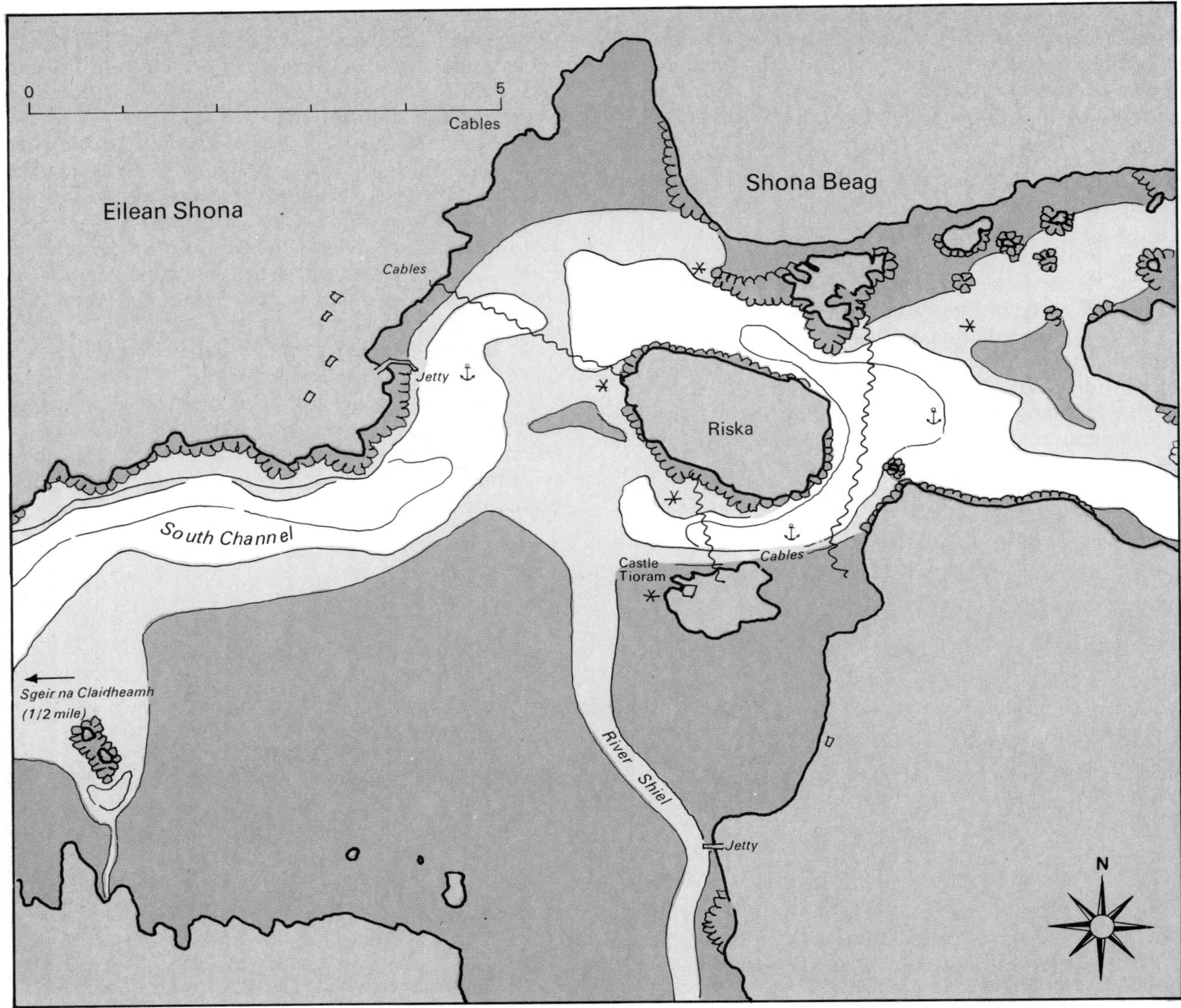

Loch Moidart

Further east most of the loch dries, with a narrow channel following the south shore. It can be explored with a dinghy or shoal-draught boat with the aid of the old chart *531*.

Supplies

The nearest stores are at Acharacle, over two miles by the road south of the castle. Phone box ½ mile along the same road.

Castle Tioram is well worth visiting; note that the spit joining the island to the mainland covers at HW.

Loch Moidart – north channel

56°48′N 5°52′W

The main difficulty here is to identify correctly the rocks at the entrance. Pass between the two Sgeir dhu's (their suffixes mean 'east' and 'west' although they are north and south of each other) heading for an islet close to the south shore. Thereafter keep in the middle of the channel, but closer to the south side as the bar is approached. The bar has a depth of 1.8 metres and the tide runs strongly over it. Anchor as far up the inner basin as depth allows. A drying bank prevents access to the main part of Loch Moidart except for dinghies and very shallow-draught boats at HW.

If there is any sea running, entering – and particularly leaving – this anchorage could be a matter of some anxiety.

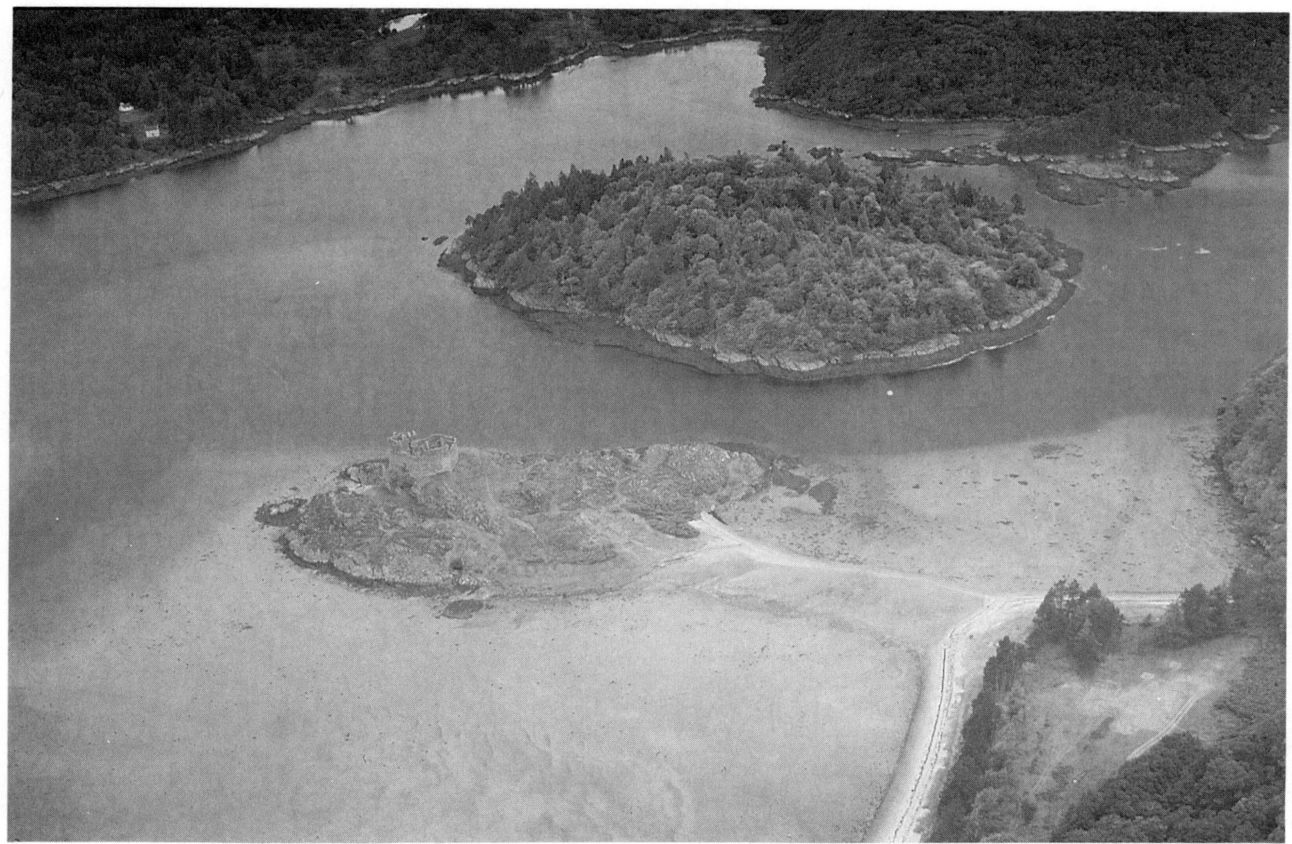

Loch Moidart – Riska and Castle Tioram from the south.

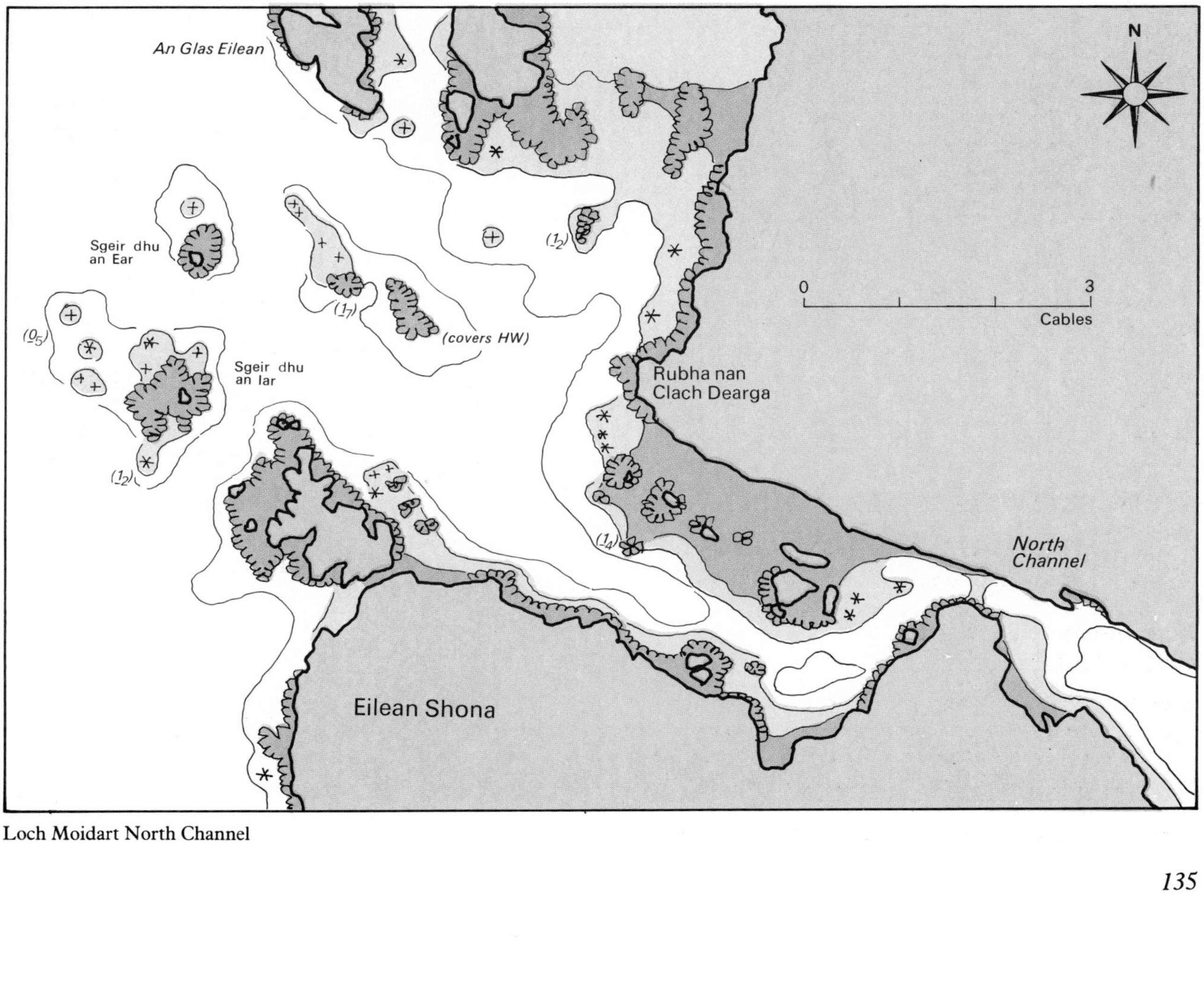

An Glas Eilean
Sgeir dhu an Ear
Sgeir dhu an Iar
(covers HW)
Rubha nan Clach Dearga
North Channel
Eilean Shona
N
0 3 Cables

Loch Moidart North Channel

Sound of Arisaig

56°51′N 5°50′W

This is the main inlet on this part of the coast with an entrance two miles wide between Rubh' a' Phuill Bhig on its south side and a group of islets near the Arisaig Promontory on the north side. The south shore is clean outwith a cable from the shore, but there are many rocks above and below water up to a mile off the north side.

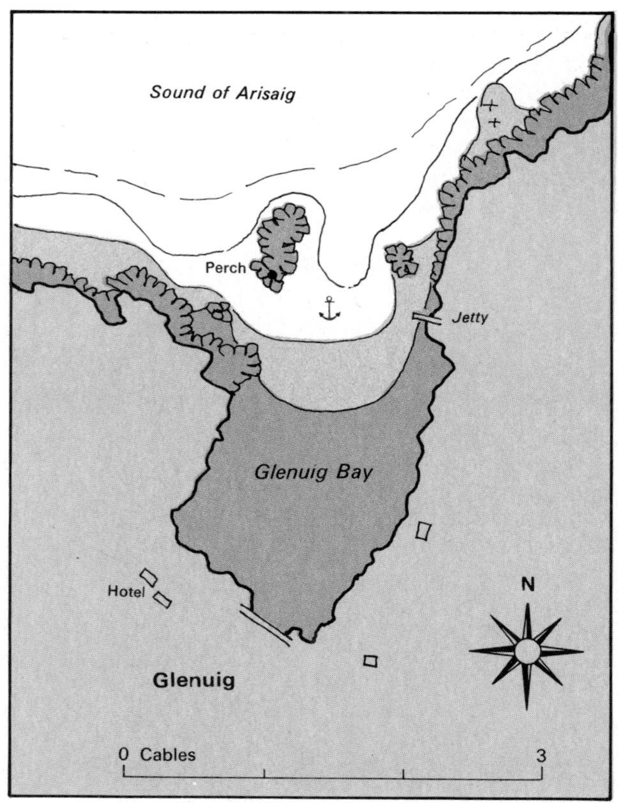

Glenuig Bay

Tides

Constant +0022 Oban (−0508 Dover).

Height in metres

MHWS	MHWN	MTL	MLWN	MLWS
4.8	3.5	2.6	1.6	0.5

Approach

Eilean an t-Snidhe, 10 metres high, 1 mile south of the Arisaig Promontory must be identified. Pass at least half a mile south of it to avoid various submerged rocks. If you want to pass north of this group keep the north end of Eigg bearing 300° just open of Eilean a' Ghaill, which lies off the Arisaig Promontory, north of Eilean an t-Snidhe.

Gulnare Rock, at a depth of 2.7 metres, is a mile east of Eilean an t-Snidhe, and Astly Rock, least depth 0.9 metres, is 1½ cables south of the Borrodale Islands.

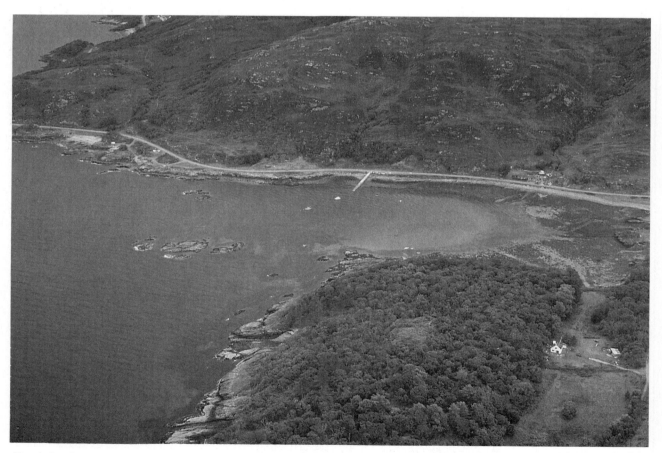

Glenuig Bay from northwest.

Both of these are avoided by keeping the north end of Muck open south of Eilean an t-Snidhe 265°.

Priest Rock off the mouth of Loch Ailort is cleared on its west side by keeping the summit of Sidhean Mor, the highest hill on the north side of the sound, open west of the end of Ardnish Peninsula on the north side of Loch Ailort 031°.

Anchorages in the outer part of the sound

Glenuig Bay (56°50′N 5°49′W), 1¼ miles east of Rubh' a' Phuill Bhig, provides some shelter but the rocks in the mouth of the bay all cover and do not provide much protection from any sea from west or north-west.

A perch near the south end of the west rock marks the north side of a passage between the rock and the mainland.

There are several moorings and the jetty is used by a ferry to Eigg; anchor between the jetty and the west rock, clear of the approach to the jetty.

Hotel, shop, *Calor Gas* 1 mile up the glen. Phone box.

On the north side of the sound several inlets provide occasional anchorages, in particular Port nam Murrach, Port a' Bhathaich, and Port Doire na Drise. The approach to each of them is straightforward with chart *2207*.

Borrodale Islands

56°53′N 5°49′W

A string of islands on the north side of the sound providing some, although not complete, shelter. The best anchorage is at Druimindarroch at the north end of the group.

There is (or should be) a perch on a drying rock 1 cable west of the south end of Eilean nan Cabar; if it is not seen keep closer to the islet west of Sgeir Ghlas and after passing the islet steer north for a cable to clear the rock.

To enter by the north of Eilean nan Cabar keep closer to the mainland than to the island to avoid Rafter's Reef which dries about halfway across this passage from the island (Cabar is translated as 'rafter').

Anchorage

Anchor in the bay north of Eilean nan Cabar clear of moorings and clear of a submerged rock off the east point of the bay.

Loch nan Uamh

56°53′N 5°46′W

At the head of the loch (56°53′.5N 5°44′W) there is a deep anchorage on the east side of Eilean Gobhlach or, in southerly winds, on the north side of Ard nan Buth.

The pool east of Eilean a' Phuill may be entered by keeping towards the east side to avoid a drying rock in the middle of the entrance.

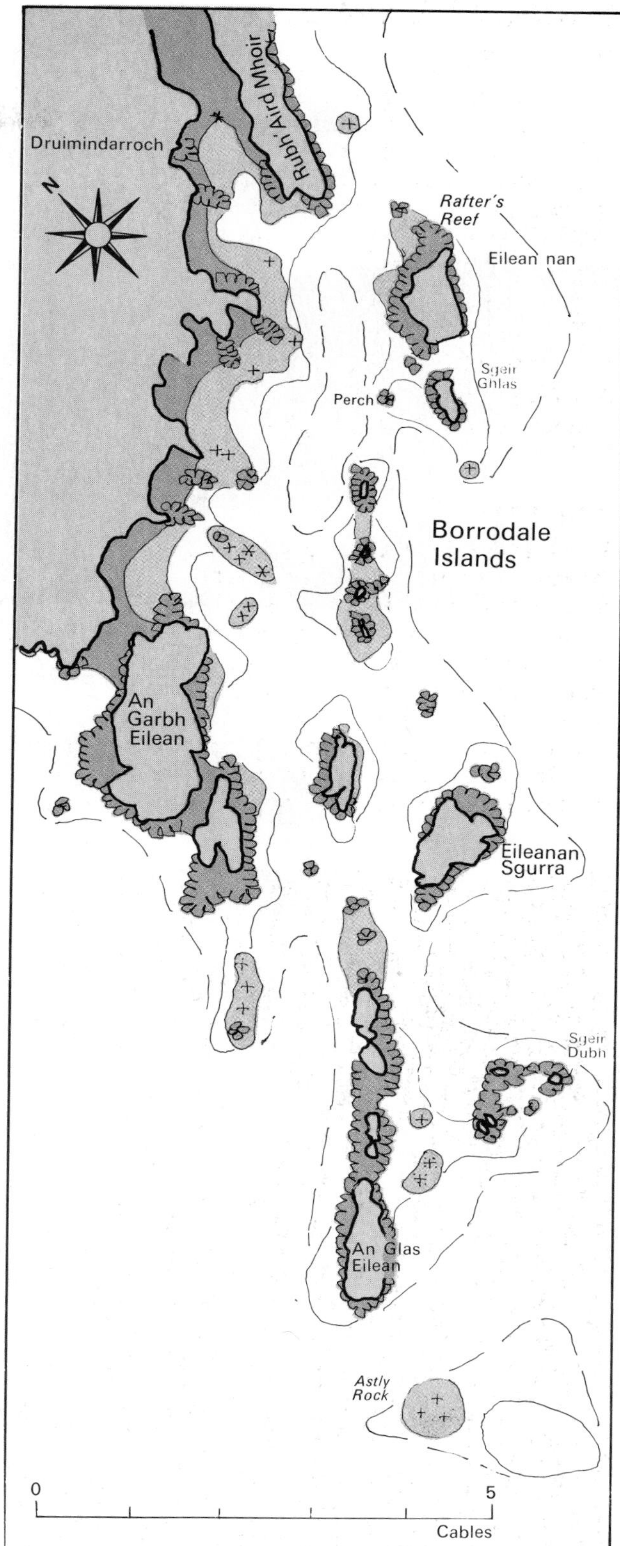

Borrodale Islands

Loch nan Uamh – Eilean a' Phuill anchorage from the east. Eilean Gobhlach is beyond the drying rock in the middle of the entrance to the pool.

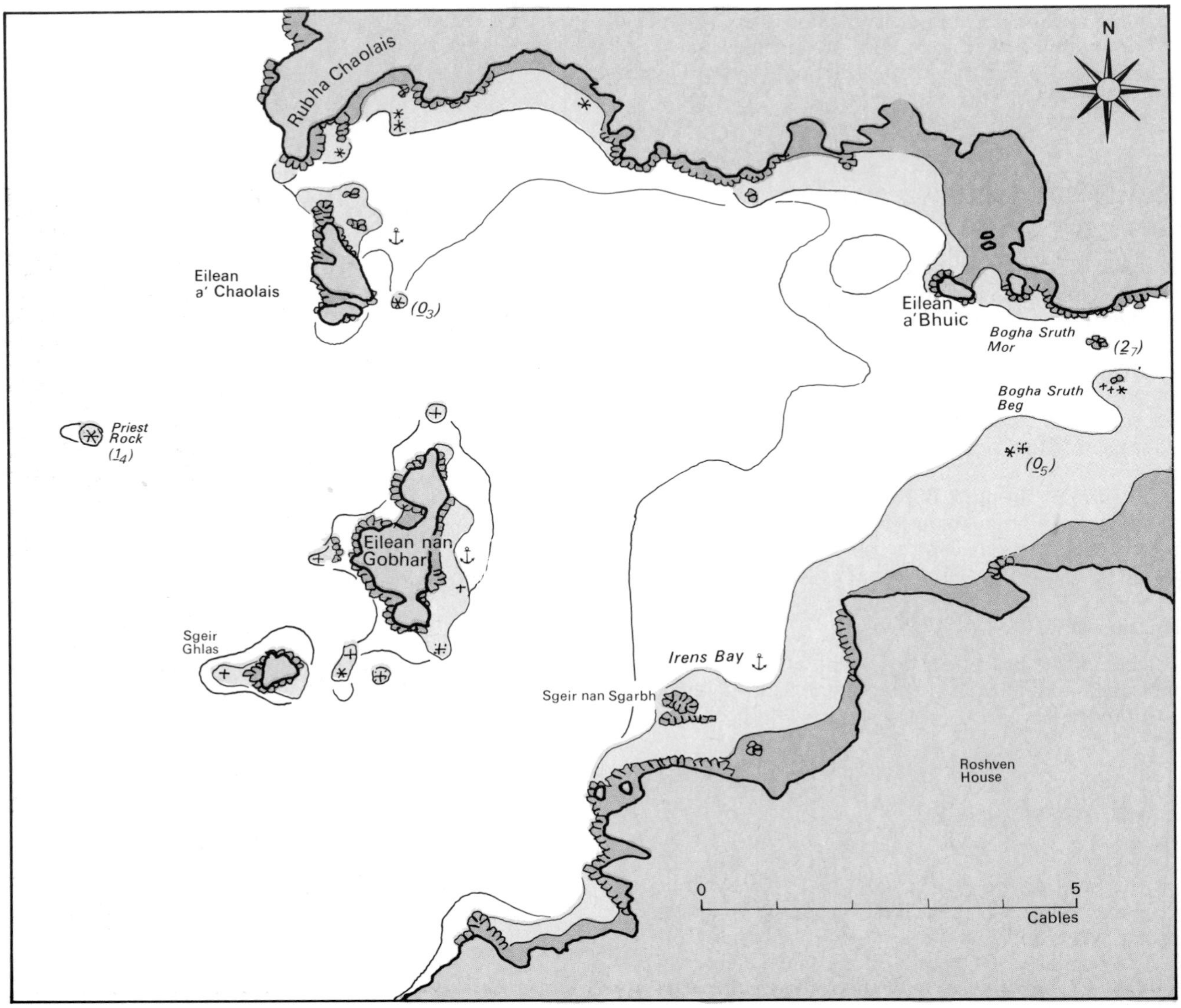

N
Rubha Chaolais
Eilean a' Chaolais
(0_3)
Eilean a'Bhuic
Bogha Sruth Mor
(2_7)
Bogha Sruth Beg
(0_5)
Priest Rock
(1_4)
Eilean nan Gobhar
Sgeir Ghlas
Irens Bay
Sgeir nan Sgarbh
Roshven House
0 5
Cables

Loch Ailort entrance

Loch Ailort

56°51′N 5°46′W

The outer part of the loch is fairly open, but Eilean nan Gobhar (Goat Island) and Eilean a' Chaolais at the mouth of the loch provide some shelter and the outer anchorages are quite easy to approach. There are quite heavy overfalls around the islands when the ebb tide runs against a strong westerly wind. Winds between south and east produce heavy squalls from the mountains.

Navigation of the middle part of Loch Ailort is as difficult as any in this chapter, with the usual crop of drying rocks, and islets difficult to identify. Beyond the narrows, 2½ miles from the entrance, mountains close in on either side.

Dangers and approach

Priest Rock, 4 cables WNW of Goat Island, dries 1.4 metres and there is no good clearing mark for it. In the passage north of Goat Island there is a submerged rock ½ cable north of the island.

The most straightforward entrance is by the south of Goat Island. Keep over a cable south of the island to avoid drying rocks south and southeast of it.

The narrow passage north of Eilean a' Chaolais may be used in quiet weather, but note drying rocks up to a cable northeast of the island.

Anchorages

Goat Island (Eilean nan Gobhar) provides the best shelter in westerly winds off a stony beach on its east side. This is a traditionally regarded as the most suitable anchorage to run for in heavy weather, although it would be unlikely to be comfortable. The wind funnels through a gap in the middle of the island. There is a submerged rock ½ cable off the south end of the beach.

Eilean a' Chaolais, close east of the island. A drying rock southeast of the island is cleared by keeping Sgeir Ghlas touching the west side of Goat Island. In quiet weather anchor anywhere in the bight northeast of the island, but note drying rocks up to a cable northeast of the island.

Irens Bay off Roshven House in light offshore winds; anchor well offshore between Sgeir na Sgairbh and the northeast point of the bay, as it is very shoal.

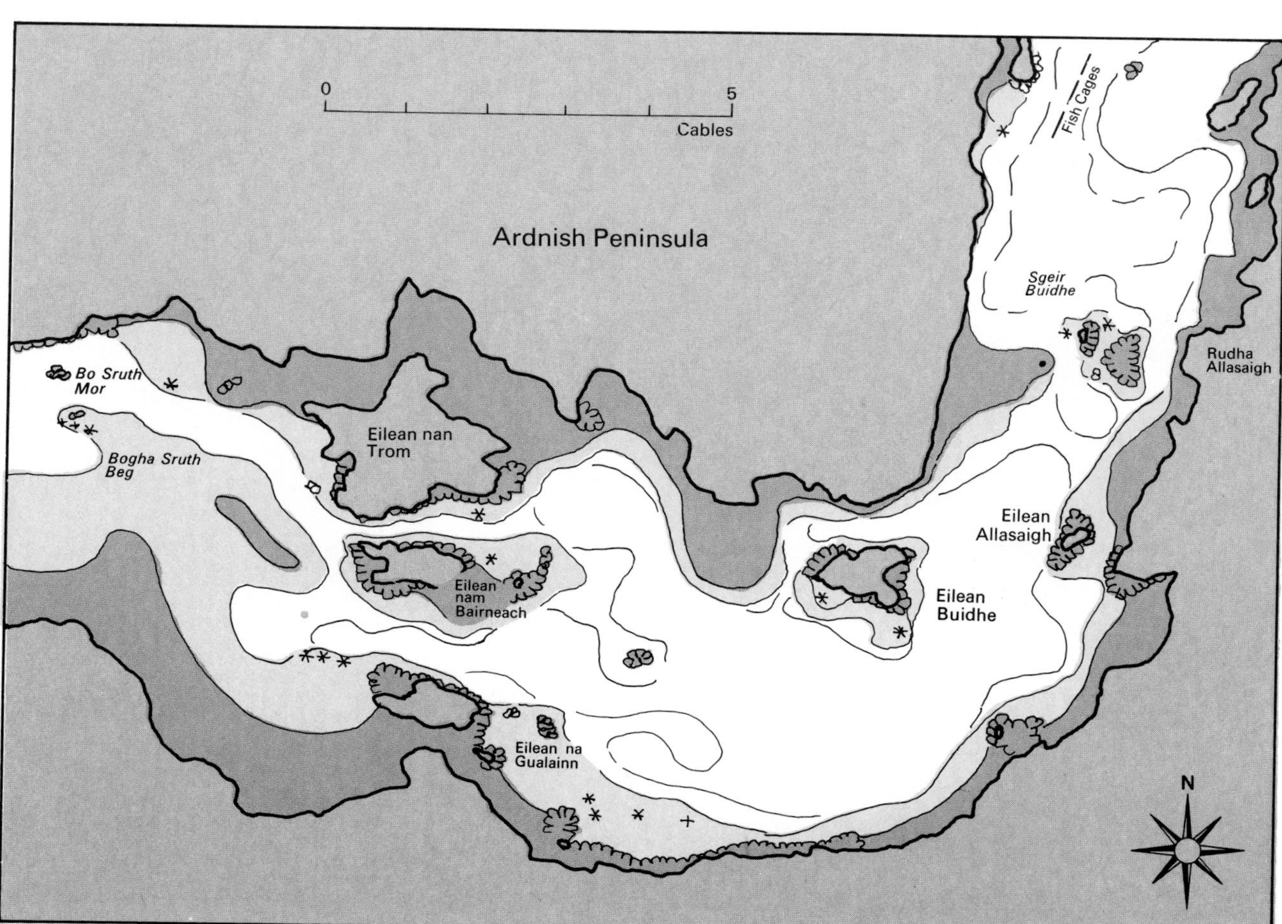

Loch Ailort – middle part

Loch Ailort – middle part

56°51′N 5°44′W

The pilotage here is only less alarming than Loch Moidart or Loch nan Ceall because the islands in the mouth of the loch provide some shelter. About ¾ mile east of Goat Island the loch narrows to one third of a mile wide. The south side of the channel is shoal and drying, with rocks drying 0.5 metre about mid-channel. Eilean a' Bhuic is west of the north point of the entrance to this channel.

Near the north shore Bogha Sruth Mor and Bogha Sruth Beg cover about half-tide. Bo Sruth Mor to the north is slightly higher than Bo Sruth Beg.

In the next mile the channel twists between shoals and drying rocks.

Approach before half-flood so that the Bogha Sruths are visible, and pass between them. If both are covered there is enough depth to pass north of Bogha Sruth Mor within ¼ cable of the shore.

After passing these rocks head for the southern half of Eilean nan Trom; then bring the east end of Eilean na Gualainn in line with the west end of Eilean nam Bairneach 140°, to pass between a drying rock west of Eilean nan Trom and a drying bank a cable further west.

The channel between Eilean nan Trom and Eilean nam Bairneach may be taken; a line to clear the drying reef a cable east of Eilean nam Bairneach is the north end of Goat Island touching the south point of Eilean nan Trom 272°.

Alternatively pass west of Eilean nam Bairneach, keeping ½ cable off that island, and follow round to pass midway between Eilean nam Bairneach and Eilean na Gualainn. After the east end of Eilean na Gualainn is passed, its north point in line with the most northerly point of the south shore 278° leads south of Bogha Druim a' Loch.

There are no regular anchorages here – nor for that matter at the head of the loch – but if your taste for rock-dodging hasn't been exhausted, the following will guide you through the upper part of the loch.

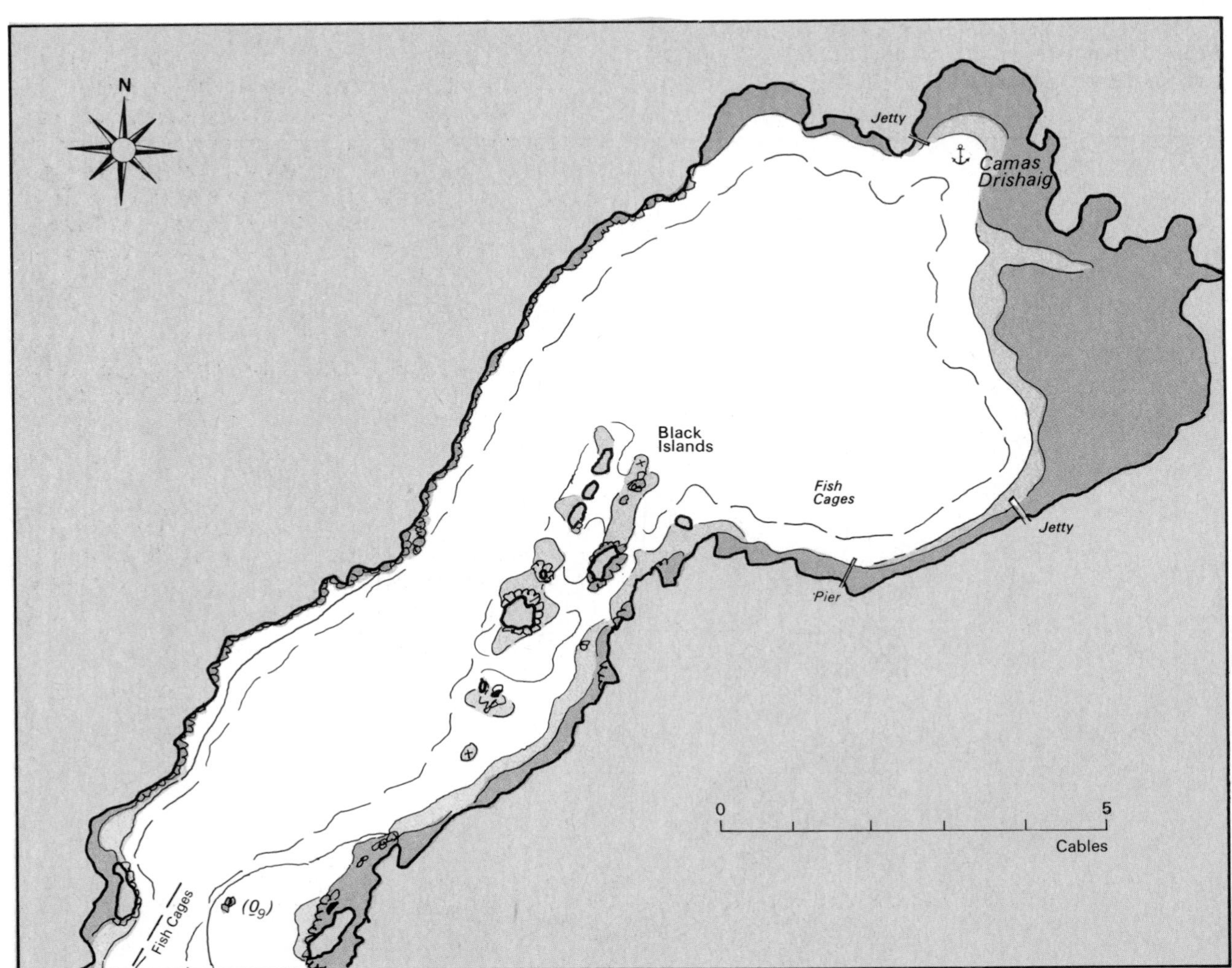

Head of Loch Ailort

Loch Ailort; the narrows from northeast.

Head of Loch Ailort

56°52′N 5°41′W

Keep at least a cable south of Eilean Buidhe to avoid a drying rock, pass about ½ cable northwest of Eilean Allasaigh and steer towards Rudha Allasaigh, 3 cables further NNE. Pass about ¼ cable off the point of Rudha Allasaigh to avoid a large area of rocks which cover at HW, ½ cable from the shore.

The spit on the west side, west of these rocks, has a boulder at its outer end which covers above half-tide. If the boulder is visible, an alternative course is to pass about 30 metres east of it, heading NNW.

About 4 cables further north a rock in the middle of the loch dries about 1 metre; it is midway between two tidal islets, one on either shore. A line of fish cages is moored off the west shore here.

Half a mile further northeast the Black Islands (Eilean Dubh) are on the southeast side of the loch. A survey of 1860 shows moderate depths among them, with a bottom of sand as well as some rock. Note the submerged rock 1 cable south of the most southerly rock above water, and a drying rock ¼ cable off the east shore.

The head of the loch is a deep basin about ¾ mile across with an extensive fish-farming industry. The east side of the basin dries for about 3 cables and the most suitable anchorage is at the mouth of Camas Drishaig on the northeast side of the basin.

Loch nan Ceall (Arisaig Harbour)

56°54′.5N 5°55′W

One of the most intimidating entrances of any anchorage on the West Coast. As the Admiralty *West Coast of Scotland Pilot* put it in 1934: 'This tortuous channel, being full of rocks, is dangerous to enter, and as the islets in the vicinity are low and inconspicuous they are of no assistance in fixing the position of a vessel.' The beacons, which have been restored by Murdo Grant, make the entrance channel possible for a stranger – once he has found the entrance.

Charts

A detailed chart is believed to be being prepared; until it appears a photocopy of a very obsolete chart, *2817*, provides the greatest detail.

Tides

Tidal streams run strongly in the entrance channel, particularly for 1½ hours either side of LW when the banks on either side of the channel are uncovered and the flow is concentrated within it.

Constant +0030 Oban (−0500 Dover).

Height in metres

MHWS	MHWN	MTL	MLWN	MLWS
5.0	3.8	2.9	2.1	0.7

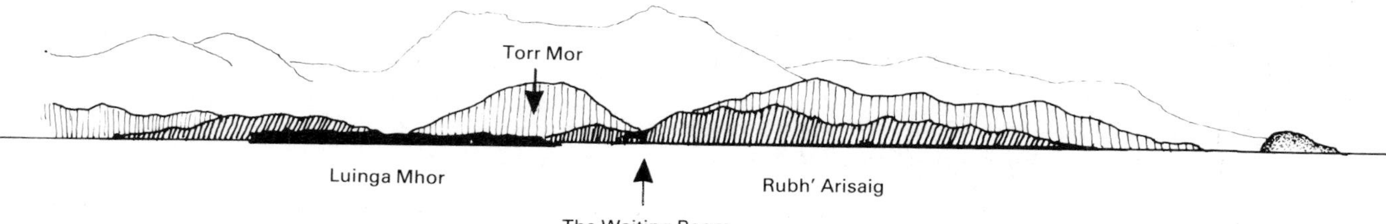

Loch nan Ceall approach from west.

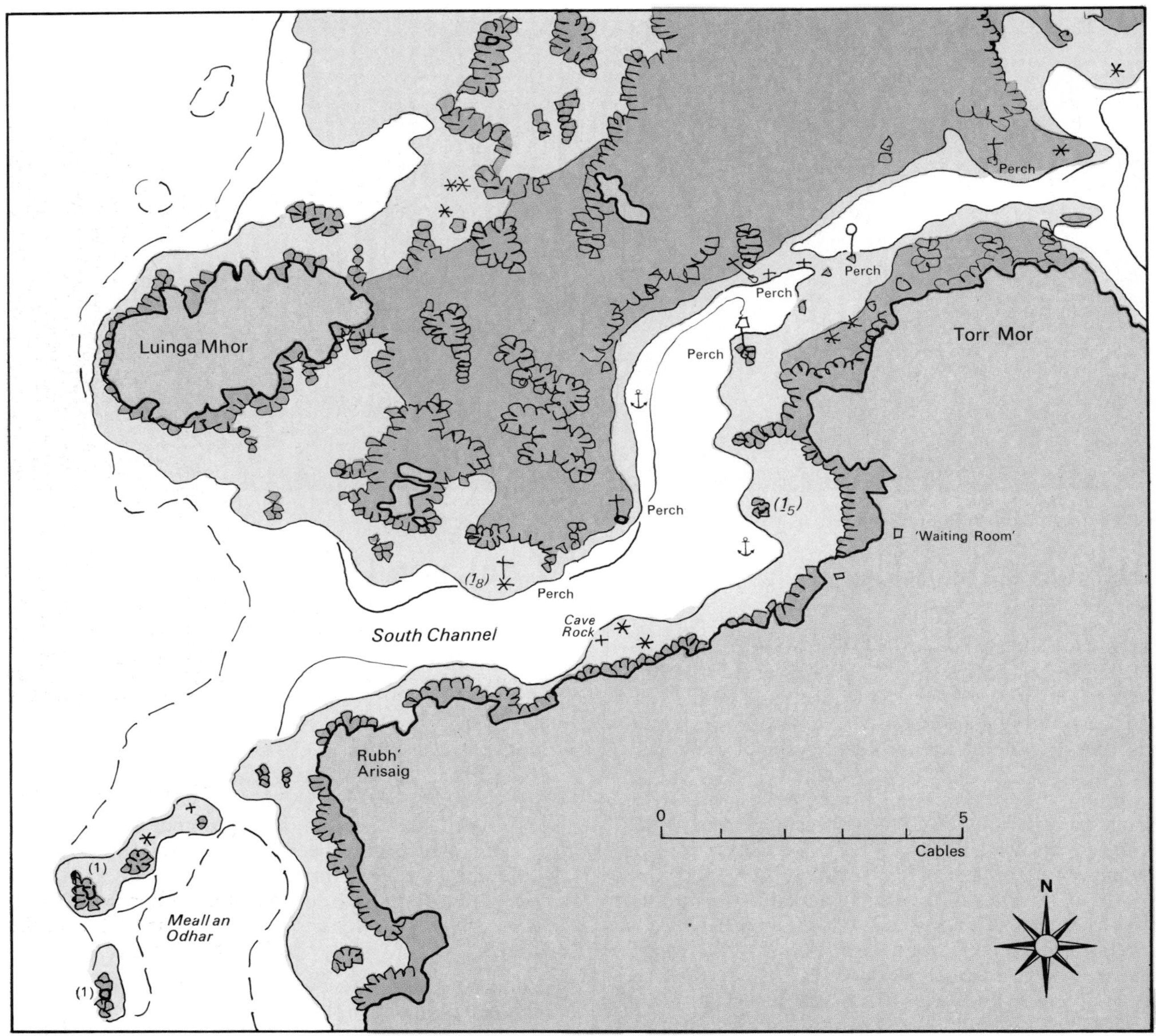

Loch nan Ceall (Arisaig) entrance

Identification

The north Point of Muck (not Eilean nan Each, northwest of Muck) in line with the southeast point of Eilean Chathastail, southeast of Eigg, 256° leads to the north side of entrance. In poor visibility note that Luinga Mhor is low and flat. Rubh' Arisaig stands up rather more and has a patch of white paint on its end, which usually shows up well.

Dangers and marks in the approach

Meallan Odhar are a group of rocks up to ½ mile WSW of Rubh' Arisaig. The outermost rocks are 1 metre high.

On the north side of the entrance rocks drying up to 3.7 metres extend over a cable south of the line between Luinga Mhor and the islet 3 cables ESE of it.

2 cables southeast of the islet is the first perch with an orange cross at the top, marking a rock drying 1.8 metres which extends at least 10 metres south of the perch.

A second perch with a crossbar is 2 cables ENE of the first. The rock which it marks covers at HW springs and extends about 20 metres south of the perch. This perch is smaller than the first, and if you are leaving at HW, take care not to miss it and make for the outer perch.

Cave Rock nearly 2 cables south of the second perch and about a cable off the south shore, dries at LW.

The Waiting Room (so called because it used to provide shelter for passengers waiting for steamers) is an inconspicuous grey cottage ½ mile east of the second perch.

Approach

From south keep at least a cable off Meallan Odhar and off the north side of Rubh' Arisaig, and pass a cable south of the two perches described above.

Loch nan Ceall and Rubh' Arisaig from southwest.

A bearing of 080° on the Waiting Room under a prominent dip in the hills immediately behind it leads clear between the dangers in the entrance.

From north it is essential to identify Luinga Mhor and pass southwest of it; yachts have in the past mistaken the passage and attempted to enter north of the island – with disastrous results. Steer southeast towards the north side of Rubh' Arisaig until the perches and the Waiting Room are identified, and pass a cable south of the perches.

Anchorages

Temporary anchorage can be found either ¼ mile west of the Waiting Room or in better shelter NNE of the second perch on the west side of the channel.

Loch nan Ceall – the first perch on the left. The Waiting Room is just right of the gap to the right of Torr Mor, ahead.

The second perch, towards HW.

The entrance channel

For most of the next mile the channel is from ½ to 1 cable wide between drying rocks and sandbanks, of which the most prominent are marked by four more perches, two to be left on either hand. These may be difficult to pick out at HW when little of them is showing, or at LW when they are hidden among the labyrinth of rocks. Each perch seems to appear in a surprising place in relation to the previous one. Make quite sure that each perch is the one you think it is; both

Loch nan Ceall – the second perch, with the third beyond the tip of the reef.

Loch nan Ceall – the third perch at HW.

those on the starboard hand have special topmarks. Not one of the perches is on the extreme end of the rock which it marks.

The third perch, 3½ cables NNE of the second, with a truncated cone topmark and a white reflective sign below it, is left to starboard.

The fourth perch with a crossbar, a cable NNE of the third, is left to port.

The fifth perch with a diamond topmark above an open circle, 2 cables east of the fourth, is left to starboard. Between these two perches the bottom is shallow and rocky with depths of less than 1.5 metres, and the passage should be avoided by boats of deeper draught near LW springs.

The sixth perch, with a crossbar, ¼ mile ENE of the fifth, is left to port. For a further two cables there are drying sandbanks on either side, with a drying rock on the north bank; this north bank extends south of a direct line to the next perch. Keep a careful check astern at this point to make sure you are not being set off course – especially if you are so rash as to try to enter against the ebb.

Arisaig Harbour

56°54.5N 5°51′W

Arisaig village is at the east side of a basin, about 1½ miles from the sixth perch. South of the village is a group of low cottages, and south of them again several detached houses among trees. From a point ½ cable south of the sixth perch steer for the cottages and keep them bearing 090°.

Another perch is ½ mile east of the sixth, on a rock drying 2.4 metres, 1½ cables off the north shore of the basin. Pass ½ cable south of this perch to avoid a rock which dries 0.6 metres, 1 cable south of it, and continue to head for the cottages.

Anchor clear of moorings off the pier in the northeast corner of the basin, and clear of the approach to the pier which is used regularly by a passenger boat.

The inlet at the pier dries at LW springs; yachts may go alongside on a rising tide if access is not needed for the *Etive Shearwater*. Two white posts at the head of the inlet kept in line lead between reefs at the entrance. Trailed boats may be launched at the head of the inlet (ask first).

Camas an t-Salainn in the southeast corner of the basin has several moorings in it but it may be possible to find space in which to anchor. Approach from north to avoid rocks shown on the plan.

From the entrance channel, looking east. The final perch is on the rock on the left with the village beyond the reef behind it, and the group of cottages on the right.

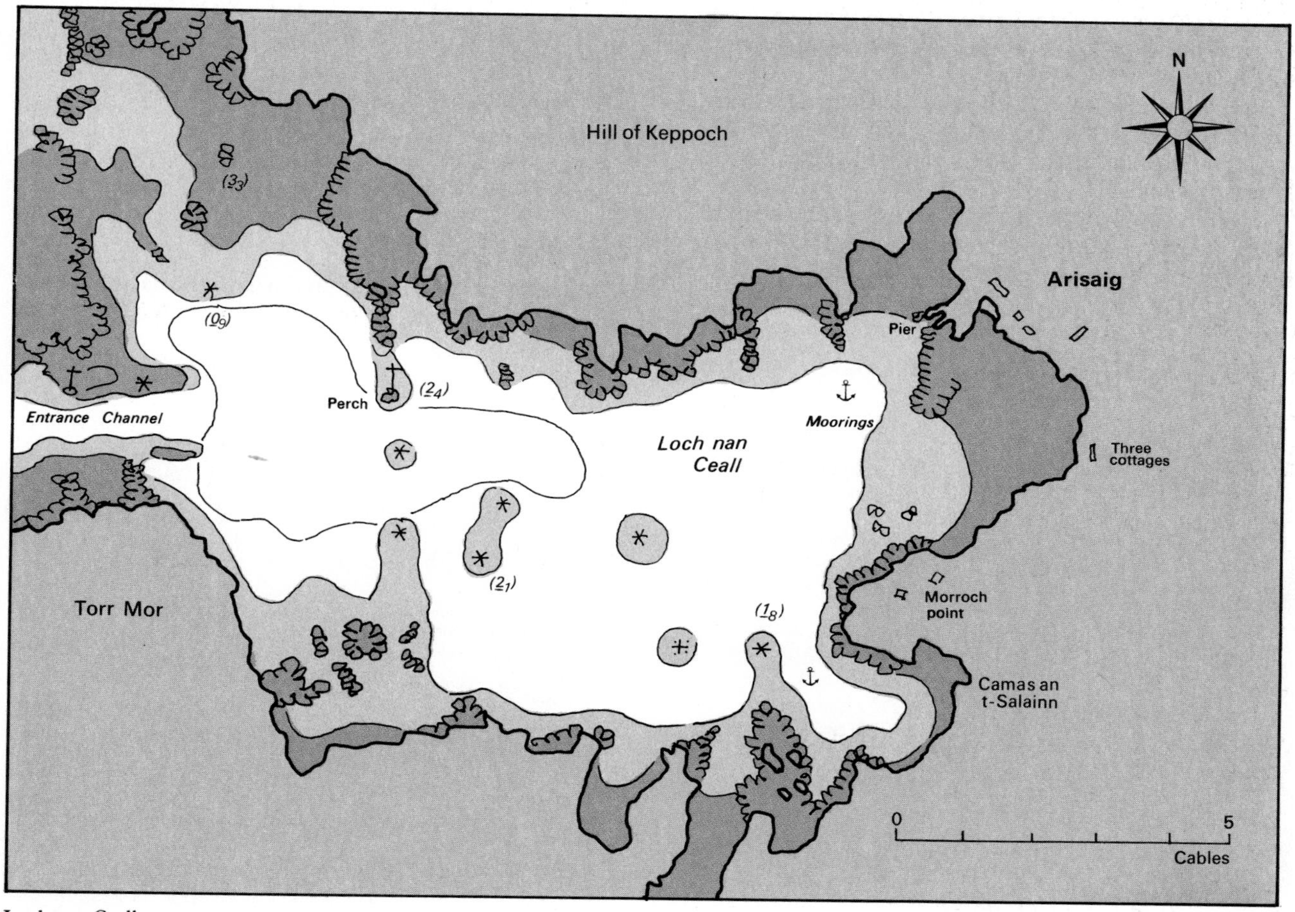

Loch nan Ceall

Services and supplies

Moorings, repairs, diesel, petrol, *Calor Gas*, water at pier. New slipway, 1987. Shop, hotel, restaurant.

Communications Post office, phone box, train and bus to Mallaig and Glasgow. Arisaig Marine, ☎ Arisaig (068 75) 224 or 678.

North Channel

North of the skerries in the entrance is the North Channel, of which the current Admiralty pilot drily observes, 'it is seldom used, even by vessels with local knowledge'. One of my more adventurous friends took my 35-foot ketch through this passage – and told me about it afterwards (he is now skipper of a large motor yacht in the Mediterranean). It would be impossible to provide pilotage notes; use the old chart if you must try it.

Passage notes

North of Loch nan Ceall there are drying rocks over a mile from the shore; in poor visibility keep outwith the 15-metre contour or set a compass course to avoid the risk of following the coastline in among the rocks.

Morar River

56°58′N 5°50′W

A river estuary 5 miles north of the entrance to Loch nan Ceall with a winding channel, mostly with a depth of less than 0.5 metre, between inviting banks of white sand, which feature regularly in Tourist Board brochures. The entrance has a bar on most of which there is no more than 0.2 metres and the position of the deepest part varies.

The slightest swell would make the entrance hazardous even to a shoal-draught boat except perhaps during the last quarter of the flood.

A keelboat might find a place to lie afloat at the most northerly point of the channel at neaps, otherwise it is only to be considered by owners of twin-keel and shoal-draught yachts.

Several yachts are kept on moorings at the head of the estuary, but there must be many occasions when the sea on the bar makes it impossible to go out.

Supplies

Shop, hotel, garage, post office, phone box.

Mallaig

57°00′.5N 5°50′W

A busy fishing harbour and ferry terminal, and possible future base for offshore oil operations, at the south point of the entrance to Loch Nevis, 7½ miles north of Loch nan Ceall. Its main attraction is the wide range of services, but yachts have to take their chance among working boats. For an overnight anchorage Arisaig is preferable unless you think the entrance is too difficult. Mallaig used to be very uncomfortable in northerly winds but the new extension to the Steamer Pier may provide more shelter.

Glaschoille, on the north side of Loch Nevis, 4 miles from Mallaig, is more peaceful in northerly winds.

Charts

2208 (1:50,000) and plan (1:7,500) on chart *2534*.

Tides

The constant is +0030 Oban (−0500 Dover).

Height in metres

MHWS	MHWN	MTL	MLWN	MLWS
5.0	3.8	2.9	2.1	0.7

Approach

If you have VHF R/T, call up the harbourmaster before entering for advice as to where to anchor or berth alongside.

Morar from northwest.

Mallaig from northeast. The new breakwater is in the middle of the photo; Rubha na h-Acairseid beacon is at the extreme right.

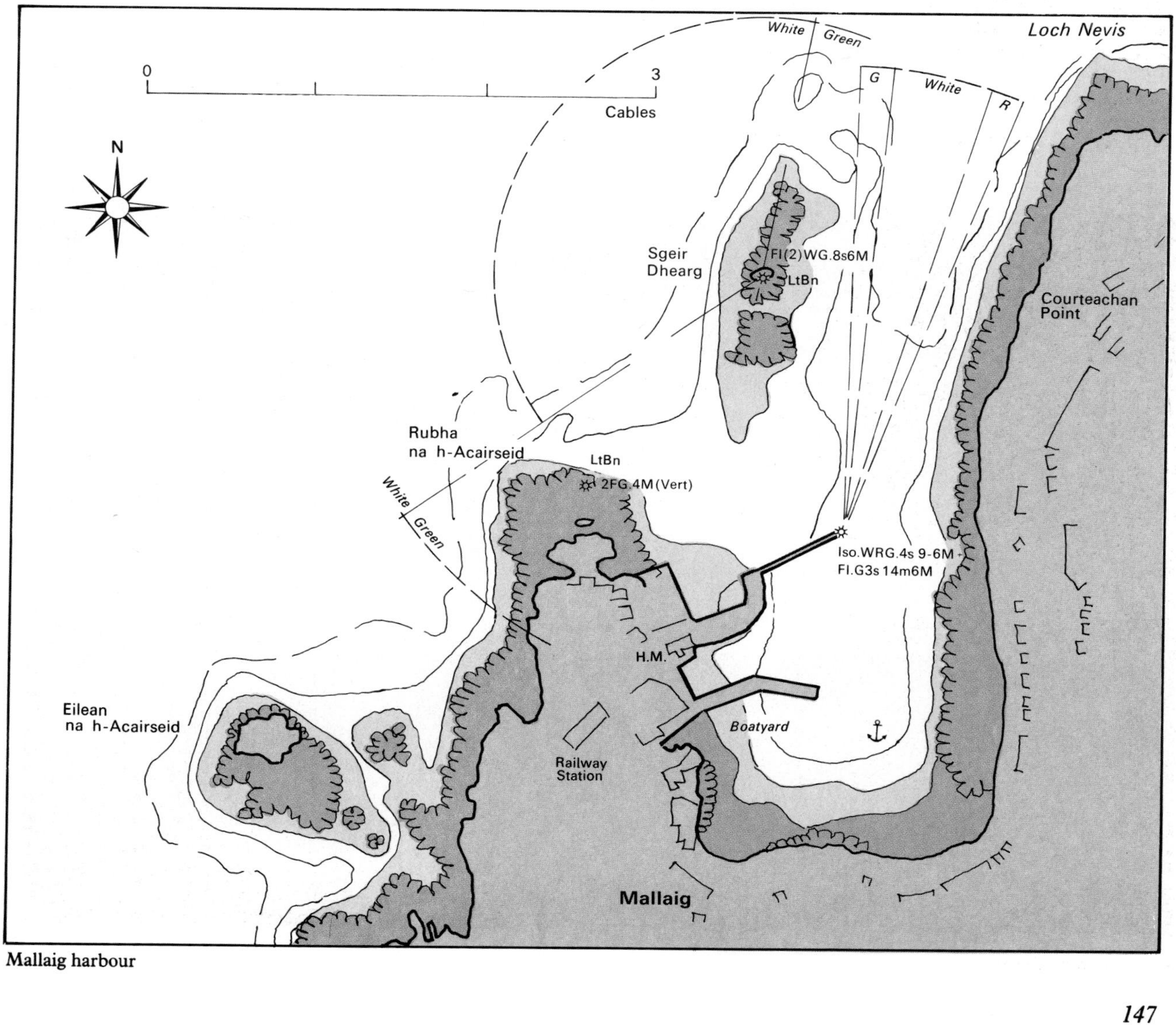

Mallaig harbour

From south and west Eilean na h-Acairseid and large industrial buildings on Rubha na h-Acairseid, ENE of the island, help to identify the entrance in poor visibility. Keep at least a cable offshore, or outwith the 5-metre contour until you have identified the small light beacon on the reef north of Rubha na h-Acairseid (not to be confused with the grey stone beacon on Sgeir Dhearg). Do not turn to enter the harbour until you see the Steamer Pier extension north of the light beacon 115°. Pass between the small beacon and Sgeir Dhearg, keeping closer to the south side.

From north pass between Sgeir Dhearg and the mainland.

Lights

At night the lights may be difficult to identify against the lights of the town.

Sgeir Dhearg Fl(2)WG.8s6m5M
Rubha na h-Acairseid 2F.G(vert)5m4M
Steamer Pier extension Iso.WRG.4s9–6M, with a separate light Fl.G.3s14m6M

From south or west approach in the white sector of Sgeir Dhearg light and pass between it and the 2F.G(vert) light, closer to the latter to avoid the south end of Sgeir Dhearg.

From north pass into the green sector of Sgeir Dhearg light and into the white sector of the Steamer Pier light.

Anchorage

Anchor in the southeast corner of the harbour or as directed by the harbourmaster. There are many moorings and the bottom is foul.

Supplies and services

Boatyard, engineer, diesel, petrol, *Calor Gas*, water at pier. Chandler and chart agent. Shops, including chemist and butcher, bank, hotels.

Communications Train and bus to Glasgow, ferry to Skye, post office, phone box.
☎ all Mallaig (0687)
Harbourmaster 2154
Boatyard (Henderson) 2304
Chandler and chart agent (Johnston Bros) 2215

The Small Isles and Ardnamurchan looking north.

VIII. The Small Isles

The Small Isles are the group of four islands between Ardnamurchan and Skye, each inhabited by a small community and each of very different character. Only Canna, the most northwesterly of them, has a good sheltered anchorage and it makes an ideal staging post on the way to the Outer Hebrides.

Charts

The only charts showing the Small Isles in any detail are *2207* and *2208* at 1:50,000. Even these don't include the whole of Canna; *1795* does, but at 1:100,000. Ordnance Survey map *39* neatly covers all the Small Isles at the same scale.

Tides

On the west side of Eigg the constant averages +0022 Oban (−0508 Dover).

Height in metres

MHWS	MHWN	MTL	MLWN	MLWS
4.7	3.5	2.6	1.6	0.5

Among the Small Isles the flood stream runs generally northwestwards and northwards, and both flood and ebb reach a rate of 4 knots in places, particularly east of Eigg, between Muck and Eigg, and around the rocks between Canna and Hyskeir. There are heavy overfalls wherever there are relatively shallow banks. Steep seas are reflected off the west point of Rhum in strong westerly winds.

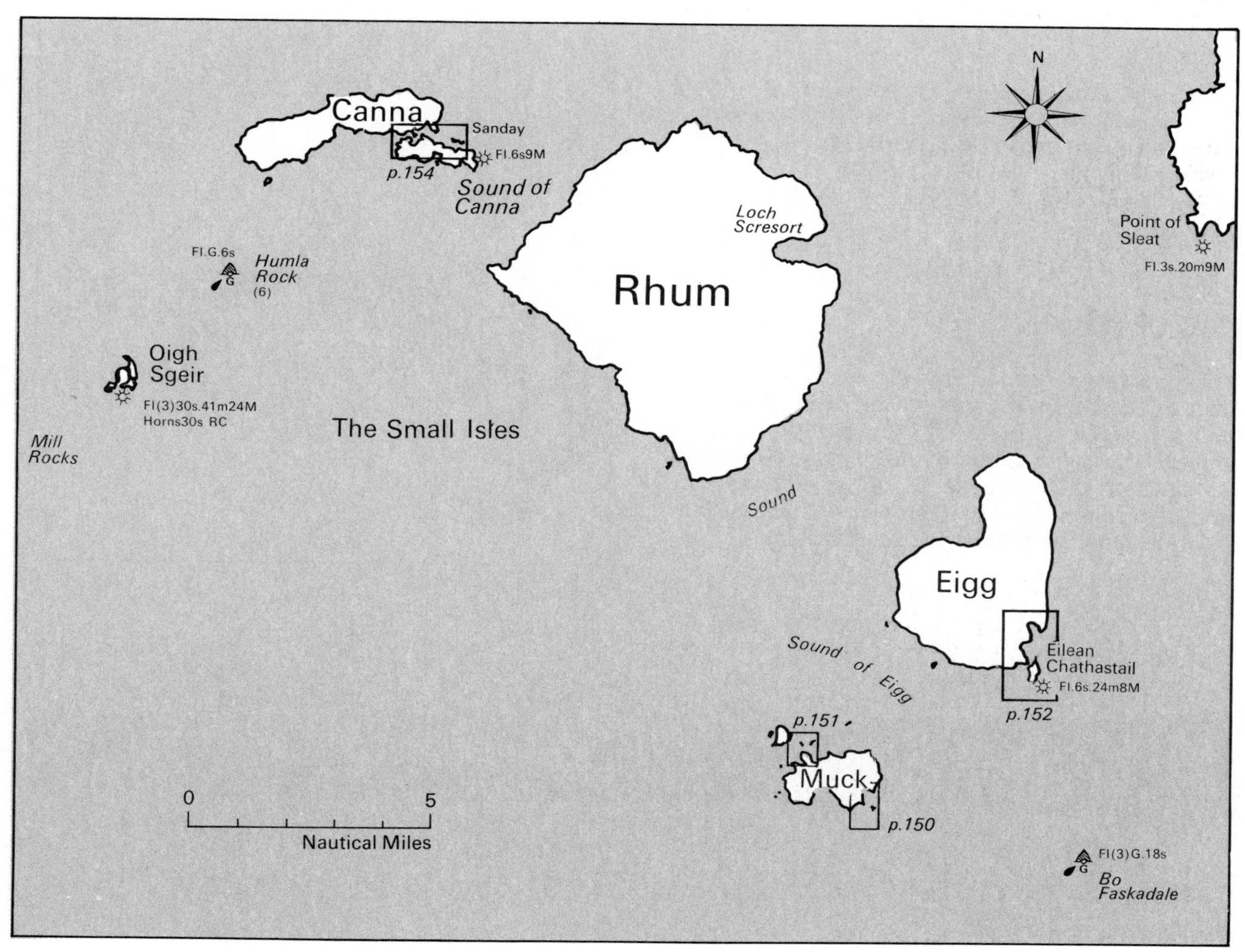

Among the Small Isles the streams turn approximately as follows: north-going stream begins −0530 Oban (+0130 Dover); south-going stream begins +0100 Oban (−0430 Dover).

Dangers

There are so many drying rocks up to ¼ mile off the shores of the Small Isles that the chart must be carefully studied before approaching the shore.

Banks and rocks east and southeast of Eigg and Muck are described in the next chapter.

In the passage between Muck and Eigg, 6 cables north of Muck, Godag is a group of rocks of which the most southerly is above water, with rocks drying and submerged up to 3 cables further north.

Southwest of Canna there are several rocks between Canna and Hyskeir (Oigh Sgeir) and there is some doubt as to the completeness of the survey here.

Marks

The best identification is the shape of the islands themselves. Rhum is high and mountainous; Eigg has the long ridge of the Sgurr lying on an east–west axis at its south end which from the east looks like a detached rock pinnacle.

Good use can be made of transits of the edges of any two islands, and this is particularly valuable as there are several magnetic anomalies in the area.

Lights

Ardnamurchan lighthouse LFl(2)30s55m17M
Eigg (SE point of Eilean Chathastail) Fl.6s24m8M
Canna (E end of Sanday) Fl.6s32m9M
Hyskeir (Oigh Sgeir) Fl(3)30s41m24M
Bo Faskadale buoy 6M NE of Ardnamurchan Fl(3)G.18s

Isle of Muck

Muck has been run successfully as an agricultural estate by the McEwen family for very many years. It is the least visited of the Small Isles, partly because of doubts about the shelter of its anchorages. However it is a most attractive place in an undramatic way and, short of a failure of the weather forecasts, one anchorage or the other should provide good shelter.

Port Mor

56°50′N 6°13′W

At the southeast side of the island, Port Mor is the main harbour, but the rocks at the entrance do not completely prevent any sea from south. Small shoal-draught boats may find space to dry out in complete shelter behind the L-shaped stone jetty at the head of the inlet.

Port Mor is identified by its houses.

Approach

The entrance is between the above-water rock Dubh Sgeir, which has rocks drying ½ cable all round it, and Bogha Ruadh which is the end of a drying reef extending ¼ mile south of the east point of the inlet. The leading line is not easy to make out but must be positively identified before entering.

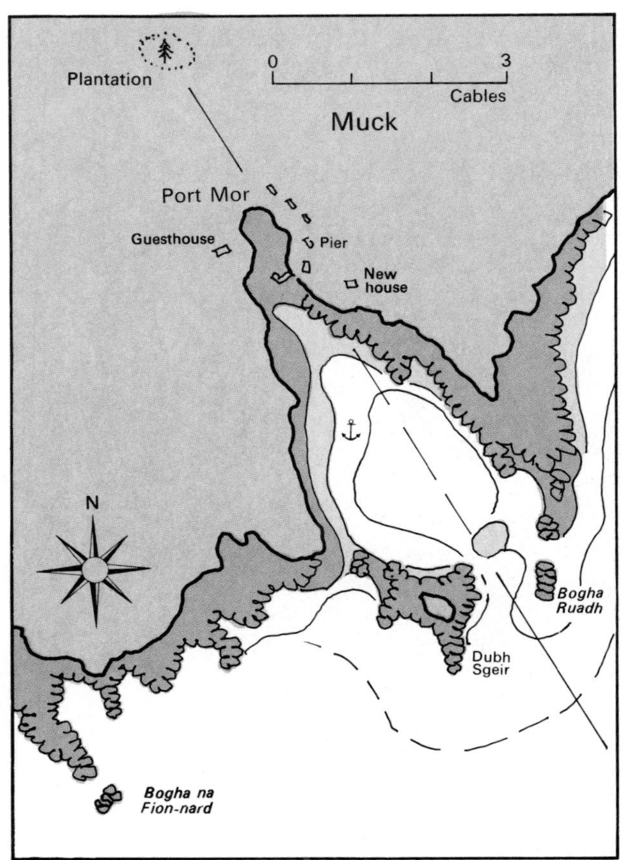

Port Mor

Muck, Port Mor approach.

The leading line is the middle of a group of trees on the hillside beyond the head of the inlet over the gable end of a cottage at the pier 329°, but there are other houses which could be mistaken for the cottage, which is hidden from a yacht coming from the east until almost on the line.

From east or northeast, keep the east shore of Muck open of the west shore of Eigg until the leading line is identified, to clear Bogha Ruadh.

Anchorage

Anchor clear of moorings and drying rocks on the northeast side of the inlet.

No supplies. Phone box near the pier. The new guest house can provide meals if arranged in advance.

Gallanach (Bagh a' Ghallanaich)

56°51'N 6°15'W

The entrance to this bay on the north side of Muck is obstructed by drying reefs, but these only offer limited protection from seas from the north.

Tides

Tides run at 4 knots at springs in the Sound of Eigg, between Eigg and Muck, and on the west side of Muck, but less strongly across the mouth of the bay itself.

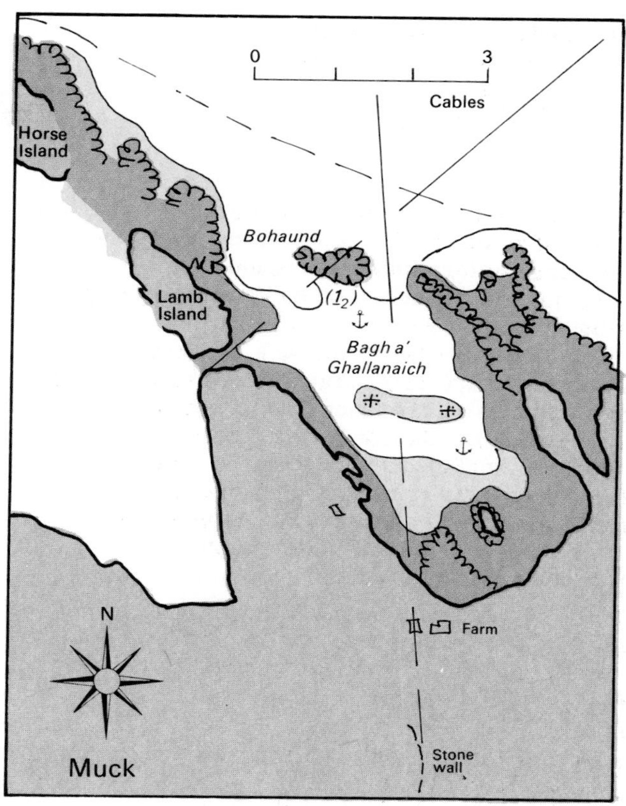

Muck, Gallanach Bay.

Approach

From east pass south of Godag, the detached rock 6 cables north of Muck, as there are drying and submerged rocks ¼ mile north of it, and head for the north end of Horse Island (Eilean nan Each). The gap between Lamb Island (Eilean Ard nan Uan) and Lamb Point, immediately south of it, appears as a square notch in the skyline. When this closes, head for the south end of Lamb Island, keeping the gap closed, to clear the reef on the east side of Gallanach Bay.

The second leading line is a yellow barn with a curved roof on the west side of the farmhouse ahead, in line with a conspicuous dyke (stone wall) on the east slope of the hill beyond; this leads between Bohaund and the reef to the east.

About 2 cables south of Bohaund is a shoal with rocks awash at either end. Pass round either end of the shoal, or above half-tide over it, and anchor north or northwest of the tidal islet towards the head of the bay.

Isle of Eigg

Eigg is the most easterly of the Small Isles and is large enough to have a substantial population, most of whom live at the northwest side of the island. The main anchorage (56°53′N 6°08′W) is at the southeast side, in the channel between Eigg and Eilean Castle (Eilean Chathastail), but its shelter is not very good, except for shoal-draught boats which may be able to use a drying boat harbour.

The anchorage is identified by reference to the Sgurr, a prominent ridge rising to a peak at its east end. Eilean Castle is 35 metres high, grass covered, with a white light beacon on its southeast side.

Tides

Constant averages +0022 Oban (−0508 Dover).

Height in metres

MHWS	MHWN	MTL	MLWN	MLWS
4.7	3.5	2.6	1.6	0.5

The tide runs strongly through the anchorage, the flood running northwards, turning south 2 hours before HW. Off the east side of Eigg streams run at 4 knots at springs, causing a heavy sea with wind against tide, and making the approach from east difficult.

Dangers

Drying rocks extend for a cable south and southwest of Eilean Castle. North of Eilean Castle there is a line of drying reefs. The entrance from east is between Garbh Sgeir, marked at its north end by a perch with a triangular topmark, and Flod Sgeir, marked on its east side by a perch with a circular topmark. These perches have recently been restored but their existence should not be relied on.

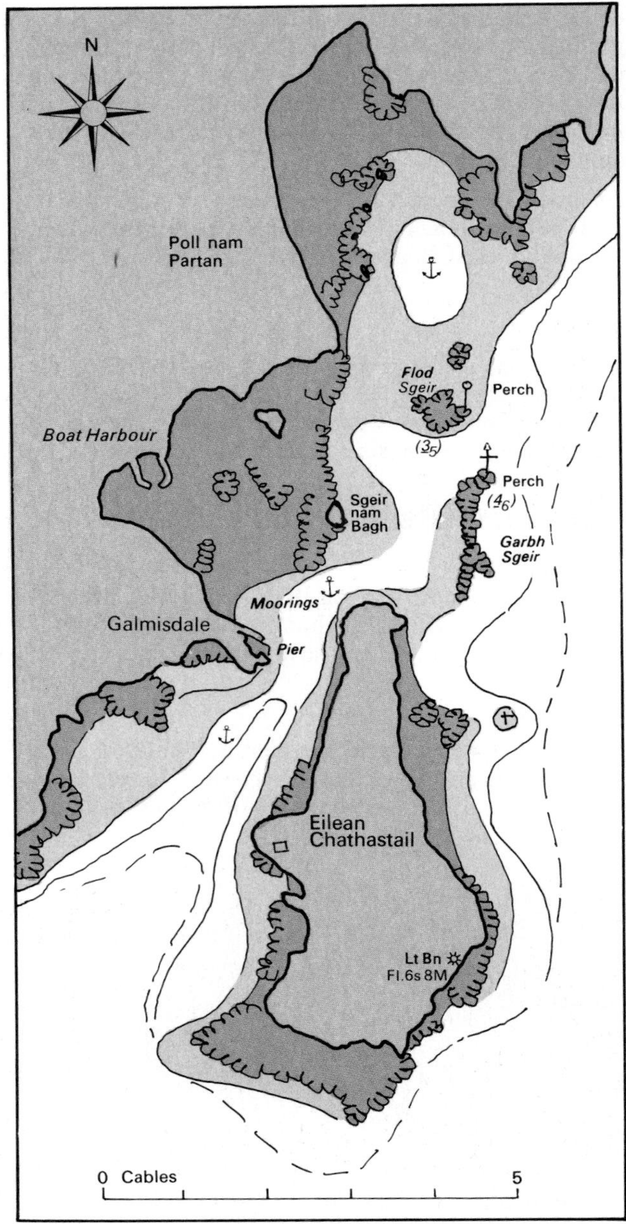

Galmisdale

Approach

From south the approach is the more straightforward, but keep more than a cable off Eilean Castle to avoid the drying reefs. Rubha na Crannaig, the east point of Eigg, open west of the north point of Eilean Castle 028° leads clear of the reefs at the southwest point of Eilean Castle. Reefs also extend from the south side of Galmisdale Point.

From east the perches marking the passage between the reefs must be identified. Pass between them and head southwest for the above-water rock Sgeir nam Bagh, then south towards Galmisdale Point.

Eigg – Flod Sgeir at low tide.

Eigg – anchorages from the north shore of Poll nam Partan.

Eigg – Garbh Sgeir and Flod Sgeir.

Anchorages

South of Galmisdale Point clear of reefs drying 1 cable from northwest side, and also clear of the strong tide in the narrows.

North end of Eilean Castle There is not usually space near the jetty owing to the moorings, but owners of quite large boats claim to be able to find (or make) room for themselves. There is a risk of fouling ground tackle, and one recent visitor had to call for a diver from Mallaig to release his anchor. Shoal-draught boats may be able to anchor inshore of the moorings, or dry out in the boat harbour at the head of the bay.

Otherwise anchor as convenient between Eilean Castle and Sgeir nam Bagh, avoiding the reef drying SSW from Sgeir nam Bagh, and also avoiding obstructing the passage which is used by various ferries.

Poll nam Partan, ½ mile north of Eilean Castle, has just enough depth for medium-sized yachts, but no more than 0.5 metre in the approach. Enter at a suitable rise of tide between Flod Sgeir and Eigg, keeping the east side of Sgeir nam Bagh in line with the west side of Eilean Castle. Anchor on sand clear of rock or weed, easily visible in the clear water, wherever depth and swinging room can be found.

All of the above anchorages are only safe in moderate weather.

Laig Bay on the northwest side of Eigg provides occasional anchorage.

Supplies and services

Diesel, water, *Calor Gas*, coffee shop at jetty; phone box on its northwest side. Post office and shop 2 miles along road to Laig. Ferries to Mallaig, Arisaig and Glenuig. Isle of Eigg Estate, ☎ Mallaig (0687) 82428

Isle of Rhum

The largest of the Small Isles, Rhum is spectacularly mountainous. It is owned by the Nature Conservancy Council and used for research into the breeding of red deer, with a sideline in white-tailed sea eagles. Access is limited to two marked trails from Loch Scresort, on the east side of the island. Permission to go beyond these limits has to be be arranged in advance, and is only given to members of recognised climbing clubs. Landing is only permitted at Loch Scresort, and dogs may not be taken ashore.

Kinloch Castle, built in 1903, is preserved with its original furniture and a working orchestrion, (a type of mechanical organ). For a few years efforts were made to run the house as a hotel but this has ceased. Tours are arranged on certain days (at present Tuesdays and Thursdays).

Dangers

Off the north point of Rhum there are several drying rocks up to ¼ mile from the land; these are avoided by keeping outwith the 15-metre contour.

At the west point of Rhum drying reefs extend 1 cable from the shore, and any sea from the west is reflected and becomes particularly steep and confused.

Loch Scresort

57°01'N 6°16'W

An inlet over a mile long on the east side of Rhum, shoaling very gradually towards the head, subject to violent squalls in strong westerly winds, and swell with easterly winds.

Drying reefs extend nearly ¼ mile from the south shore at the entrance, and there are drying rocks close inshore on the north side.

Approach

Keep well off the south shore on entering, and anchor off the concrete slip on the south side of the loch, or northeast of the stone pier further in.

Supplies

Basic stores at shop. Phone box and post office.

Isle of Canna

Canna is the most westerly of the Small Isles with a well sheltered natural harbour, often used by yachts on passage to the Outer Hebrides, as well as by fishing boats for which a buoy has been laid in the middle of the harbour. Its climate is better than its neighbours, having no mountains to the west, and it has white sandy beaches. Canna has been presented to the National

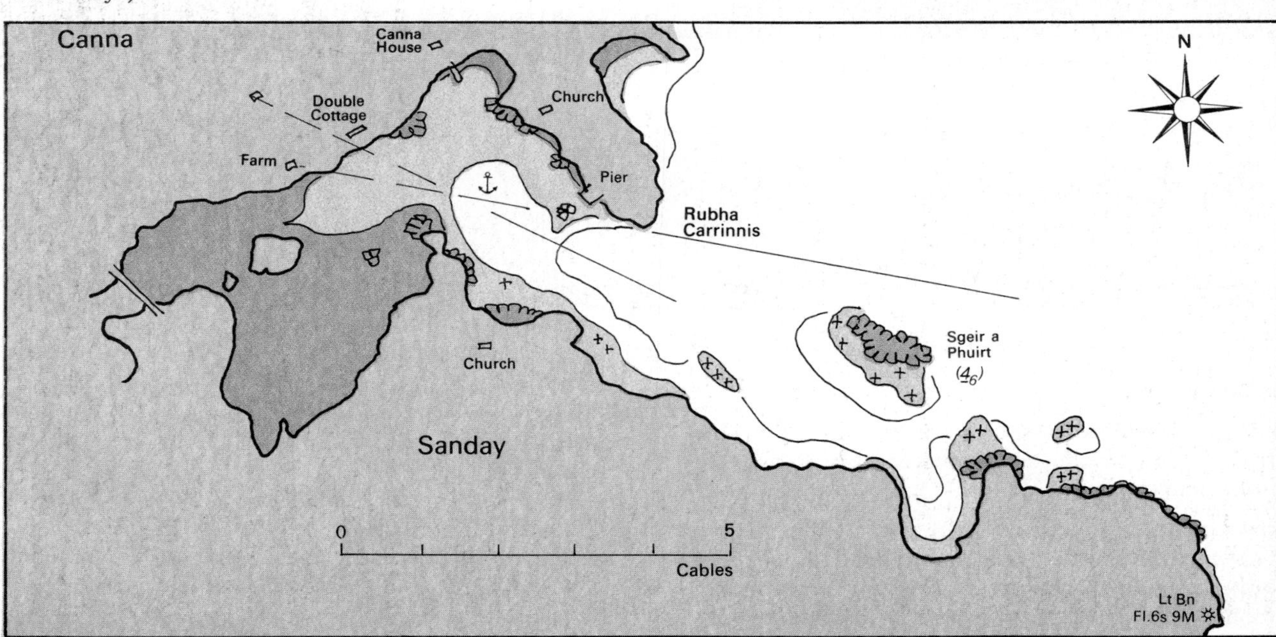

Canna Harbour

Trust for Scotland by John Lorne Campbell, its owner for many years.

Canna Harbour

57°03′N 6°30′W

Dangers and marks

Rocks off the coast of Rhum are described above. The north side of Canna is clean beyond a cable from the shore. Between the south side of Canna and Hyskeir there are several rocks for which chart *1795* must be consulted.

There is an abnormal magnetic variation east of Compass Hill at the northeast point of Canna.

The east point of Sanday on the south side of Canna Harbour is marked by a small but conspicuous white light beacon.

Sgeir a' Phuirt, an extensive reef between the light beacon and the harbour entrance, dries 4.6 metres, 2 cables north of Sanday.

Inside the harbour on the southwest side of Rubha Carrinnis, the north point of the entrance, is a wooden pier. West of the pier is a drying rock, with a shoal spit southwest of it. The harbour shoals gradually towards the northwest shore, with a clean sandy bottom.

Approach

Identify the farm towards the west end of the harbour and keep it in line with the south side of Rubha Carrinnis to lead north of Sgeir a' Phuirt. Keep to the south half of the entrance to avoid the rock west of the pier. This rock can be avoided by keeping a conspicuous cottage on the hillside open southwest of the southwest end of a pair of cottages on the shore.

Lights

Sanday light beacon Fl.6s32m9M is obscured between 061° and 152°. There are no lights to lead into the harbour.

Anchorage

Anchor wherever there is enough depth; a good guide is to bring a prominent white stone cross in the churchyard on the northeast side of the harbour under the summit of Compass Hill.

On most nights the harbour fills with fishing boats about 2300 hours, and they leave again about 0300. Show a good anchor light, and if you use a tripping line, secure it inboard.

Land below the church on the northeast side; the stone jetty in front of Canna House is private.

No supplies. Phone box and post office at the pair of cottages on the northwest side of the harbour.

Canna Harbour from ESE. The farm, double cottage and cottage on the hillside are quite easily identified.

Canna Boat Harbour

Between the west end of Sanday and the south side of Canna, this harbour provides a temporary anchorage in very quiet weather. There are many rocks in the approach and Sgeirean Dubha, 2 metres high, in the middle of the entrance, is the key to the problem. A rock which just dries, 4 cables southwest of the entrance, is cleared by keeping Sgeirean Dubha in line with the summit of Compass Hill bearing 051°. Pass between Sgeirean Dubha and the rock northwest of it which covers at HW.

Tarbert Bay

57°03′N 6°32′W

A mile west of Sanday, southeast of a dip in the skyline of Canna. Identify Haslam, an islet 3 cables off Canna, rather closer to the west side of the bay than to Sanday. Keep at least ¼ mile off Haslam and approach the bay keeping closer to its west side than to Haslam. Anchor towards the northeast side of the bay, clear of rocks.

Hyskeir (Oigh Sgeir)

56°58′N 6°41′W

A group of low islets 5 miles southwest of Canna with a white lighthouse 39 metres high. It is only rarely visited by yachts and it is not recommended as there is almost no shelter. The lighthouse is now unmanned.

Dangers and marks

Between Hyskeir and Canna, Humla Rock, 5 metres high, has a green conical light buoy (Fl.G.6s) on its southwest side. There are submerged rocks and shoals around Humla, and between that rock and Canna. The usual passage from Ardnamurchan to the Minch is between Hyskeir and the Humla buoy.

Mill Rocks, 2¼ miles southwest of Hyskeir, have depths of less than 2 metres. For a further 3 miles southwest seas break in strong winds owing to the uneven bottom.

Approach and anchorage

The north point of Eigg just open of the south point of Rhum 085° leads 1½ miles south of Mill Rocks.

To anchor at Hyskeir the following course has been followed: pass 1 cable west of the north end of Hyskeir and steer 170° to keep open the narrow channel between the largest islet and the next islet to the west to avoid a drying rock in the bay northwest of the lighthouse. The landing place is on the east side of the channel. Although this course has been taken successfully in the past, it certainly should not be assumed that there are no other rocks around. There are many rocks off the south end of the channel.

Hyskeir from southeast. The drying rock northwest of the lighthouse shows clearly. Dark patches suggest other submerged rocks.

Appendix

I. CHARTS AND OTHER PUBLICATIONS

The Imray chart *C65* at a scale of 1:150,000 covers all the places in this volume, with the exception of Canna and the north part of Rhum. It is available at most chandlers and from the Clyde Cruising Club, usually folded, but for any boat which has a large enough chart table it is better to order a flat copy, or one laminated in plastic.

A general chart for the whole west coast of Scotland is Admiralty chart *2635* at a scale of 1:500,000.

The following Admiralty charts relate to the waters covered by this volume. Some of these are essential, and the more you have, the less your pilotage will be fraught with anxiety. The relevant Ordnance Survey maps are also listed.

Chart	*Title – areas in Chapter 1*	*Scale*
2169	Approaches to the Firth of Lorne	75,000
2326	Loch Crinan to the Firth of Lorne	25,000
2320	Loch Crinan	7,500
OS55	Lochgilphead	50,000

Chart	*Title – areas in Chapter 2*	*Scale*
2169	Approaches to the Firth of Lorne	75,000
2386	Firth of Lorne – southern part	25,000
2387	Firth of Lorne – northern part	25,000
1790	Oban and approaches	10,000
2171	Sound of Mull and approaches	75,000
OS49	Oban & East Mull	50,000

Chart	*Title – areas in Chapter 3*	*Scale*
2378	Loch Linnhe – southern part	25,000
2379	Loch Linnhe – central part	25,000
2380	Loch Linnhe – northern part	25,000
	Loch Leven Narrows	10,000
5076	Loch Etive (upper part, fathoms)	24,320
2372	Corran Narrows	10,000
	Approaches to Corpach	6,250
OS41	Ben Nevis	50,000

Chart	*Title – areas in Chapter 4*	*Scale*
2171	Sound of Mull and approaches	75,000
2390	Sound of Mull	25,000
2474	Tobermory Harbour	10,000
2392	Sound of Mull – western entrance	25,000
2394	Loch Sunart	25,000
OS49	Oban & East Mull	50,000
OS47	Tobermory	50,000

Chart	*Title – areas in Chapter 5*	*Scale*
2169	Approaches to the Firth of Lorne	75,000
2171	Sound of Mull and approaches	75,000
2652	Loch na Keal and Loch Tuath	25,000
2771	Loch Scridain	25,000
2617	Sound of Iona	25,000
OS47	Tobermory	50,000
OS48	Iona & Ben More	50,000

Chart	*Title – areas in Chapter 6*	*Scale*
2171	Sound of Mull and approaches	75,000
2474	Loch Eatharna (Arinagour)	10,000
	Gott Bay and Scarinish Harbour	15,000
2475	Gunna Sound	25,000
OS46	Coll and Tiree	50,000

Chart	*Title – areas in Chapter 7*	*Scale*
2207	Ardnamurchan to Sound of Sleat	50,000
2208	Mallaig to Canna Harbour	50,000
2534	Mallaig Harbour	7,500
OS47	Tobermory	50,000
OS40	Loch Shiel	50,000

Chart	*Title – areas in Chapter 8*	*Scale*
2207	Ardnamurchan to Sound of Sleat	50,000
2208	Mallaig to Canna Harbour	50,000
1795	The Little Minch	100,000
OS39	Rhum & Eigg	50,000

Order charts early so that you have time to order more, if it looks as though your first choice was not enough. There are Admiralty chart agents throughout Britain, and in most other countries. Chart agents on the West Coast are:

Crinan Boats, Crinan ☎ (054 683) 232
Nancy Black, Oban ☎ (0631) 62550
Seafare, Tobermory ☎ (0688) 2277
Johnston Bros, Mallaig ☎ (0687) 2215
Kelvin Hughes, Glasgow ☎ (041) 221 5452

Don't rely on buying charts locally without ordering in advance – they may not be in stock. Some other chandlers stock Admiralty charts, although sometimes at a higher cost.

Imray, Laurie, Norie & Wilson Ltd are Admiralty chart agents and will supply charts by post; Wych House, The Broadway, St Ives, Huntingdon, Cambridgeshire PE17 4BT, ☎ (0480) 62114, Telex 32496 Kelouk G.

Some charts which have long been discontinued provide much more detail, at a larger scale, than any now published for the same area. Two of particular interest are *531* (Loch Moidart), and *2817* (Loch nan Ceall – Arisaig). Two other large-scale plans are *3608* (Loch Aline and Loch Corrie), and *3015* (Loch na Keal, Mull). All older charts, particularly the fine Victorian engravings, show more detail inshore and on land than the current publications, although they may be less accurate. Old charts should only be used to supplement current ones, not as a substitute for them.

Photocopies of old charts – of editions not less than 50 years old, for copyright reasons – may be obtained from the National Library of Scotland Map Room Annexe, 137 Causewayside, Edinburgh 9, ☎ (031) 667 7848. They can provide either a single photographic copy of the whole sheet, or more quickly a patchwork of A3-size pages.

Current charts show much less detail ashore than older charts, and Ordnance Survey maps at a scale of 1:50,000, or Bartholomew maps at 1:100,000 help to fill in the picture.

Although the coverage of Admiralty charts is extremely good, there are two areas where there is no adequate large-scale chart. Coll and Tiree are shown on *C65*, and Coll with part of Tiree on *2171*, but for the whole of both islands at a larger scale OS map *46* will be found helpful.

Part of Canna is on chart *2208* at 1:50,000 and all of it on *1795* at 1:100,000, but it is neatly covered, with all of the

Index of Admiralty charts for the west coast of Scotland

Small Isles, on OS map *39*; this can be used in conjunction with chart *2208* and the new Imray *C66*.

Loch Linnhe is very well covered, but for a brief visit you may find OS maps *41* and *49* sufficient, in combination with *C65*.

A set of 50 sketch charts published by the Clyde Cruising Club is available from chandlers or direct from the CCC at SV Carrick, Clyde Street, Glasgow G1 4LN. These charts are convenient to use because of their size, but the relevant Admiralty charts should also be carried.

The Clyde Cruising Club *Sailing Directions and Anchorages* are also available from the CCC at the above address.

The Admiralty *West Coast of Scotland Pilot* (NP 66), with supplements up to date, is a most valuable publication.

The Admiralty tidal stream atlas for the *North Coast of Ireland and West Coast of Scotland* (NP 218) is very useful.

Tide tables are essential, preferably for Oban and giving heights of each high and low water. These can be had as a separate publication from local chandlers, yacht centres and boatyards, as well as chandlers in Glasgow, or you can have the full *Admiralty Tide Tables* Vol. 1 (NP 201) or Brown's, Macmillan's or Reed's Almanac.

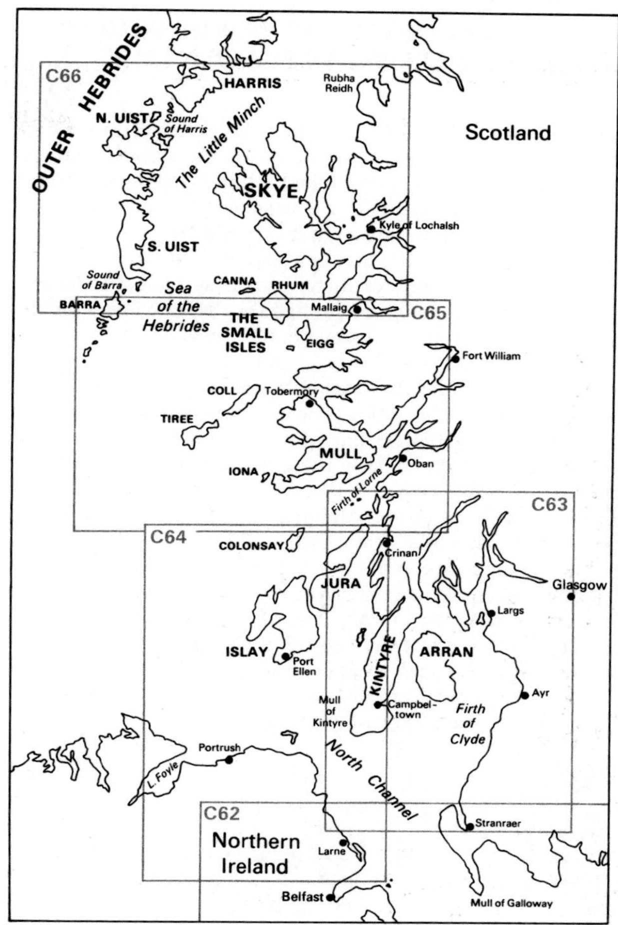

Index of Imray charts for the west coast of Scotland

II. GLOSSARY OF GAELIC WORDS WHICH COMMONLY APPEAR IN PLACE NAMES

Many varieties of spelling are found, so it is as well to search for possible alternatives; variations of the same word are listed together but usually at least have the same initial letter. Many words beginning with a consonant take an 'h' after the initial letter in certain cases; notably in adjectives the genitive and the feminine gender and genitive cases of nouns, so that most of the words below could have an 'h' as the second letter.

There is no possibility of guiding the reader on pronunciation except to say that consonants followed by an 'h' are not often pronounced, and that 'mh' and 'bh' at the beginning of a word are pronounced as (and of course in anglicised versions often spelt with) a 'v'. *Mhor* is pronounced – approximately – *vore*; *claidheamh* is something like *clayeh*, and *bogha* is *bo'a*.

Some names, particularly those of islands ending in 'a' or 'ay', are of Norse origin. Anyone at all familiar with French and Latin will see correspondences there, for example Caisteil – also Eaglais and Teampuill.

Many words are compounds made up of several often quite common parts, frequently linked by *na/nam/nan*. The following are the most usual forms of words which commonly occur in Gaelic place names. They often set out to describe the physical features and so give some clues to identification. Some of them occur almost everywhere; most lochs have a Sgeir More and an Eilean Dubh, or vice versa.

Gaelic	*English*
a, am, an, an t-	the
abhainn (avon)	river
acairseid	harbour (acair = anchor)
achadh (ach, auch)	field
allt	stream, burn
ard, aird	promontory
aros	house
ba	cattle
bairneach	limpet
bagh ('bay')	bay
ban	white, pale; female (ban-righ = queen), as noun: woman
bealach	narrow passage
beg, beag, beaga	small
ben, beinn	mountain
beul (bel)	mouth of (belnahua = mouth of the cave)
bodach	old man
bogha (bo')	a detached rock, usually one which uncovers
breac	speckled (as noun: trout)
buachaille	shepherd
buidhe (bhuidhe, buie)	yellow (also: pleasing)
bun	mouth of a river
cailleach	old woman
caisteil	castle
camas	bay
caol (a' chaolais)	narrow passage (kyle)
caorach	sheep
ceall, cille (kil...)	monastic cell, church
ceann (kin...)	head
clachan	usually a group of houses (clach = stone)
claidheamh	sword (hence 'claymore' = great sword)
cnoc (knock)	rounded hill
coire (corrie)	cauldron, hollow among hills, whirlpool
craobh	tree
creag	cliff, rock (crag)
darroch	oak tree
dearg ('jerrig')	red
deas	south
dobhran	otter
donn	brown (dun)
druim	ridge
dubh (dhu)	black, dark, (disastrous)
dun, duin	fortified place, usually prehistoric
each	horse
ear	east
eilean (or eileach)	island
fada	long
fir, fear	man
fraoch, fraoich	heather
garbh	rough
geal	white
gille	boy
glas	grey (sometimes green)
gobhar (gour)	goat (gabhar = she-goat)
gorm	blue
gamhna	stirk, year-old calf
iar	west (easily confused with Ear)
iolair	eagle
keills, kells	church
kin... (ceann)	head of
liath	grey
mara	sea
meadhonach	middle-sized
meall	lump, knob
mor (more, mhor, vore)	large, great (often only relative)
muc, muck	pig (often a sea-pig = porpoise or a whale)
na, na h-, nam, nan	of (the)
naomh (nave, neave)	holy, saint
...nish (ness)	point of land
poll, puill	pool
righ ('ree')	king
ron, roin	seal
ruadh	red, reddish
rudha (rhu)	point of land, promontory
sailean	creek
sgeir, sgeirean (skerry)	rock, above water or covering
sron	nose (as a headland)
sruth	stream, current
tigh	house
tober	well
traigh	beach
tuath (or tuadh)	north
uamh	cave

III. QUICK REFERENCE TABLE OF PROVISIONS, SERVICES AND SUPPLIES

Place, grouped in sequence of chapters	*Diesel*	*Petrol*	*Calor Gas*	*Water hose*	*Water, nearby*	*Chandlery*	*Charts*	*Boatyard*	*Moorings (vis)*	*Moorings (l/t)*	*Pontoon berths*	*Launching place*	*Provisions*	*Hotel*	*Restaurant*	*Showers*	*Laundrette*	*Bank*	*Refuse disposal*
Crinan	●	●	●	●		●	●	●			●		●	●	●				●
Ardfern	●	●	●	●		●	●	●	●	●	●	●	●	●	●	●			●
Craobh	●		●	●		●		●			●	●	●	●	●	●	●		●
Kilmelford	●	●	●	●		●		●	●	●			●	●					●
Balvicar	●			●					●	●			●						
Cullipool															●				
Easdale													●						●
Loch Feochan	●			●		●		●	●	●			●	●	●				
Gallanachbeg	●		●	●		●		●		●						●			
Oban	●	●	●	●		●	●	●			●	●	●	●	●			●	●
Ardantrive	●		●	●		●		●	●	●									
Dunstaffnage	●	●	●	●		●		●	●	●	●	●	●		●	●			●
Connel		●											●	●					
Port Appin		●											●	●	●				●
Ballachulish		●											●					●	
Onich	●	●	●		●								●						
Corran		●											●						
Fort William	●	●											●	●	●			●	●
Corpach	●			●	●	●		●	●	●			●						●
Craignure	●	●	●										●	●					
Loch Aline	●	●		●				●					●	●	●				
Salen (Mull)		●							●				●	●	●				
Tobermory	●	●	●	●		●	●		●				●	●	●		●	●	●
Salen (Sunart)			●		●	●			●			●	●	●					
Strontian		●	●										●	●					
Bunessan	●	●	●	●		●		●	●	●			●	●		●			
Fionnphort													●						
Iona					●								●	●					●
Arinagour	●	●			●				●				●	●	●	●	●		
Scarinish	●												●						
Glenuig			●										●	●					
Arisaig	●	●	●	●		●		●	●	●		●	●	●	●	●			
Morar	●	●											●	●					
Mallaig	●	●	●	●		●	●	●					●	●	●	●			●
Eigg	●		●		●								●						

Sailmaker Owen Sails, Tralee Bay, Benderloch, by Oban, Argyle PA37 1QR. ☎ (063 172) 485/255. Between Lochs Etive and Creran.

Compass adjusting information Bill Grant, 2 Adelphi Villa, Nursery Lane, Oban PA34 5JA. ☎ (0631) 63452.

Index